Curse of the Tomahawk

by

James B. Miller

July 4, 2012
James B. Miller

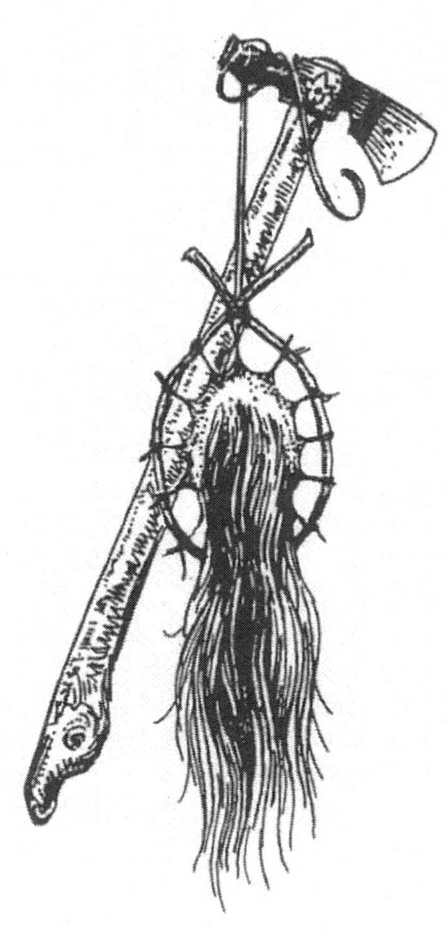

One of the mighty warriors of the "Six Nations."

Curse of the Tomahawk

This book may be ordered **online or at any fine bookseller.**

ISBN: 1448664527
ISBN: 978-1448664528

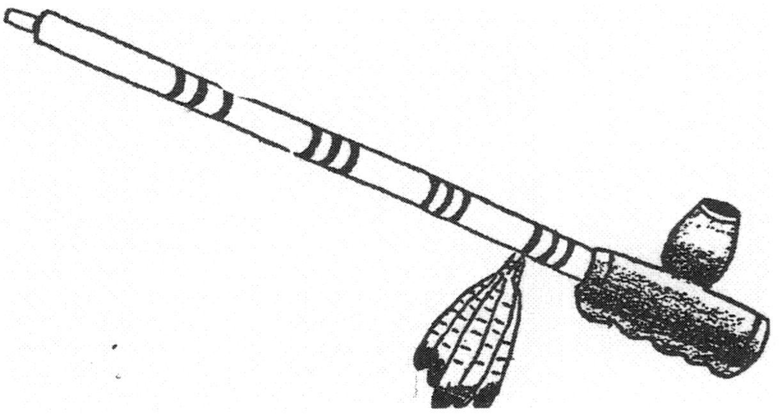

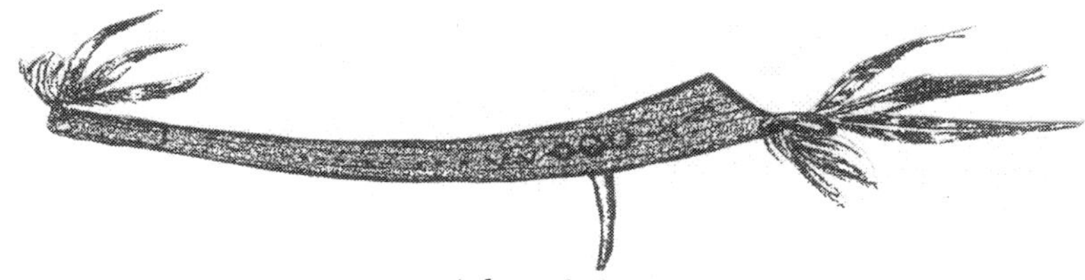

Acknowledgments

This is a work of fact, not fiction. All places mentioned in these pages actually exists or existed. You can follow the trail of history and walk in the places where the people in these pages once walked. The people mentioned in these pages actually lived and performed their duties in the roles in which they are portrayed. All the letters quoted in these pages were written by the actual people. This story is based on fact and on real people. Of course I took certain artistic license in telling their story, but I drew from facts the story of this important, yet overlooked, expedition of the great American Revolution.

I would like to mention all of the following organizations which helped in my painstaking research: the Tioga Point Museum, the Spalding Memorial Library, the Towanda Public Library, the Bradford County Library, the Pennsylvania State Archives, the Osterhout Free Library, the Muncy Historical Society and Museum, the Luzerne County Historical Society, and the Gettysburg Public Library.

As a Revolutionary War re-enactor I would like to thank and dedicate this work to all of my band of brothers.

This is my way of keeping history alive.

But most of all I thank and dedicate this work to my *father*, my daughter *Angela,* and my grandson *Cayleb.* I love you all very much.

Author's Note

This is addressed to all who live along the West and the Northern(or Main) Branches of the great Susquehanna River. You need only to look in your own backyards to see where many trails of history passed. Along the banks of the Susquehanna many Indian maiden walked hand in hand with their beau, dreaming of the future amid the beauty of the surrounding mountains. For thousands of years many of their like hoped and lived in the beauty of these mountains. Many a warrior hunted, married, lived, and fought for many untold generations. Here the mighty Susquehannocks lived, mentioned in Captain John Smith's writings on his escapades in the New World. Here Etienne Brule, the scout for the great French explorer Champlain came to meet with the great Susquehannock warriors at Carantouan, or Spanish Hill, a full five years before the Pilgrims landed at Plymouth Rock. Here in these mountains and along the Susquehanna the Mahican, Delaware, Nanticoke, Shawnee, Conoy, Muncy, Tutelo, Saponie and mighty Iroquois tribes of Native Americans lived, to name a few not lost to the ages. Here Connecticut settlers set out to carve a new haven for themselves in the wilderness, fighting numerous wars and skirmishes with the Indians and their fellow white men alike. Here they fought the Pennamite-Yankee War over a period of some forty odd years. Here they fought numerous battles of the American Revolution. Here many a family suffered. Some in triumph. Some in bitter defeat. Here many Indian and white man struggled, all with the hope of a new day in their hearts; all of them thinking of more than themselves and always of their posterity. Yes, we were very much on their minds. Should not they be on our minds for but a moment, for but a whisper in time?

They do whisper across the ages not to be forgotten, as well they should, for their story is unparalleled in the annals of American history. Stop and listen to the whispers across the ages. You may be surprised. Listen to those whom planted the roots of this country. Our ancestors knew of those roots. They were those roots. Their story is a true American story. Their story is all of ours, each and every one.

Do not forget them, or we shall forget a part of ourselves.

James B. Miller, May 4, 2009.

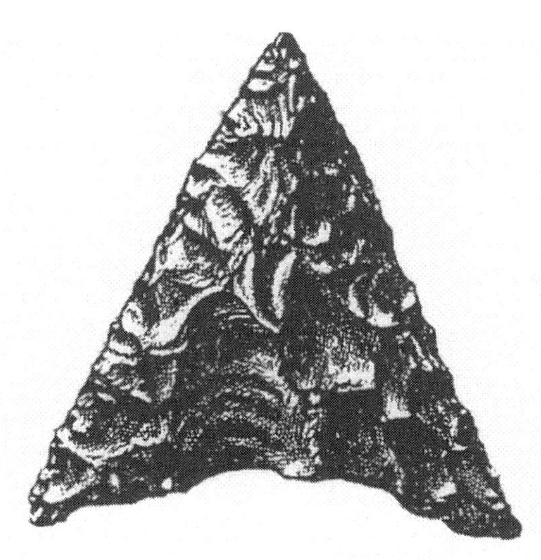

Thos. Hartley

Chapter One

August 4, 1778

The vast forest stretched across the ancient mountains, only broken by the mighty Susquehanna River winding its way through them. The thriving trees blanketing the face of the timeless land harbored and sheltered the life scrambling beneath them for eons. Eons that stretched into ages. Ages which had witnessed each of the lives with a patience born of the earth itself.

Of all whom lived before in the dark folds of the forest none seemed as resilient as people. They cut threads of trails through the tapestry of the endless forest. Their quaint hamlets and villages draped the river banks every now and then, slightly scaring the land, and the ages, forever.

Into this forest and ancient order of Native peoples others came from lands far across the seas. They blew as a new wind; a cutting wind which caused the Native peoples to fear it would forever change the nature of the land. These newcomers' hands turned in a different way. Their hearts felt in a different way. Their minds thought in a different way. Their passions led them in a different way.

The Native peoples tried to stand against the prevailing wind which bore the newcomers, but these newcomers burned with a fever few had ever witnessed. So they had given them battle; a terrible battle, which would have driven a lesser people of lesser passions away forever. The Battle of Wyoming.

But these newcomers, these Wyoming* settlers, let the fires born of their passions fuel every aspect of their lives. These passions led them back to the land. Their land, which the Native people and Tories had driven them from nary a month before. The passions born of the terrible Battle of Wyoming pulsated through both peoples' veins along with their deep love for the land.

This clash of passions between the Wyoming settlers and Indians along with their allies, the Tories {conservative Americans who did not rebel against their God-given sovereign}, had not ended with the Battle of Wyoming. Like its part in the larger Revolutionary War, it would never end until the heart of the last Wyoming man beat no longer, and his blood seeped into the ground which he so cherished.

Most of whom tried to stand against the Six Nations and their allies lay on the fields of Wyoming still to this day, left to their fate. This thought haunted each the men's minds tramping along the trail back to Wyoming, but onward they tramped. White knuckled fists clenched a varied assortment of firelocks in their ragged, but determined, column of men. Tri-cornered hats bobbed along with round hats, slouch hats, and mere handkerchiefs; their headgear as varied as the clothing upon their backs.

No noise sounded in the still air but the tired shuffle of their feet lest it betray their presence to their foe, who might be watching from behind any tree, bush, or large rock.

Every shadow received due attention from those on the flanks, for the memories of that cruel battle but a month ago still remained fresh, something they feared not even time would erase. Thus, every noise from the shadows triggered a new response, a new fear, only to be quelled by the flight of

**Wyoming at the time of the American Revolutionary War is considered to be the area along the Susquehanna River from Tioga Point (present Athens, Pa.), to present Nescopeck, Pa.*

some startled animal. Though tempted by the thought of their meager and stale rations to fell the many elk, turkey, squirrels, and deer, not a shot rang out from among them. Hunger, a burning sense, but nonetheless a sense of life, pulsed through their veins but their minds forbade such actions. They need not be told for the hundredth time by their colonel of the importance of reaching the valley as stealthily as possible. Once they gained their former home their colonel planned to announce their presence to the world. Tories beware! The Six Nations beware! Wyoming is back! But the threat of ambush remained too omnipresent to be treated without due regard. This lesson they all carried from that bloody field of death at Wyoming.

Familiar sights along the trail triggered visions of happier and more hopeful times, times now clouded by the memories of that awful retreat. But a few weeks ago some of these very men struggled along the trail to the sanctuary of the settlements along the Delaware with their terrified children and distraught wives in tow. Their visions fueled an unquenchable desire for revenge in their famished souls.

They had trod this ground in defeat. Now they trod it in defiance to reclaim their homes, their lives, their land, and their dignity. No one would pry their feet from the ground once they regained a foothold on it again; no one.

It is true the empty and hollow feeling of doubt haunted their minds from time to time, but they need only to glance at their fellows to quell it. The stern continence in each man's soul beamed through his eyes. Fear quailed against it. It reaffirmed the defiant spirit burning within each of the men. John Jenkins did look to Obadiah Gore marching beside him. The aged, but still keen eyes of Luke Swetland, did turn to his old friend Isaac Tripp. Moses Brown did look to his fellow veteran of many battle, Ira Stephens. Nathan

Denison did turn to Zebulon Butler.

Something within the looks reaffirmed the spirit which cursed through all of their veins. It, the spirit of the pioneer, failed description in the spoken word; it could only be felt by those of the same spirit. This spirit spat in the face of reality and allowed certain people to rise above seemingly insurmountable odds and emerge victorious. So strong did this spirit burn in this new people-these *Americans*-it seemed destine to enrich and inspire them until their hands stretched across the entire continent only to be checked by the south seas.

All upon the continent, even some fellow Americans, did not share this spirit. These others scorned and called the pioneers and their so-called spirit mere folly. These words, spoken by some even in their home state of Connecticut, also pulsated through their bodies from their tired feet to their aching heads. You have lost! Why play the senseless fool? Gather your losses and return home! Leave the forest to the savages! Have they not beaten you enough?

But these words, spoken around warm hearths in far away hamlets along the coast rang hollow to these men. Some spoke, others acted. Those whom only spoke rarely understood the doers, the ones whom not only spoke, but acted upon the words.

The Wyoming Valley, this beautiful and pristine place seemingly graced by the hand of God, must be reclaimed. It must be salvaged. Too much blood and too much life had been sacrificed for it to be disregarded. The land lay drenched not only with their sweat but quite literally their blood. Their life's blood. This made it unquestionably theirs. The promise of Wyoming far outweighed the horrors of war. A war which also threatened their critics by their safe and warm hearths. Better it be fought here, by men of such spirit, than by those whose comfortable lives absolved them of the sacrifices war demanded.

Their land-therefore their lives-lie in the hands of their enemies, the British Crown, the Six Nations, and the hated Tories. They must march to retrieve it and fight for it again if need be. Others, the talkers, need not understand it. They, too overcome with reason, would never understand anyway, but the doers, such as General Washington, understood and promised relief. In this man they found trust and faith. The rest of the nation may scorn them, but men cut from the same fabric understood. And for now they need be the only ones to understand.

The tired pace of the troops suddenly livened. Heads perked up from rising chests. Eyes scanned the burned remains before them. They all silently filed around the desolate farmstead on the trail ahead of them. Men spread out among the surrounding trees, firelocks at the ready to strike against any unwary foe. But to their dismay no Indians haunted the forest around the sight of the cruel act.

A lone horseman slowly trotted around the charred remains, his lower lip rising in disgust. His mount's feet trampled the litter of iron pots, bits of broken but once prized china, torn open featherbeds, and other implements of a once prosperous and promising life. He reined his mount to a stop beside the carcass of a rotted beef, the animal's legs jutting straight in the air from its half devoured chest. The rancid smell nearly gagged him. He looked to the trail of wolf tracks leading from the carcass to the dense woods beyond. A low grunt of disgust crept through his tightened jaw.

A lone wolf suddenly cried in the still air, seeming to answer his scoff but perhaps just venting its outrage at being interrupted in the middle of its feast.

Alert eyes darted in the direction of the sound,

gripping their rifles in their white-fisted knuckles. If the wolf, a warrior of opportunity, much like their adversaries, showed itself it would breathe its last. But the dark folds of the forest did not betray its presence.

Everyone stood, each looking in the direction of the eerie howl, wondering if it be an omen of what would be or not. Some muttered a prayer on a whisper. The horseman grunted a disapproval and reached for the pistol in his belt.

The lone howl erupted into a chorus of howls, seemingly instigated by the painted demons' of the forest Gods themselves. The horseman raised his pistol in the air and fired, his mount prancing anxiously about until his stern hand tightened its reins. The howls slowly faded with the retreating wolves. He smartly reined his horse about to face the wide-eyed men surrounding him.

He glanced about, gauging each of the men's continence by their eyes. He nodded, slowly placing the spent pistol back in his belt. "Men," he finally said, breaking the uneasy silence, "look about you! Need I remind you Bullock's here is a good nine miles from the valley proper! Look at the devastation! I hope it will only harden your resolve as it has mine!"

A few nods answered his words but no one spoke.

He pushed his hand down on the pommel of his saddle and turned his tall frame about in it. He looked at the charred remains, silently thankful no telltale human skeletons lay among the devastation. He wondered of his own home and turned about again.

"Lieutenant Jenkins!" he shouted. "Mr. Hollenback!"

Two men immediately stepped forward from the milling soldiers.

Dozens of eyes followed them.

"Yes sir, Colonel Butler," both said at once, snapping

to attention in front of him.

"Each of you are to assemble ten men of choice and reconnoiter the valley, you Jenkins, from the north, and you Hollenback, from the south." He stopped and gazed over his shoulder at the remains of the farmstead again. "If you encounter any of the devils do what you may," he added. "The rest of us shall make our way to the river common and meet you there. Now be about ye work, the day grows long."

Both men momentarily raised their right hands to the brims of their hats before smartly turning to face the eager faces already pleading to be included in their number. With nods and pointing fingers the two quickly filled their ranks. Both hastily formed their chosen men in line and checked their accoutrements and weapons. In another moment they scrambled away from the farmstead, one party in one direction, the other in the opposite direction. Dispirited and soulful eyes watched their departure.

"Do not worry," Butler admonished them. "There shall be sport for ye all before this matter is settled, that I grant ye! Now prepare to resume the march! This is but the first step. But with each step beware, watch the shadows for the painted devils, for our enemies may lurk all around us, for the sun has not set on their empire yet. The *curse of the tomahawk* prevails, I fear, so look sharp! With providence's help we may prevail and strike their hearts a fatal blow, thus putting an end to it all, for I fear it may be the only way to a true and lasting peace! So onward, for our wives, our children, our homes, and our dignity!"

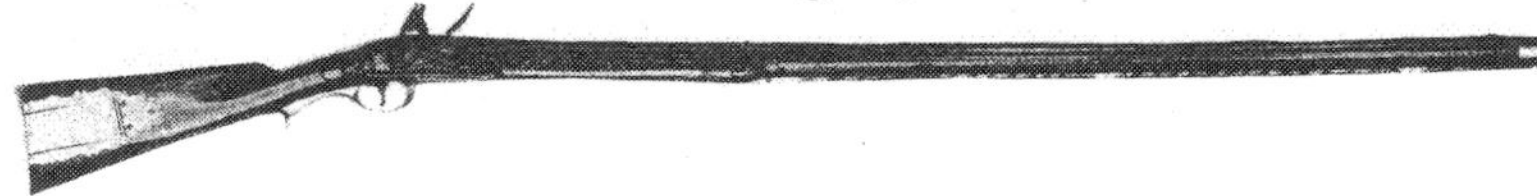

Chapter Two

Matthias Hollenback locked his eyes on the top of the mountain to his front and trotted with all his might toward it. Knowing Colonel Butler and the rest of the men to be starting directly behind him, he wished to clear their van with all due haste. He tasted the air and with darting eyes scanned all around him. No doubt plagued his mind with concern for the men following, for he knew each, and trusted their keen eyes.

They trotted with nary a word passing between them. Each man knew of the hunt and shared his fellow's ardor for it. They received the honor of being the first patriots to step upon Wyoming soil again.

Woe to the enemy they encountered, regardless of their number.

Each silently followed Hollenback's lead, though a Pennamite by birth, a Yankee heart beat in his chest. A trader and quite an ambitious soul, his energies and undying faith in Wyoming endeared him to everyone. The blood spot on the shoulder of his shirt from a wound not completely healed from the late battle, aggravated to bleed again by his spirited trek to regain Wyoming only endeared him more to the men following him.

Finally gaining the top of the mountain he stopped. All gathered around him and gazed down at the green valley below. The Susquehanna glistened in the sun, likening it to a silver thread winding through the green tapestry of God's earth. Crests of white water surged against its silver face from the rapids known as Nanticoke Falls below them. An eagle glided on the gentle breezes along the mountain opposite them. Beautiful, but their eyes did not seek out the beauty, but those whom trampled it.

Hollenback gripped his hat in his hand and wiped his brow. "None are about, as I see, but keep a sharp eye about just the same," he said. He lifted the pan of his rifle up to his front and checked it for powder. "Be sure that your flints are sharp and your firelocks are ready for sport!" he added. He pointed down the side of the mountain and to the small clearing at its foot. "We'll make our way down there and then turn north, if ye see any of the rats, let them have it!"

Spreading out in a wide line, each man a few arm lengths from the other, they descended into the valley. They moved silently, as always, and all jumped when the boom of a turkey taking to flight sounded in the air. A few angry curses followed the bird in its haste. Hollenback, forcing a swallow down his dry throat, motioned them to a stop beside a large boulder protruding from the mountainside. The clear ground around the rocks offered a slight reprieve from the forest and a vantage point from which to gaze upon their objective. He waved his men just to the edge of it, hoping their rough and dirty homespun clothes helped camouflage them from any wary eyes along the river.

"Cast your eyes about," he said, painfully aware of the

late hour. The sun already touched the top of the mountain behind them. The deep breaths and pants of his men added to his apprehension. The mountain proved steeper than he anticipated. Nonetheless, much more ground needed to be covered.

He muttered a curse under his breath for forgetting a spyglass in his haste. Looking to the sea of green blanketing the mountains it would have definitely proved very helpful. A particularly rapid series of pants turned his attention, as well as the others, to the older man in their rear. The man, having a good ten years of age over the rest of the party, now showed it. Purely exhausted, he leaned against a tree.

"Look smart, my dear man," Hollenback said.

The man bowed his head. "Spirit's willing," he said, panting, "but it plays hell on the body sometimes, is all." He looked around to see if anyone shared his humor. Stern eyes gazed back at him, all but Giles Slocum. He rubbed his hand on a bare spot on the trunk of a tree beside him. "Damn them porcupines," he said, "destroy many a good tree if left to it. Gnawing at this one I see. They'll gnaw and gnaw for months and next thing you know the tree ain't leafing no more 'cause it's dead. I durst say it's a fact, it is."

Hollenback raised an eyebrow to the man and shook his head. Some men would say anything in tense moments. Their chatter seemed to ease their nerves. He remembered hearing men blabbering away in the heat of the battle at Wyoming, loading, blabbering, and firing. But to him it made no difference, as long as they continued firing. He never took any stock in such, but knowing what Slocum had endured on the battlefield he let it pass.

Slocum paid no heed to their indifference. Being out here played on a man's soul. If a memory lightened the moment, so be it. "Damned porcupines," he continued, letting a smile grow on his face. "Never forget the night Grandpa Tripp come yelling out of the privy in the dead of winter." He let a laugh escape from his chest. "Got quilled he did, no lie, some of you might remember if you have a mind to. Grandpa Tripp yelled enough to wake up Ester clear up in Tioga, I grant you. Yelled like a stuck pig! Damn porcupines like the salt left by drippings and such around the hole, you know. Anyways, Grandpa howled all the more when old Hooker Smith yanked them quills. Weren't in his foot neither!"

Smiles cut through the stern looks about him. A few chuckles filled the air.

"Yes," Hollenback said, "there's a time and place for such stories, but now isn't one of them." He looked at the grins growing on the hard-faced pioneers. "Let us be about our business lest we get stuck!"

Slocum nodded his head with the others who appreciated his brand of humor and choked down his urge to laugh again. He lifted his rifle and moved away from the tree, giving the bare spot on the tree one more quick rub. "Damn them porcupines," he muttered to himself under his breath.

"A quill's nothing compared to a spear," Hollenback scolded him.

Slocum said no more, but took his place by the others scanning the river bottom below.

Hollenback's eyes seemed the keener. He looked about intensely, with no passing glances, but a careful yard by yard survey of the area. No shadow or bush escaped his eye. The potential danger of ambush demanded all his senses be sharp. He cursed himself once again for forgetting a spyglass. What of it? He countered the thought after another moment. So be it. All of them carry full powder horns or full cartridge boxes and plenty of lead. He, nor any of his men, will fall to the savage today. This time it's their turn.

Finally satisfied nothing occupied the valley below save a few wolves, deer, or elk, he motioned his men forward again. "We see nothing, but have ye firelocks at the ready nonetheless, who knows what lies in the shadows," he said. Another turkey snapped to the wing in their front. Rifles followed it in an instant. They just as quickly lowered with anxious eyes toward their captain.

"It's fine," he said, "I'm glad ye be so keen as to drop anything that wears a feather!" He noticed the shadows becoming deeper. The sun sank further behind the mountain. "Let us make for the river with all due haste for that is where we shall find some sport if there is any to be had." He glanced back to the few older men. The more eager eyes seemed to be the younger ones. "If ye be young and fleet of foot be at it, we shall follow."

That is all the word the younger men needed. They spilled down the mountainside in a rush against the setting sun. Twigs cracked and a few stumbled, but none stopped for a second. None stretched farther ahead than young Solomon Bennett. Becoming lost in the momentum of the race he burst into a clearing at the bottom of the mountain well ahead of his comrades. Thorns in his arms and legs burned for his attention. He lowered his rifle to tend to them when a slight movement in the corner of his eye caused him to instinctively raise it again.

His jaw dropped at the sight of three tall warriors of the forest. In another instant he lifted his rifle to his shoulder. Barely breathing, his hand cocked back the hammer of his rifle in the stunned faces of the warriors.

The warriors stared at the white apparition bearing down on them in a moment of stunned disbelief. From what magic did this white demon appear out of the thin air? They stood astounded, two froze in the motion of loading a freshly killed deer into a beached canoe while the third stood with a slight bundle in his hands. He looked down at the three rifles at his feet.

He reached down when suddenly a powerful blue and white puff of smoke exploded full into his face. A sudden and tremendous force threw him backwards against his stunned comrades. Red spurted from his upper chest and bathed the canoe. Twisting, he rolled in pure agony through the hands of his friends and into the swirling Susquehanna. The canoe followed him.

Whoops and yells mixed with angry curses echoed down the mountain. A mad rush descended the mountainside. A mad rush of Yankees. Crashing footsteps along with the curse of *Copperheads! Copperheads!* assaulted the air of the once peaceful forest. The fury rained down the mountain.

"I got 'em! I got 'em!" Bennett screamed back up the mountain. He stood wide-eyed while furiously trying to load his rifle. "Come quick! Come quick!"

More roars answered him.

The braves' eyes darted all around, to their rifles, to the canoe, and to their flailing comrade in the swirling water. The larger of the two let out his own wail and madly gestured to the canoe, breaking his fellow's gaze at the rifles. Reaching out with one of his huge hands he grabbed the canoe, all the while urging the other to follow his lead in his own tongue. In a fit of frustration the other brave yanked his tomahawk from his belt and flung it with all of his strength at the wide-eyed white demon.

The demon quickly ducked, watching the weapon fly harmlessly into the brush behind him. In one mad motion the white demon rammed the ball in his rifle home.

The braves, knowing but a few seconds separated them from another assault, wildly paddled the canoe across the river, flinging the deer into the swirling waters. The brave in the rear flung his paddle from one side of the canoe to the other, paddling for dear life itself. His larger partner struggled to hold onto the wounded man and fight with his free hand against the water. He finally let out a loud grunt and lifted the wounded man from the water, spilling him into the canoe. His hands quickly gripped a paddle.

A hail of lead whizzed through the air all around the canoe. Splinters flew from near misses striking its rail. Little gouts of water surrounded it. The braves bowed their heads and paddled, praying to reach the shore before one of the mad demons' shots buzzing through the air stung them.

Hollenback raced down the mountain, anxious that his order to advance pell-mell might not meet with disaster. What a fool! He thought to himself, going against your better judgment and all. He listened to the rifles bark below, trying to gauge the amount of men engaged by the sound. Finally reaching the foot of the mountain, he burst into the clearing, much relieved by the sight before him.

All of the men fired from any position, standing, propped against a tree to steady their aim, kneeling, or lying flat on the ground. Each hastily rammed a new ball home as quickly as possible and fired again. Smoke hung over the small clearing.

Hollenback let out a deep sigh of relief and spurted to the front of the men, peering through the smoke. Two braves madly dragged a third up from the far shore, struggling to escape the deadly hail of lead. He instinctively raised his rifle and fired. Peering through the smoke he witnessed the warriors disappearing into the ever present folds of the forest. He knew nothing could find them now.

"That's it boys!" he yelled. "They're gone, once they gain the sugarbush you'll never find them!"

"To hell with that!" one of them yelled, firing blindly into the trees on the opposite shore.

"That's enough!" Hollenback scolded him. "Have ye enough powder and lead in your pouch to fight the entire Six Nations?"

"No, but I'll damn sure put a hurting on the red-skinned devils I sees!" the man countered.

"You may play easy with your life on your own but not while ye are under my command!" Hollenback said. He stared deathly at the man, leaving no doubt of his sincerity.

The man lowered his rifle and spat on the ground. "Rifle's about fowled anyway," he said, lowering the weapon. "Damn Continental powder anyways! Colonel Stroud kept all the damn good powder for his own use at Fort Penn anyhow! He didn't want to waste none on some damn fool Yankees braving the forest as to get back their land. Stroud don't care no how! Ain't his land! Damn Pennamite rascal!"

"They must've come out for their canoe just as we started down from the rocks," a man reported, lifting some broken branches up from the shore. "Had it hid under these. Man, they are cunning devils, never know when they'll pop up or where they'll be at."

Hollenback nodded. He hoped the man's appraisal of their enemy struck home with his men, for every word rang true. He lightened the mood with a smile to young Bennett. "Ye did well, is it ye that hit the one?"

"Yes sir," Bennett said. With beaming eyes he nodded his head, giving a quick acknowledgement of the praising eyes around him.

Another man raised one of the Indians' abandoned rifles up in his hands. "These ain't no trade rifles," he said.

"They're good ones, made proper and with care, look at the furniture about them."

All gathered around, each thinking, but not saying, what they feared. No doubt the weapons came from the battlefield at Wyoming.

"Any of ye recognize them," Hollenback asked.

Shaking heads answered him.

"Looks as if your prize will float away, boy," a grizzled looking buckskin-clad man said, pointing his rifle barrel across the river. The canoe waggled just on the edge of the far shore. The current played at it, threatening to carry it away any second.

Bennett looked over at the finely made birch bark canoe and groaned. His imagination ran wild visioning the treasure within it. He looked over to Hollenback in anticipation.

"Damn," Hollenback said. "I wouldn't boy, but hell, ye have a right to it. It's up to ye."

"Sweet damn!" Bennett said, hastily stripping off his shoes and shirt. "Can't let it pass."

Everyone followed him to the edge of the shore. He stripped off his buckskin trousers and waded out into the water.

"Here boy!" one of them called to him, reaching out with a knife. "Put this between your teeth, just in case."

Bennett eagerly grabbed it and bit down onto it. Turning, he dove into the water, swimming with all his might against the current.

"Everyone load and stand ready," Hollenback ordered the rest of the men. "If anything so much as a damn chipmunk shows itself over there blister it!"

All watched with their weapons raised. Soon the boy lifted himself up to the edge of the canoe and plopped down into it. The motion caused it to finally release its precarious hold on the shoreline and drift into the swift current toward Nanticoke Falls.

Bennett quickly lifted a paddle and plunged it into the water. In no time a sea of congratulating hands welcomed him back on the riverbank. He had won the first victory back at Wyoming and he had the prize to prove it. All seemed well and right for a fleeting moment, but each man took little stock in the feeling. As Colonel Butler said, this is just the first step.

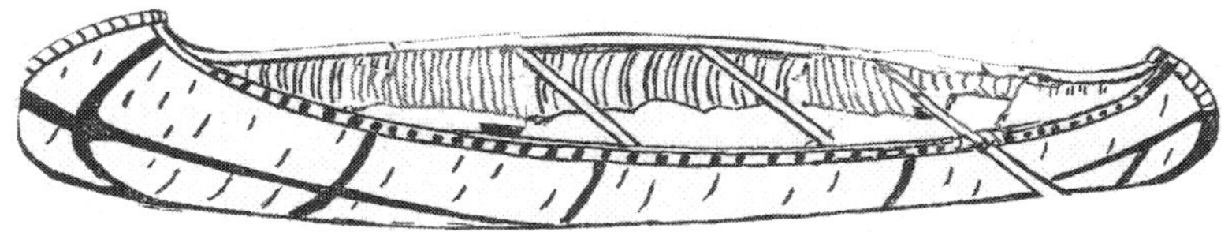

Chapter Three

Men trailed into the river common at Wilkes-Barre. Their anxious eyes soon turned to dismay at the sight before them. Nothing stood all around but the charred remains of many a home save the lone cabin they now naturally gathered around. Stunned men fell into a daze, realizing the full brunt of their enemy's power and awful resolve. Some milled about aimlessly, trailing their rifles in limp hands. They stared at places once alive in their hearts. Homes that sheltered and birthed many a child within their walls. The community which once harbored all of their hopes and dreams of the future lie devastated before them. It seemed all their dreams lie in the ashes. The flames had destroyed more than mere dwellings. They had destroyed lives.

Zebulon Butler rode his horse slowly around the streets. His mind also raced with memories. He paled by a huge elm tree by which many of his family, friends, and acquaintances, had spent many a summer day beneath its shade, talking and sharing hopes and promises of a better tomorrow. Tomorrow, yes, always tomorrow. They had built a haven before in this wilderness; they could build it again! The grain still stood high in many of the fields, no doubt left by the enemy for their own future use. It would soon ripen and with it the enemy might return. No! Too many relied on the grain; among them those whom planted it in the first place. Without it many faced poverty and destitution.

He suddenly perked up in his saddle and trotted over to the cabin. Lifting his hand, he pushed against the charred timbers of one of its corners. It creaked but still stood firm. The noise brought a few of the curious but still sullen men to him. "See," he said to them, slapping his hand smartly on his thigh, "it's charred, but at its heart it's still solid! Not unlike us! It is not much, I grant ye, but it is something."

The men looked down and slowly walked back toward the front of the cabin. A few others struck flint to start a fire in a pit by it. They bent down and blew on the tinder, ever mindful of the growing shadows and ignoring their prancing colonel.

Butler let out a huff and approached his old friend Denison, whom stood leaning sorrowfully against a tree, staring at the men attempting to start the fire. He had never seen the great-hearted man so crestfallen. "Come now Nathan," he said, "the fields are still full, the grain, the harvest, don't forget it. It will bring a new beginning from these ashes. Is that not why we braved the forsaken wilderness to return? We cannot leave it to the Tories and Indians! We cannot leave it to the damn Pennamites!"

"Ashes," Denison muttered through his hand over his mouth, "all is ashes and forsaken."

Butler leaned down and looked closely into his eyes. Could this be the staunch defender of the valley? If his spirit lay devastated what of the men? He must do something before the grief disabled all the men and with it all hope. "Get a hold of yourself, dear friend, we are all alone out here. We must stand strong as an example or all will be lost," he said just loud enough for his friend to hear.

Blank and empty eyes stared back at him through long strands of sweat drenched locks of hair underneath a frayed and worn slouch hat. “But all is lost,” Denison said, neglecting to brush the hair before his eyes out of his sight. “We have barely enough provisions to return to Fort Penn. It was all I could do to procure the arms this rabble has, many of them I durst wonder will shoot straight at that. I had to fight Stroud hand and foot for every piece! These men are brave, but not fools. Perhaps it is all folly. What are we to do if Indian Butler returns with but a third of his number?”

“We’ll stand and fight and have that rascal’s hair before all is done!” Butler said.

“Bold words,” Denison said, “I have heard them before, from Lazarus Stewart’s lips, no less.”

Butler’s eyes widened at the mention of the brash captain whom had insisted they march out and meet the enemy in the battle while he and Denison cautioned against it, preferring to wait for reinforcements. He was a brave man and had fallen on the field of battle; that honor should never be taken away from any Wyoming settler’s memory, but to insinuate he himself had acted as brashly cut deeply into his sense of pride.

“I shall never speak ill of any of those dead upon that field, for all died with honor,” he said. “But we cannot just lay down and die. It shames us as well as their memory.”

“I arrested him and would have tried him if you would not have intervened when you did,” Denison said. “You of all people, the irony of it all.”

“I would not have marched out as I did but for his influence, it’s true,” Butler said, “but no one is to blame but I. Not ye or anyone. I would have fought properly and waited for Clingman, Franklin, and Spalding, and sent the militia out to draw the rats into the awaiting regulars, but that is that. Nothing can be done about that now and as I said I honor those brave souls, now and forever. That is all I shall ever say of the matter." He looked up to the darkening sky and let out a long sigh. " Now my man, it is for us whom live to honor their wishes and reclaim what they have given all for, for their children, wives, and yes, for us, all of us."

The stirring words had little affect. Denison rubbed his face and collapsed down against the tree. "What are words in the face of this?" he asked.

Butler looked anxiously around at the others. If he lost Denison, he lost all. He clenched his fingers down tightly on his saddle horn, searching his mind for something to reinvigorate his ragged ranks. His frustration turned to anger, but he swallowed hard against it. His eyes fell to his ragged clothes. Thorns and scrub brush had ripped his trousers, shirt, and fine waistcoat to shreds. His body began to burn with scratches, bruises, and aches. He let out a gasp and shook his head, he himself surrendering to the feeling of despair sweeping over his fellows. His head fell to his chest, letting his hat fall to the ground. He looked at it but presently felt sapped of all energy to dismount and pick it up.

Suddenly a roar erupted from the river's edge. Men perked up from the fire and looked toward the disturbance, ready to meet the new threat. They all formed a hasty line and leveled their firelocks toward the riverbank.

"Hold on up there!" a voice shouted. "It is I, Mathias Hollenback! And we have returned with a right smart prize, too!"

The rifles dropped. The excited men of Hollenback's party rallied amongst their fellows, so alive and full of spirit they did not seem to notice the crestfallen faces greeting them. They rambled up to the fire and plopped down several turkeys, all wearing wide eyes and smiles from ear to ear. In no time the jubilant men spread their feelings through the others. Congratulatory remarks to Bennett filled the air.

Butler and Denison watched from the tree, both feeling a little shame, but nonetheless more than when a bright eyed John Jenkins poured into the party with his men. He and Hollenback met and grabbed each other's arms up to the elbow, profusely shaking them. Smiles beamed across their faces.

"There is the answer," Denison said, slowly rising and walking to the group. He looked back over his shoulder and waved to Butler behind him. "That is the spirit of Wyoming! Let us never lose it again, dear friend!"

Butler nodded, letting a wide grin grow across his face. He kicked his heals into his mount's flanks and spiritedly rode to the cabin. "Well now, men," he said, "let's get to it!" He flung one leg over the saddle, forgetting all about his aches and jumping down from the saddle. Slapping his mount on the rump and he sent it toward the good English grass on the green while he rolled up his tattered sleeves. He marched right through the men and entered the cabin, stopping only to snatch a pine knot from the fire. He shone it all around the interior of the cabin and jammed it into a space in the chinking in the walls.

"Small, but it'll do for a start," he said. He grabbed at one of the charred logs and pulled it down. "This'll need replacing straight away, but the rest seem sturdy enough. Some of ye get to work on that while the rest get to felling trees for a good stockade to greet Indian Butler if he shall be foolhardy enough to return. That is," he said, looking to the two young subalterns, "unless you two can suggest a better place to stockade."

"No," both of them said, "all is razed or burnt that we have encountered."

"So be it," Denison said, grabbing an axe and heading for the tree line. "We'll make do for now, but I grant ye we shall soon erect a new fort that shall never fall against those painted rats again!"

A chorus of newly invigorated huzzas rang out.

Wyoming lived once again this night. The spirit pounding through the men's veins gave promise it would never fall again.

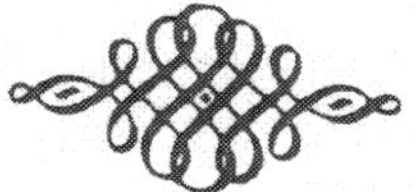

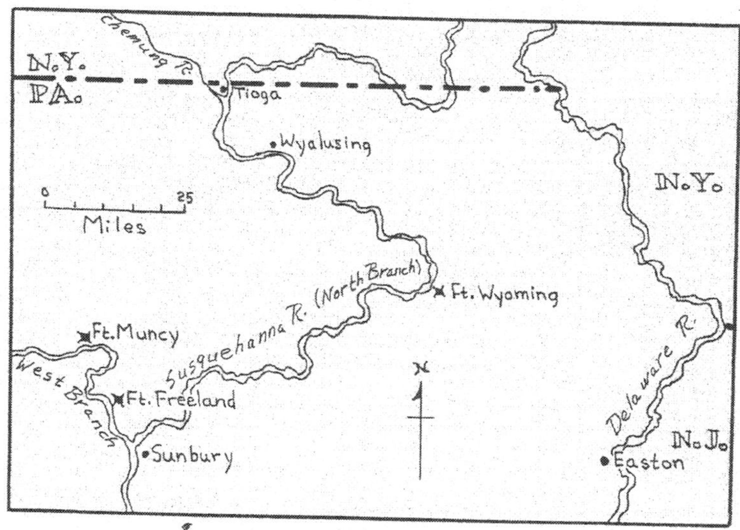

Chapter Four

Zebulon Butler darted out of the half-finished stockade, mounting his readily saddled horse. His spine tingled with the sound of the lively shots ringing from the north. He looked back and waved at the men who hastily dropped their axes and grabbed their cartridge boxes, shot bags, powder horns, possible bags, and firelocks. With a wave forward of his hand they ran up the road, each quickly checking their weapons while they trotted, knowing they must be ready to fire in an instant.

To their relief the shots lessened the closer they approached to the disturbance. Butler thought of the earlier alarm. Though less lively than the sound of this one it had chased off quite a few feathered and painted heads in the tree line. But nonetheless the threat seemed ever growing. No doubt they had returned in larger numbers.

He rode down to the huddled group of men in a small clearing, intensely eyeing the tree line which commanded their attention. He reined his mount to a stop, pulling a pistol from his belt. "Where are they?" he shouted to the men.

"They've scattered again," Robert Carr answered, lowering a spyglass from his eye. "Don't know their number but they fired a volley and scampered off!" He nodded his head toward the man next to him.

The man looked up at Butler, fingering a fresh hole in his hunting shirt. "They nearly got me," the man said, "but I've still got my hair, thank God!"

Butler nodded, turning to acknowledge the first man from the fort to come rushing up to them. "Slow down,

Lord," he said, "they've scattered again."

Lord Butler's eyes beamed at the sight of his father tall in the saddle. He let his pride swell across his face, regardless of the others. "Yes, Father," the teenager said, slightly relieved, but on the other hand anxious for the opportunity to prove himself as brave as the fine figure of his father. He took a few steps to the front of the men, gripping his rifle tightly in his hands. He eyed the entire tree line and looked back up to his father. He nodded his head to the others who formed around him.

"Yes, scout the wood," Butler said, looking up to the setting sun, "but do not go far, all must retire to the fort when the sun sets, to be out here unprotected is the truest folly and I will have none of it." His words cut off the protests from the men. He wished all saw the importance of building a haven before trying to round up the stray cattle and livestock milling about the forest. But these men would not be ordered, he well knew, they must be lead. Though the nightmare of the late Battle of Wyoming haunted him, to his mind brought about by the adherence to the New England ideal of democracy, he left well enough alone.

He cast a sour eye to Captain William Hooker Smith, commander of the remnants of the devastated Twenty Fourth Connecticut Militia Regiment, who came rushing up, panting and huffing and trailing his musket behind him.

"They've gone," Carr reported to his portly commander.

"Yes," Smith said, "I see, see that all foraging parties return to the camp soon, the day grows long." He glanced up at Butler, knowing he had precluded the headstrong colonel's orders.

"Very well," Butler said, turning his attention to the regulars, whom he did command, "Captain Spalding have your men, except those on scout, return and continue their work, it is of utmost importance that the stockade be finished with all due haste! The growing frequency of the enemy precludes the fact. I only wish others gained the same insight."

Hooker Smith rubbed his sweating brow. What did he want him to do? After all, everything these men owned in the world sat in these ashes. Who could stop them, or blame them, for trying to salvage all they could, anyhow? "Yes," he said, "and all those who can should assist Captain Spalding's men, for as the good colonel says, it is of great importance."

Butler gave Smith a slight bow of his head, knowing his affirmation to be the best he could offer at the moment. They all turned and trod back to the camp, keeping a close eye on the bushes and tree lines along the road. Distant thunder clouds boomed in the distance. Forks of lightning flashed in the growing darkness. With each closing boom the colonel's words echoed in the militiamen's minds.

Butler noticed the affirming looks cast at him from the ranks and gazed back at the angry flashes of light in the dusk. "Thank you providence," he muttered under his breath. If his words proved inefficient, he knew nature's warning rang loudly in the men's hearts and souls.

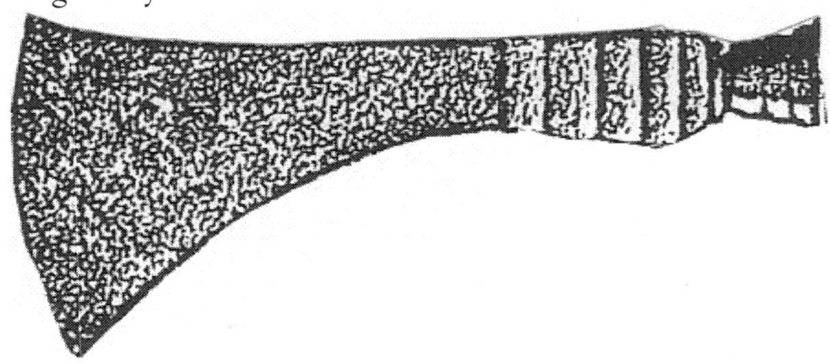

Chapter Five

Colonel Butler leaned back in his hastily repaired chair. It creaked and he immediately leaned forward again, taking heed of its warning. His eyes beamed in the flicker of light from the pine knot jammed in the chinking between the logs of the cabin's walls. He gazed down at the paper in front of him, listening to the sound of the soldiers working on the stockade by firelight just outside the cabin. A last roar of distant thunder from a fast moving storm rolled through the air, making him pause and wonder of providence. He bowed his head, mouthed a quick prayer and opened his eyes to the paper.

Picking up his quill, he slowly dipped it into an ink well of soft maple bark ink and began writing:

"Camp Westmoreland, August 5, 1778
To the most honorable Colonel Hartley,
Fort Augusta, Sunbury,

I arrived at this place yesterday with about sixty Continental troops and about forty militia. We discovered two small parties of Indians yesterday, and fired at them, and discovered two other parties this day. What numbers there is about is uncertain. If your honor should think it consistent to have some part of the troops under your command advance as far up the river as this place, or as far as you should think proper, I think it will be a means of keeping the savages from murdering and robbing the inhabitants of these frontiers.

Colonel Butler,
commanding, Camp Westmoreland"

He put down the quill and quickly folded the paper. Hastily sealing it the best he could, he called over his shoulder for Captain Carr.

The half-opened door of the cabin creaked fully open. Carr shuffled through it, removing his hat.

"As you and Mr. Goss have so graciously volunteered to run dispatches between I and Colonel Hartley, here is the first," he said, handing him the letter.

Carr immediately grabbed it and carefully placed it in the haversack slung over his shoulder.

"Be ever mindful of your surroundings," Butler said, "you know of these cunning savages and their Tory brethren. Being of the sea as ye once were, I have no doubt of your judgment and skill of navigating any storm, but this storm is unforgiving. These dispatches must not fall under the enemy's eyes, nor you, my good man, nor Goss, so be most careful but act with all due haste."

"Yes sir," Carr said, slightly bowing his head. "We shall depart directly."

"I have told Captain Spalding to issue you each a brace of pistols as well as the best rifles we have," Butler said. "See him before you depart."

Carr nodded and disappeared into the shadows beyond the door. It crept closed after him.

Butler rose from his chair and paced about, pondering their situation, and wondering if he had not just sent two fine men to their deaths. Visions of the late battle flashed through his mind, causing him to clasp his hands tightly behind his back and bow his head. He closed his eyes tightly against the thoughts and many faces flashing through his mind's eye. Faces he would never see again. Faces he had commanded. "No, my children!, No!" he blurted out in a moment of reflection and agony. For one awful heartbeat he rode along the line of battle again, beseeching his men to stand fast against the terrible onslaught. "Just hold fast for a few more volleys and they shall break!" He had no doubt, now, nor then, of his words. Oh, cruel hand of fate, why must such good men suffer and die to establish providence's hand in this unforgiving wilderness? Why? Why? He found himself speaking aloud in his anguish and quickly choked down the words lest someone should hear.

The door slid open, exposing his wide-eyed son, Lord. He looked around for a quick moment, searching for the specters to whom his father spoke, but seeing no one, he reckoned they lay in his father's mind. Ghosts dwelt in the soul as well as the mind.

"I have sent Captain Carr and Goss to Fort Augusta," Butler said, noticing his son's stare out of the corner of his eye. "Command does weigh heavily upon a man's soul, son, oh, what General Washington must endure in his beleaguered mind! You must remember to always be on the guard against such feelings, and not dwell on them too long, for they shall carry you down, son."

"Yes, Father," Lord said. He slowly sat the trencher he held down on the table. It overflowed with beef, mutton, corn, and carrots, all fresh and colorful. "You must eat, as everyone else has. Food is aplenty again, what with the rounding up of strays and all. We were right to return. The fields are full and it shall be a fine harvest, thanks to the enemy's oversight. And do not worry of Carr and Goss. I myself made sure they left armed to the teeth, woe be the savages they encounter, if any. My scout alone brought in five sheep and two bullocks!"

Butler ran his hand through his hair, suddenly embarrassed. A commander must not reflect too much on the past, but must learn from its mistakes and take strength from its triumph, he thought to himself.

He sat down and dug into the bounty, hoping the feast to relieve some of his angst. "Hartley's entire regiment has been ordered up here, you know," he said through heaping mouthfuls, suddenly realizing how famished he actually felt. "Brodhead's already about the West Branch. Spirit, my boy, that is what we all possess, despite our little differences. We must not look with such suspicion on the West Branch settlements, despite their destruction of the Charleston and Judea settlements, and the fact they are mostly from the Jerseys and Pennsylvania. We all have a greater enemy at the moment and he must be overcome if we are to have any-thing. I am sure they share the same sentiment, especially men of such caliber as Hartley." He took a long drink of rum from a wooden noggin. "Ah, we must start a distillery as soon possible after the fort, for a man must have drink!"

"We have fully three hogsheads full," Lord said. "For we must not thirst."

The door creaked again, revealing a much improved Nathan Denison. He strode across the room, holding his own trencher full of meat and corn. "The corn is a bit green, but good, by jingo!" he said, plopping down on a blanket by the hearth. He also took a great gulp from a noggin. "I think we shall be fine, Zebulon, the longer we stay, the better things are looking."

"Huzza to that, Nathan," Butler said, raising his noggin in toast, "huzza to that!" Silently he thought to himself of the small parties of militiamen absenting themselves from the work of raising the fort on their own whim. He also reflected on the complaints of a few opportunistic individuals plundering what little property which remained after the late battle. He knew all weighed heavily on maintaining this post;

until the harvest at least. Things must change in order to protect their prosperity. Children's bellies depended upon it. Widows needed it. Future generations needed it.

No, things needed changing, and let those who opposed good order be damned. The cries of the dead and the living beseeched him and he heard them loudly in his mind. He knew all men of good sense would follow his lead. He only hoped the actions he now decided upon would not drive a wedge through the independent spirit he also cherished. He took another long drink and swallowed hard against his new thought, knowing to survive they needed discipline. He prayed it would only strengthen their resolve rather than diluting it.

Chapter Six

Captain Spalding woke with a jolt just before dawn. His mind flashed with the thoughts that had burdened him all night. It made for a restless sleep at best. Sweat already dripped from his brow. The humid air seemed stagnant and he looked around at the restless men lying all about him. They lay in every conceivable position in the crowded stockade, some on blankets, others on deerskins, or on furs, but most on the bare and hard mother earth.

He stretched and rose next to the wall, gazing out through a loophole in it. Nothing stirred outside the walls. He wiped the sleep from his eyes and stumbled over to the entrance of the stockade with its half-finished gate leaning next to it. The lone sentry perked up and raised his rifle in salute.

"No need for such, Stephens," he said, putting his hand on the man's shoulder, "too early in the morning."

"Fine sir," Stephens said over the echo of multiple snores. A few lip smacks and snorts filled the air, many with a disgusting swallowing sound afterwards.

"They sleep hard," Spalding said, "as they live." He scratched his head, looking toward the embers of the nearest fire pit. He slung his haversack around to his front and pulled a noggin from it. "Is there any coffee in that pot?" he asked Stephens.

"Should be, but it's been sitting all night," he said. "Do you want me to make it fresh?"

"No, my man, you are fine." For the first time he noticed Stephens' swelled lip. His mind flashed with the altercation between he and Brown last night.

Stephens noticed his stare. "Yes," he said, "but you should see Moses' eye!" He turned and faced the gate again, looking to the green beyond it and to the trees. "But at the most, I can't blame him. A good half dozen or so left the fort last night, playing what mischief who is to know?" He bowed his head, feeling he may be speaking out of line, but someone had to say something. "Some returned neglecting my challenge and mocking my demand for the parole. It is hell, especially for someone like Moses who is denied to even look about his cabin while others range freely." He shook his head. "But his curses, and threats to leave the ranks as soon as his enlistment expires in but a few weeks, played heavily on us all. So much so I couldn't contain my rage."

Spalding sat silently, letting Stephens ease his conscience through his words. It did upset him, though, seeing such close friends who had endured so much in the past two years without a word of discouragement between them come to blows. Tensions did run high here at Wyoming. The fact kept him restless all night.

"Still," Stephens said, turning to look at the captain, "it was just a soldier's fight. I should hope no charges shall be pending, what with all we've been through. It was hard on Moses to leave his wife and two infant sons back at Fort Penn after what they had endured in Forty Fort in the late battle. There is much charity in Fort Penn for them, but who is to say how long that may last. It plays heavily upon his nerves."

Spalding nodded at Stephen's defense of his friend even after the harsh words spoken between them last night, not to mention the blows. Their friendship, forged from Millstone, New Jersey, to Valley Forge and beyond could never be lessened by mere harsh words. He found strength in their brotherhood.

"It is not as either of us are *fist bullies,"* Stephens added. "You of all people should know that, for we have both served you faithfully through this whole terrible tragedy, this Revolutionary War."

Spalding's eyes perked up at the mention of the new word for the war. He had heard a few say it before and he liked the ring of it, for it sounded true. He also suppressed a smile at the thought of the small-framed man considering himself a bully of all things. He made up his mind instantly, answering his conscience that had plagued him all night. "Yes, I know my good man, and all both of you have contributed should not be forgotten, by this, or future generations," he said. He shrugged his shoulders. "If Moses deems it necessary to leave the ranks at the expiration of enlistment, so be it. He, as well as you, have earned it."

"No sir," Stephens said, "but my family is safe in Connecticut. I shall remain where my duty calls and see this thing out, but if I were Mose," he added, "I might see things differently." A loud crashing sound turned his attention to the gate. He lifted his rifle and gazed out into the early morning light only to lower his weapon at the sound of distant laughter and whoops of triumph, in English-Yankee English.

He shook his head. "Something must be done, sir, with all due respect."

"I know," Spalding said. He sat down the tin pail of coffee and rose from the fireside, brushing back his hair with his hands and tying it with a leather strip. His eyes rolled in deep thought and he marched toward the cabin door, pushing it aside and walking into it unannounced.

"Captain Spalding," Butler said, slowly rising from the fireside. He gazed back down at the flames and turned to the captain again. He rubbed his freshly shaven face and straighten his tattered clothes. He looked over at Denison, who also sat next to the fire. “We were just about to call you,” he said, “glad to see you up and about after all of your’s and your men’s efforts yesterday. Smashing job, by the way, after this day the fortifications should be complete, then we shall see about a larger, more formidable fort.”

“Yes sir,” Spalding said, “but as for morale and the general well-being of the whole settlement, something must be done. We must have order to rebuild our homes, our communities. It must be so if we are to entice any of the others into returning!”

“Yes, yes, my dear man,” Butler said, “do not get yourself into a tizzy.”

Spalding rolled his eyes and let out a gasp full of frustration. Denison just watched him, taking a long inhale from the clay pipe between his teeth. He smiled and let out a long trail of smoke. Butler strode over to an improvised desk and nonchalantly picked up a lone paper. He whipped it sharply in the air and handed it to the upset captain.

Spalding held it up to a small window and read it. He soon nodded his head in affirmation. “It is just,” he said, handing the paper back to Butler. “Something had to be done, I too, see no other way.”

“Oh, keep it fine sir,” Denison said. “We talked half the night, we did, and finally came to the same conclusion.”

Spalding shrugged his shoulders and looked at the paper again.

“You are to address the men with this new decree,” Butler said. “We must have them assembled at once.” He rolled his eyes at an upsetting thought. “Have you seen Captain Smith?”

“No sir, barely anyone is astir after last night.”

"Well we shall see to that, let them have this for breakfast!" With that remark Butler carefully placed his hat on his head and led the others through the door. Few eyes greeted them in the early morning light, save Stephens at the gate, smiling on being relieved from guard duty, and a few others walking toward the gate with a pick and shovel.

"Here, Captain Smith!" Butler called to them, causing them all to stop and curiously turn about to face him.

"We," Smith said, "are about something which shall prove a pleasant surprise, fine sir."

"Yes, well, about that, we all have a few surprises this morn," Butler said. "Beat the drum and assemble your men. Are they all about?"

Smith cocked an eyebrow and slowly gazed about the stockade. He raised his lower lip. "Most, I suppose," he said. "We're out to dig up the four pounder! Wrapped it tight and buried it at the time of the battle lest the enemy capture it too. I know just the spot!"

Another officer, listening but a short distance away, darted toward them. He curiously rubbed his right hand. "What? The cannon? I wanted that damn thing brought to Forty Fort in the late battle and you buried it?" he asked, shaking his head.

"Now Jenkins," Butler said, "it was probably best at the time. We had no ball for it, anyhow, and no carriage."

"Best for whom?" Jenkins asked. "Just the report of the damn thing would have spooked many of them. They call it thunder death! It was a damn fool thing to do, is all. Could have loaded it with stone, lead balls, or such!"

"Yes, but what is past is past," Butler said. "We can only learn from the past. Is not that right, Captain Smith?"

"Yes, I suppose," Smith said, looking wide-eyed at Jenkins storming away from them. No one dare argue with the man on his knowledge of the Indians, for he knew them better than anyone after being their captive for months.

"Yes, now," Butler said, "about your men."

A sharp slapping sound cast their attention toward the gate. Stephens sharply presented his arms and stared eagerly at the colonel.

"Yes, my man, have you something to say?" Butler asked. "Have not you been relieved?"

"Yes, sir," Stephens said, "But begging your pardon, sir." He looked anxiously to Captain Spalding.

"Go ahead, Stephens," Spalding said with a nod to Colonel Butler.

"The others, of the militia, sir, they range freely with no regard for proper order and such," Stephens reported, adverting his eyes from Smith's sour gaze. "But all that have been about in the night have returned sir," he added, "for the moment at least."

"Yes, well we shall soon see about that, we shall," Butler answered. He nodded to the drummer.

The drum immediately beat a lively call to assemble. Men rose, some grumbling, some much less enthusiastically than others, but soon they all stood in a meandering line in the cramped stockade.

Butler strode in front of them, his hands clasp tightly behind him, looking all the part the regal commander. He eyed each man. Some shook their heads while others just ignored him.

"What are ye about?" a voice filtered from the ranks behind him, "ye are no Washington."

He turned and glared back in the direction of the insult, his eyes blazing with anger. "Officers!" he shouted, "see to your men, look smart! We, my fine lads, are no longer a rabble! And damn it things are going to change!

Attention to orders!" He marched over to Captain Spalding, waving at him to read the letter aloud.

Spalding cleared his throat and waited for the grumbles to die.

Butler paced behind him, fit to be tied.

Spalding lifted the paper and began speaking:

"Detachment Orders, Camp Westmoreland, August 7, 1778

"Our present situation appears rather dangerous and alarming, and as our whole interest and the little remaining prospect of our crops depends on our maintaining this Post and keeping possession of the country, therefore every person will consider himself under the strongest tie and obligation to do his utmost in the defense of the place against our common enemy. And as it is impossible that we can make ourselves formidable in any degree without submitting ourselves to good order and discipline, therefore the martial law is to be strictly adhered to, and obeyed as well by the militia as the Continental troops and all who join the detachment under Colonel Butler.

"The pernicious practice of strolling about in small parties, and absenting themselves without leave, is not only hurtful to good order but dangerous; therefore the Colonel forbids it in the most strongest manner. And because complaints have been exhibited that some evil persons have been plundering and making waste of what little private property has escaped the merciless hands of our common enemy, the Colonel forbids, in the most positive manner, any kind of plundering or making waste of property-as killing sheep, swine or poultry; or in any manner injuring the interests of any man- as removing hidden things out of their places; unless it be such as is taking damage, and then try to bring it into store, where it may be taken proper care of.

"For [the] future the guard is to be relieved at six o'clock in the morning, and the roll [is] to be called twice a day: morning and evening. It is expected that the officers will be particularly attentive

to see that the above order be complied with; and the non-commissioned officers required to enjoin it on the soldiers, and give early information of all breaches that come to their knowledge. And all who are found guilty of the breach of this order may expect to suffer the consequences of the martial law in their cases.

Officers of the day-this day, Lieutenant Gore; to-morrow, Lieutenant Pierce."

Spalding eased the letter down and stood at attention, suddenly regaining his military bearing. His scanning eyes noticed an abrupt change in the stance of the men. The days of lack discipline faded in each of the eyes staring back at the blistering eye of Butler. He meant every word of the order; that fact could not be mistaken.

Spalding stepped back and gave way against the wall of the cabin in the crowded stockade. Butler took a step forward, not muttering a word. For all he cared his order said it all. Now he would stand and give them a moment to digest it under his steely eye.

A cry, echoing through the woods to north, interrupted his stance. At first it faded only to return a moment latter from another direction, but closer. One after another the war cries sounded from every direction; but none at the same time, and only after the previous cry faded. The men stood firm, but each gazed out of the corner of his eye up to the lush and green mountains from which the cries sang their eerie chorus. Hard eyes melted with concern, but still they stood still under the menacing eye of their commander. No one would ever move again; that is without orders.

The sentry, the only man outside the gate, paced nervously about and raised his rifle. He pointed the barrel in the direction of one of the cries. The closer they sounded the more agitated he became, looking back into the stockade at his frozen comrades. None offered a word. None came to his aid.

A near cry sounded just to his left, over a slight knoll. He raised his rifle and fired, cursing the spine tingling noise. "Shut up you murdering savages!" he shouted at the top of his lungs. He looked back into the stockade. No one moved. "What has overcome everyone?" He wondered aloud. "The murdering devils are about! Can't you hear?!?"

"Relieve that man at once," Butler said, turning smartly and walking toward the cabin. "Smith, be about that cannon! And be damn quick about it!" he called over his shoulder before entering the cabin.

"They are just about their games," Spalding said, stepping to the front. "Just trying to spook us. Follow your orders and all shall be fine, now officers, take charge of your men."

Chapter Seven

"Paxtang, Pennsylvania, July 12, 1778
Supreme Executive Council of Pennsylvania,
Philadelphia

"I write you this letter with reluctance, as I am certain it must give pain to any man of sensibility. I left Sunbury, and almost my whole property, on Wednesday last, July 8. I never in my life saw such scenes of distress. The river and the roads leading down it were covered with men, women, and children flying for their lives-many without any property at all, and none who had not left the greatest part behind. In short, Northumberland County is broken up. Col. Samuel Hunter only remained, using his utmost endeavors to rally some of the inhabitants and to make a stand, however short, against the enemy. I left him with very few-he had not 100 men on whom he could depend. Wyoming is abandoned-scarce a single family remained between that place and Sunbury when I came away. The panic and spirit of flight has reached even to this place-many having moved even out of this township-and almost everyone is thinking of some place of greater security.

"For God's sake-for the sake of the country-let Colonel Hunter be reinforced at Sunbury. Send him but a single company if you cannot do more. Something in the way of charity ought to be done for the many miserable objects that crowd the banks of the river-especially those who fled from Wyoming. They are a people, you know, I did not used to love, but I now most sincerely pity their distress. The women and children, in general, are now removed out of Northumberland County, and I cannot but hope that the men will most cheerfully return with fresh troops that go up that way."

William Maclay"

Quite a letter indeed, the man sitting at the desk thought while watching the same Colonel Hunter mentioned in the lines stand solemnly and watch Colonel Brodhead and his regiment march out of the gates of Fort Augusta to continue their trek to Fort Pitt. He watched the other regal men standing by him. General De Haas stood stoically, his mind apparently on other matters; no doubt on the small parties of militia he had dispatched up the river to replace Brodhead's men. The taller, somewhat more dignified man next to him stood watching with a hard eye of concern. The hard-eyed man, General Potter, occasionally turned to either of the other officers to make some comment. His eyes gazed back to the man watching them through the window only once, then turned back to the troops at the gate. He pitied the man in the window.

Both of the generals' polite refusal to accept command and remain simply as private gentlemen echoed in his mind as the man turned from the widow and stared at the papers before him. On his shoulders, though a rank below both of them, fell the full weight of command. He sighed and fingered through the copies of many other letters from people beseeching the Continental Congress-or anyone-to act.

Well now they had acted. And here he sat, bewildered to say the least, finding none of the pages did justice to the true despair gripping the land. Now the weight of it all fell to him, being ordered personally by General Washington to protect five hundred miles of the frontier with but one regiment and promises of a thousand militiamen. He would not hold his breath in anticipation of the militia. That left he, a scattering of a few stout-hearted settlers, and his small two hundred man regiment. Impossible-but war played hell with the possible-and he intended to do his very best in spite of it all.

He stood and leaned against the window, gazing down at Maclay's letter and over the wall to the peek of Maclay's house but a few rods to the south. He rubbed his eyes with his free hand, eyes with a stern continence about them, as an old schoolmaster would have, but somehow warm, mysterious and deep, as like men of his caliber. His stout, yet slightly pudgy body barely filled the window. He looked as any farmer's son of Pennsylvania-not tall and commanding as George Washington, or bold and bright as General '*Mad*' Anthony Wayne-but sincere and stern. A man of the people as much as he appeared like them. But the deeper qualities of his nature shone through also, and men such as Washington and Wayne recognized a fellow of their like and called him friend. No small feat considering the standards of the two great generals. He would not let neither of them down while he still drew a breath.

He turned, biting down on his lip, and sat down at the desk. He hastily dipped a pen in ink and wrote a report to congress, confirming all the others had reported before him.

A slight knock at the door broke his concentration for a fleeting moment but he quickly regained his thoughts and grumbled 'enter' to the door.

A soldier smartly entered and stood near the door, waiting for the pen to stop its trek across the paper before speaking. "Colonel Hartley" he said, watching him fold and seal the paper with wax, "your mount awaits and the men are assembled to march."

"Very well," Hartley said, motioning to his blue regimental coat hanging by the door.

The soldier promptly grabbed and opened it.

Hartley slid his arms into it and placed his cocked hat onto his head. "Yes, Captain Walker, we have a lot to do yet,

I am afraid. We must reach Muncy and Wallis' with all due haste. We must strike at the heart of the enemy at that, also."

"Yes, sir," Walker said. The colonel's remark about having to strike at the enemy's heart echoed in his mind. Yes, the heart, he mused. He could not think of a better man to lead them than the man before him.

"But one must look before he is to leap," Hartley added with a nod of his head. "Now that Colonel Brodhead and his regiment have left the enemy may feel free to make his depredations against the settlements more freely. We must curtail his efforts on the very fringes of the frontier. Let Indian Butler show his face in these parts again and we shall show him what for, however slight our numbers, I tell you, my good man."

Walker bobbed his head in affirmation and followed the stout little man out the door. Something will be done now, he thought, noticing the gleam in the colonel's eyes. If anything, Washington and Congress had done one right thing in choosing this man to secure the frontier. In zeal, determination, and resolve few could call themselves his equal.

With men such as he, perhaps this nation will overcome the seemingly insurmountable odds and achieve victory. Something about these men shone through the dismal clouds of despair descending over the newly formed nation. Something beyond mere courage and zeal. Something that is partnered with all things born new to the world, and as all things new, be they ideas, or nations, it either possessed it or faded away.

The thing called spirit.

Chapter Eight

"Get after them! Get after them!" Colonel Hartley shouted to the men in advance of the column. Several fleet-footed men raced after the mad blur sprinting toward the tree line. Several reloaded on the run and fired at the painted devil but he disappeared into the trees, seeming to melt into the underbrush.

"Captain-Lieutenant Sweeney!" Hartley called over the heads of the men from atop his nervous mount. "Call them back, there's nothing but an ambuscade awaiting them in that underbrush."

Sweeny barked out the necessary order and waved back the disappointed squad of men. They turned about reluctantly, cursing their bayoneted muskets. Their fast-footed foe disappeared time and time again under the inaccurate fire of their muskets, almost taunting them with their easy escapes.

"Resume the march!" Hartley barked, seeming indifferent to their complaints.

"Their complaints are valid," General De Haas commented just loud enough for Hartley to hear. He edged his own mount closer and shook his head. "Brodhead had the same problem, and some of his men, as well as the militia, do have the rifle and tomahawk," he added.

"The way they dart away and disappear as a ghost into the forest is uncanny," Hartley said. He looked down at his horse. "Perhaps four legs and swan shot in every cartridge box would even the odds," he added.

De Haas grinned. He liked the idea. "Perhaps," he

said. Perhaps Congress has appointed the right man for the job, one who will adapt and make the best of the tools available to him without complaint, he thought to himself, impressed by Hartley's resilience. "Wallis' is but a mile away, up yonder," he said, pointing with his free hand up the river. "They pester those who have braved the dangers to return to harvest the crops," he said. "Nary a cabin is left standing, but the fields are unmolested."

"They left it for themselves, thinking they had rid the Susquehanna of us," Hartley said, "in that they are sadly mistaken. Instead of lessening the good peoples' resolve they have unwittingly strengthened it."

"I hope so," De Haas said, rolling an eye toward the blackened spots of ground where cabins had once stood amid the ripening fields of grain they passed. It seemed a strange contrast.

"Dreams and the hopes of good lives lay in those ashes," Hartley said. "We must do our utmost to help these people reclaim this land."

Congress had picked the right man, De Haas thought, but may have given him the improper tools. He looked at the fine blue regimentals with white facings on Hartley's men. Most already showed the rigors of frontier duty with torn cuffs, missing buttons and the like. He noticed moccasins adorning some of their feet as well as more durable buckskin britches and trousers but realized most switched from their torn britches to buckskin out of necessity. The same went for the footwear, he reasoned. These men hailed from Berks and Chester Counties, mostly farmers, merchants and trades men. They had lived much too long in the shadow of Philadelphia. He remembered from the introductions of the officers back at Fort Augusta the spattering of men in the ranks hailing from Virginia, Maryland, and Delaware, but they seemed of the same cut. Men of the same feather drew together. But these are the tools they received, he reminded himself. One must make do.

His eyes livened at the sight of the huge green lot of English grass to their front. He waved Hartley and his column toward it, leading them down the trail to a huge stone house. Charred timbers marked the burned outbuildings surrounding the stone haven. Tramped grass and embers from numerous fire pits dotted the green; no doubt the places Brodhead's men had camped.

A spirited man strode from the partially burned door of the stone house, lifting his hat from his head and grinning from ear to ear. "My, My," the man said, bowing his head to De Haas and gazing about at the men behind him. His eyes locked on Hartley. "You, my fine sir, must be Colonel Hartley!" he said, offering him his hand. "It is quite grand to see ye, and in command of such a fine lot!"

"Yes, Mr. Wallis, I presume," Hartley said. He put his hand to his saddle and slowly eased out of it. Brushing his regimental off he ran an eye over the house.

"Walls three foot thick all around," Wallis announced. "Rifle slits in every wall. Damned fools couldn't burn it, but they tried, but it, as I, am still standing." He stomped his foot on the ground. "And this is where I intend to stand 'til my bones rest in this very soil, God help me."

"Yes," Hartley said, extending his hand. "I should hope so." He liked the man's grit. It hinted at the deeper resolve of his nature. "I heard you are of the Society of Friends," Hartley said, noticing the pair of pistols tucked in his belt.

Wallis looked down at the pistols and patted one of them on the butt. "Some believe in one way, while others believe in another. I believe God will not condemn a man for protecting what is his and his own, unlike others, whom live in the safe city, us on the frontier have a more practical sense of things."

Hartley, knowing many a Quaker, for he hailed from York, found the man's warm demeanor refreshing and much different from any other Quaker he had known, save Nathanial Greene. He immediately warmed up to the man.

"Now if you and the General shall see fit to grace my humble adobe, you shall have my sincere gratitude," he said with a beaming smile.

"Well, I must say, it is good to be appreciated," De Haas said, gracefully dismounting.

"The day grows late," Hartley said, "sir, with your leave." He turned back to his awaiting officers.

"By all means, I am sorry I have no more to offer," Wallis said, spreading his hand over the green grass. "But by all means, sir, you are most welcome by us all. Lay out your camp where Brodhead had his, all about the green."

"Very well," Hartley said. "Captains take charge and dismiss the column. We shall camp here for the evening. Post a strong picket."

The men spilled from the ranks and onto the grass at their officers' behest. A black man appeared from the house and directed the men about with a warm smile to the nearest spring and whatnot.

Hartley noticeably eyed the man for a moment until Wallis ushered him into the door. Another oddity for a Quaker, he mused: the ownership of his fellow man.

Apparently this man made due and adapted to his surroundings. But De Haas seemed to have no qualms about the man and his resilience did seem refreshing. He subdued his suspicions when Wallis greeted him with a fine mug of rum. He gulped it down and sat on a bench by the table, resigning himself to work with the tools available to him.

This man carried a wealth he needed at this time; a wealth of the knowledge of the area, unsurpassed, and he would deal with the devil himself to acquire the knowledge needed to carry out his mission. A great smile stretched across his face as he slammed down the mug on the table. "Now tell me fine sir," he said, turning his attention to his host, "everything about the nature and lay of this land."

Wallis' eyes lit up at the invitation, glad to see the suspicion melt from the officer's eyes. His lively tongue rang with praise for the newly arrived colonel and his regiment, Colonel Brodhead and his regiment, the militia, and General De Haas, disarming them more and more with his charm before giving a careful summation of all he knew of the area; he being it's largest landowner and all.

Soon a lively murmur rose from the green plain. Fires flittered and the smells of a freshly roasted beef, specially slaughter by the black man for the men, filled the air. Still, men stood at intervals all along the slight rise of ground surrounding the green and the riverbank below ever watchful and alert. As comfortable as the grass seemed, the haunting realization of their ever present enemy pressed the men's thoughts. They knew somewhere out in the night many eyes watched their camp, perhaps waiting in the dark shadows to spring upon the unwary and steal away their life in a heartbeat. Every rustle in the brush received due attention. Every hoot of an owl caught a suspicious eye.

Dover, Philadelphia, Richmond, and Baltimore seemed a world away to these men, but they stood to their duty.

Their honor demanded it.

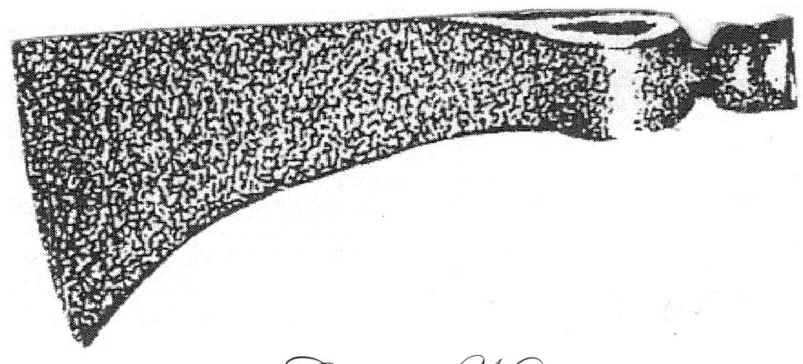

Chapter Nine

Colonel Hartley eyed the huge elm standing before him. It must be a full twenty feet around at least, he figured, pacing around it. The lumber from it alone could build a fine home. He gazed around at the other trees, just as large, if not larger, and sighed. "What vast wealth lay in this virgin land," he muttered under his breath. He ran his hands along the rough bark and remembered the great groves of towering hemlocks and white pines he had seen between Wallis' house and Sunbury. What prizes for the Navy alone! Every time he looked at the fine and straight pines he saw the masts of some future ships. The visions of sweeping grain in the lush fields flashed in his mind. Fertile and rich soil lay about these mountains. The timber alone proved enough to build so many homes it staggered his imagination. This land stretched for countless miles, each acre richer than the next. What a time to be alive, he thought. To live and breathe at the beginning of it all. The beginning of this new nation! The beginning of this *American Nation!*

"Colonel," a voice called from around the tree.

"Yes," he said, slowly peeling his hand from the bark. He straightened his clothes and took a few steps around the tree.

The man standing by the side of the tree let his eyes rise up it. "Fine timber, countless miles of it! What a harvest!"

"Yes, Captain Walker," Hartley said, "I have noticed."

"There's something of God in it all," Walker said. "And now he has brought his children to develop and prosper in its bounty. There is more to play in these times. Makes a man feel small and his complaints insignificant in the grandeur of it all."

"Yes, I quite agree," Hartley said. He looked toward a sharp cracking sound just over the ridge to their front. A huge crash sounded immediately after it.

"The harvest has begun," Walker said, "if it is just for a haven against the heathen of the forest and those whom would deny God's will."

Hartley nodded his head and walked toward the noise. "You're felling trees already?" he asked. "We just selected a place for the fort last evening."

"Haste makes waste," Walker said. "We won't let you down, sir, nor our country."

"No, I don't think you will, nor the men," Hartley said, looking at the threadbare man. The bush had played hell with all their clothing, but not their spirit. Their fleeting foe, seeming only a faint aspirition, flashed about now and then to make his presence known, teasing and mocking them. But it seemed to have little effect on the men's resolve.

Determination shone in all his men's eyes.

Determination and that new shinny *American spirit*. He felt hollow in its presence and sometimes wondered of his ability to lead such men. He had been tested by the rigors of the Canadian Campaign and the battles around Philadelphia. But this enemy seemed different and elusive. Just when you seemed to have him in your grasp he slipped through your fingers. Every tree, bush, and shadow proved his haven and he struck in the most inopportune moments, stealing a scalp and a life before disappearing again. Already reports poured in telling of new depredations. Although he assigned soldiers and militiamen to every party that went to harvest a crop it seemed futile. Something had to be done more than just defensive actions. One must strike the devils in their haven, he thought, but this time aloud.

"I could not agree more," Walker said.

"Yes," Colonel Hartley said, a bit embarrassed, "but first things first." He looked back over his shoulder at the sprawling camp around Wallis' stone house. "They need only strike in great numbers, I fear. Wyoming has taught us that, if anything."

"But we shall not leave the fort when they strike," Walker said. "And I promise you it shall be a stout fort when it is done."

"I have no doubt, my good man," Hartley said.

Walker hastened his march to the site of the new fort, anxious to show his commander what had already been completed of it. The whole area of the fort lay clear of scrub brush and surveyor's markers marked the outline of it.

Already a few logs sat in place, rising high in the sky with their pointed tops. A grunt to his rear slowed him. He turned to see Hartley cursing the stump of a sapling, turning his leg to examine his ripped stocking and bruised leg. A trickle of blood ran from the wound.

"Leggings are a must in this country," Walker said, walking back to him.

"No,no," Hartley said, regaining his composure. He felt belittled by his torn stocking in the face of the ragged soldier. "I am fine, and you are right, I am in need of a good pair of buckskin leggings." He shook his head and let a slight chuckle escape from his lips. "Damn frontier will get me yet, I fear."

Walker shook his head and quickly turned back to the fort, waving off the few salutes that greeted him. "No need for such," he said, "not while a man is working, anyways."

Hartley also waved off the doffed hats. "The Captain is right," he said, "be smart about your work." He watched the men groan under the weight of the huge logs. Even the great oxen pulling them struggled under their weight. With such logs laid with great care the fort would be strong indeed. His heart rose in his chest just watching the spirited workers. Every man sweated and gave his all to his work. Such men deserved an equal effort and commitment by their leaders.

He paced around, careful to walk wide of the men and keep clear of them. In no time he found himself standing next to another ranking officer watching the work with equal admiration.

"A fine lot of men indeed," General De Haas said. He raised an eyebrow to Hartley. "With such spirited men I think Congress has ordered the right lot to these parts. They will get the job done."

"Yes we will," Hartley said.

De Haas turned, raising his riding crop to point at the small bodies of men placed at various intervals around the area. "Look lively," he called to the nearest group within ear shot, "those devils are cunning you know!" The men nodded and pointed to a group leading some horses by ropes toward them. They called the parole. An immediate countersign answered their challenge. The men with the horses darted quickly past the sentries and headed straight for the officers, none more enthusiastically than the man in their lead.

"What is that bugger about?" De Haas asked. Noticing

the silver strand attached to the man's black hunting shirt he added, "Oh, my word, isn't that your man Carberry in the lead?"

"Yes sir," Hartley said, taking a few steps toward the man, "Lieutenant Carberry," he added.

"Sir," Carberry said, raising a quick hand to touch the brim of his hat. He wheeled the horse around full sided to face the officers. "This is fine stock!" he reported, casting a hand back to the other five horses. "I am so glad we collected them before the savages, for as I said, they are fine indeed."

"Yes they are," Hartley said. He paced around the horses, stopping occasionally to run a hand down their legs. "Fine horseflesh," he said, giving a nod to an equally approving General De Haas.

"In the state of things they are yours to do as you wish," De Haas said. "I am sure their owners have given them up as a loss, anyhow."

"This is fine, very fine," Hartley said. "Lieutenant Carberry my good man, I have already written headquarters asking permission to raise a company of horse." He smiled and looked up from the horse's legs. "And I think I have found that company's commander, Captain Carberry."

Carberry's eyes lit up at the announcement of his instant promotion. "I would be honored sir," he said. "Very honored!"

"The honor is all mine, Captain," Hartley said. "Saddles and holsters should be forthcoming, along with sabers. Now my good man be about erecting a stable and collecting more horse. Pick your men from the lot, I am sure we have men up to the challenge. I shall assist you in training as much as I can, but draw on your own experiences and those of the men. I am sure you will be equal to the task."

"We must make due with what we have out here,"

De Haas said. "Your colonel is right, four legs are needed to catch these rats once they are at full trot. They do not stand and fight in proper line as their bloody-backed allies. Let them try to run now!"

"Huzza!" Carberry and a few of his men shouted.

The general bowed his head and waved his hand. The spirited exchange of words brought stares from many eyes around the fort. None more than a pair of sullen eyes slowly tramping toward them.

"Who is that crestfallen chap?" Hartley asked, turning his head toward the general.

"Peter Smith," the General said. "Most unfortunate chap indeed. Ran his wagon full of his wife and family along with William King's family and a few other unfortunate souls into an Indian ambuscade in the plum tree thicket along Lycoming creek. A massacre occurred. Only he and a few children escaped. Happened just before Wyoming's massacre. He has taken it hard but has stuck it out." The General stopped talking, noticing the sad man approach within ear shot. He extended his hand to the glum soul.

"General," Smith said, nodding his head slowly. He shook his hand and turned toward Hartley.

Hartley watched the man eye the horses Carberry and his men led away. If the sorrowful man's eyes lit with recognition he swore he would have no qualms in releasing all of the animals to him. But his eyes remained dull and prosaic. Hartley extended his own hand.

"You must be Hartley," Smith said, locking eyes with the man. "I mean Colonel Hartley, don't mean no disrespect."

"Oh no, my dear man," Hartley said, "none taken."

Smith nodded, slowly releasing his grip on Hartley's hand. He rubbed his chin and gazed about the cleared ground and rising logs of the fort. "Not wasting no time, I see," he said. "That's good. I want to thank you soldiers for sharing your stores and medicines with the people here in these parts, greatly appreciated, by all, I assure you."

"Yes," Hartley said. "I only wish I had more. Supplies are exhausted at the moment, but I have written an express to the Council asking that more stores, especially medicine, are sent to Coxe's Town, there I will see it is forwarded here, where it is most needed."

"Well, I thank you once again, fine sir," Smith said. He gazed down to the ground, seeming to digest the colonel's words and comtenplate his next words. "If'n it won't be too much trouble," he said, looking down to Wallis' house, "some folks have said you are sending out soldiers to watch over us when we go out to the fields."

"Yes we are."

"I's got plenty of grain need'n to be reaped and cradled by my place just west of the Loyalstock, where Bull Run runs to the creek. Got young Brady, old man Van Ness, and some others pledging their help, but all would feel better if'n we had soldiers about us whilst we worked."

"No problem, my good man, I shall see to it personally."

Smith pointed over to a group of settlers filing down the trail toward the fort. A fine stock of long red hair flowed over the shoulders of a particularly large and robust man in the lead of the men. He held his rifle full to his chest, ever at the ready, even though they entered the camp. His smile and continence caused him to stand out among his stern-faced fellows.

"That there's James Brady," Smith said, noticing both the General's and Hartley's stares at the crimson-haired man. "Yep, his brother's Sam, and father's John, all are great

Indian fighters. Carry a certain air about them, they do. Well anyhow, James is the youngest, though John's the only one who carries the rank of captain, folks around these parts calls them all captain, don't pay no mind to what the proper people sees as title. Brave and fierce the whole lot of 'em. John, his son Sam, and the lesser John are fighting around Philadelphia. Proud to call them friend, each and every one, I am at that." With that Smith turned and trudged nonchalantly away, almost dragging his own beat up firelock behind him.

"Odd fellow," Hartley said. "But such is how the rigors of war play on some men's souls."

"Yes, poor fellow," De Haas added. "The people have not recovered. It is a most distracted, distressed, and confused situation. I shall do my best to see that all aide is hastened to you forthwith when I return to York."

Hartley said nothing, his eyes transfixed on Smith whom stopped on the ridge, talking most earnestly to Wallis. Though he felt great pity for the man at the same time something warned him of the man's nature. Something hard dwelt within the man, a hardness that turned a man's values topsy turvey. Such men needed to be watched, for sorrow and hardship had been known to tear a man's loyality away from its rightful moorings. He watched both of them in their animated conversation, watching Wallis' hands rise and fall in great sweeping motions only to be countered by Smith, who seemed to have recovered from his lethargic state, for the moment anyway.

"What to be a bird and hear what is being said," Hartley said under his breath.

"Yes," De Haas said, "but we must make due with the tools provided." He raised an eyebrow, seeming to share the colonel's gut instincts of warning.

They both stretched an eye to the rising logs of the

fort and down the ridge to Wallis' house within easy sight of the new fort. His arguments and hard insistance that the fort be built on his property ehoed in each of the officers' minds. Both had stood within his fine house, noticing while others lost everything only a few items showed missing from his belongings. They had sat at his fine table, drinking from pewter mugs and eating from fine plates. Surely the Indians and Tories should have taken all of it. But here it remained.

"He does share General Washington's confidence," De Haas said, sensing Hartley's aprehension. "And he seems to a have a sincere liking of you, can't be all that bad."

"Yes, but things aren't always as they seem, especially for a man of opportunity. For such a man's flag waves over whomever seems to be the victor," Hartley said. "But as you said, we must make due with the tools we have, so here Fort Muncy shall stand. It is the only proper spot if the settlements toward Bald Eagle Mountain and Great Island are to return, being mid-way and all."

Both men looked at each other and nodded, chasing away such feelings in the face of the despair now surrounding them. Their pledge remained for the people and with the people. If a bargain needed to be made with the devil for the moment, so be it. But woe to him if he proved fatal to their cause.

Woe indeed.

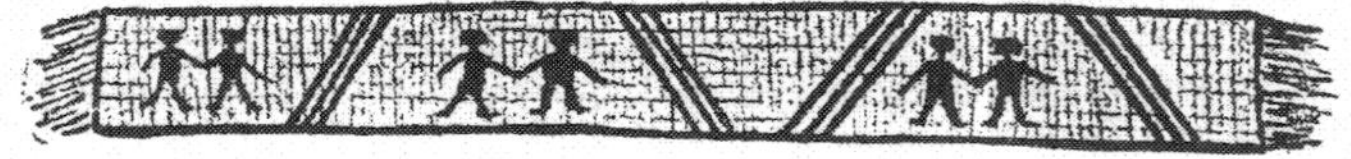

Chapter Ten

James Brady stretched his arms and walked out of the cabin door carrying his rifle with him. He wiped his eyes and listened in the deep fog slowly rising in the face of the early morning sun. Through breaks in the fog he scanned the fields. Sheafs of wheat shone from the previous day's toil. One more good day and the harvest will be complete, he thought. He mused for a moment on Peter Smith's departure with three others late last night on some trifling excuse. Odd indeed, seeing he owned the fields and all. But we must all hold together in times such as these, he reasoned. These crops would feed them all in the upcoming winter.

"You going to eat some of these victuals or not?" a voice called from the cabin door.

He looked back at the old man holding a spoon toward him. "I'll be along shortly, Van Ness," he said over his shoulder.

"I wouldn't be out there in that soup if'n I was you, alone and all," Van Ness said, turning back into the door. "You best get a move on, got seventeen others to feed, ya know, one more hungry than the next seeing how you all worked like the devil yesterday."

"I'll be along, old man, just want to look about a bit."

"Ain't nothing but the devil in that fog!"

"Then the devil will get a ball."

"And you the tomahawk!"

Brady turned, cocking an eye toward the disgruntled old man. "I'm coming if it'll shut you up!" he said. He scooped up his rifle in his hands and checked its flint before turning back to the cabin. Two others appeared in the doorway, both soldiers, hungrily eating out of their wooden noggins.

"Oh I just feel so much better having the army here and all, all eight of you," Brady scoffed as he passed them. "Best tend to your arms after you get done fillin' your gizzards."

The two men nodded, even though both held the rank of corporal. The man spoke with the air of one used to being obeyed. No wonder the others called him captain, they thought.

"You do your job," one of them said between bites, "and we'll do ours."

"I hope so," Brady snapped back to the surprised man.

"Damn if you folks about these parts ain't got eyes like hawks and ears like elephants!" the other soldier said. "If there was anything in that fog you'd know it, no doubt. But you sure are a hard lot."

"Have to be, keeps your hair where it belongs," Brady said, whisping one of his long red locks back on his head. He drew up a stool by the hearth and pulled the long black iron swivel toward him with a poker. He grabbed the spoon from the hovering old man beside him and scooped out a great helping of stew from the iron pot into his awaiting wooden noggin. Some of it spilled onto the floor.

"Tarinations," the old man said, "there's plenty, but we ain't got enough to feed the hogs!" He kicked the clumps back into the fire. They sizzled.

"Ain't no hogs about, anyhow," Brady said, "Injuns got 'em all!"

"All but a big red headed one, they did!"

"Day ain't over yet, but if'n they be brazen enough to try I'll be obliged to making them pay dearly for this scalp, I will. But if they do manage they'll have a bright red lock to guide them in the dark night."

"Ain't nothing to fun about, you cantankerous young rowdy! Now hurry up and be about your work! The sooner we's done the sooner we can get out of these parts. Gives me the willies, what with that fog and all!"

Brady laughed and grabbed a noggin of rum. "Old man's right," he said, rising up from the stool and taking a great gulp of the rum. "Daylight's burning! Let's get at it boys!" He forced down a few more great spoonfuls of stew as he rose. Disregarding the noggin to the floor, along with the old man's spoon, he marched through the door clutching his rifle to his chest like his dearest friend.

A few grunts sounded out in protest but most filed out the door behind the big red haired man. He pointed toward the cradles sitting next to the house and four men eagerly took them up in their hands.

"Well ye four be about cradling whilst us others head down to the field yonder and finish the last day's reaping. Ye soldiers see about sentry." Brady said.

Three soldiers peeled off with their militia counterparts and went about their business. The other soldiers, along with the rest of the harvesters, followed Brady down a slight hill to a field below the cabin.

They scampered to the spot in the field of the previous day's work. After nervously gazing around the fog most sat their rifles around a tree, much to Brady's disgust.

"Don't set them there fellows," he said, sitting his own weapon down a few feet away on the ground. "Spread 'em out."

Eyes rolled at him and into the fog. "You do as you see fit, Captain, but we's wants 'em up and round the tree, so we can get at them better if need be," one of them said while the others picked up their sythes and commenced working.

Brady shook his head, knowing his words fell on deaf ears anxious to complete their work and get out of the field. He grabbed his own scythe and stared at a soldier standing idily next to him. "Corporal," he said, "Haven't you best set a man yonder on that ridge?" He eyed the soldier next to him again. The soldier took the hint and slowly marched into the fog and toward the ridge without the urging of his corporal. The frontier captain's word held sway in these parts, in the art of Indian fighting, at least, perhaps not in work.

"The rest of us will spread out and form a picket line," the corporal said, more to Brady than to his men. Either way his men spread out just far enough in the fog to keep an eye on the harvesters and the trees surrounding the field.

Brady stood and watched until all placed themselves to his approval. "That'll do, now we'll put our backs to it while the sun's still hid in the fog," he said, immediately swinging his scythe in great arcs through the wheat.

The sound of the swinging scythes slid through the fog. Soldiers nervously scanned the fog, some pacing around and investigating some disturbance, but none never too far from the field. Only an occasional grunt or groan crept from their throats. The reapers made great sweeps in the field, in no time reaching the middle of it. There they stopped for just a moment to catch their breaths and wipe the sweat from their eyes, eyes soon darting toward a retreating sentry.

The sentry quickly edged near the reapers, jerking his musket up and down and motioning behind him. A spine tingling cry promptly broke the eerie silence. The sentry turned and fired, only to collaspe to the report of a dozen bright flashes in the fog.

Stark eyes looked down at the crumpled soldier and

came alive with fear. All of them ran pell-mell to the tree, their hands reaching out before them and grabbing at air in anticipation. Brady sprinted madly in front of them, trying vainly to outrun the painted devils rising from the fog. Spears struck the ground and bobbed in his wake. Flashes stabbed the fog in his direction. He ignored them all but the panting breaths at his heals. Without looking at whom followed he dove to the ground to scoop up his rifle.

He cocked, rolled over, and fired in one smooth motion, felling his prusuer. A flash in the fog sent him reeling backwards, blood spurting from his arm. His rifle flew into the wheat. He twirled and collapsed to the ground, crawling and grabbing at the stubby wheat to reach the tree. Thuds sounded in the ground all around him. The wheat flew in the air from his desperate grasp. More painted demons darted out of the fog, screaming and running toward him, seeming to ignore his frightened fellows. He siezed one of the rifles and blindly fired into the mass of painted flesh descending upon him, falling in a hail of tomahawks, war clubs, and spears.

Many hands, screaming tongues, and angry feet assaulted the writhing man. He rolled and tumbled among them, until one strong hand lifted his neck back and gripped a large handful of his red locks. In one smooth and quick motion the hair peeled from his head with an eerie wet sound. His screams rose above the chorus of war whoops.

The other white men peeled off and broke in every direction. Soldiers stumbled in the fog, only to be met by a whizzing sound by their ears and the flight of feathered spears close to their persons. They peered and fired wildly into the fog before joining their retreating comrades. Their cursing corporal met them at the edge of the field by the ridge and ordered them to stop. Hastily counting their number, he found two missing along with the unlucky sentry. Only three nervous souls stood in front of him.

"Load your weapons!" he ordered, raising his own musket toward the field. Red and yellow flashes stabbed the folds of the fog. He followed each of them with the end of his musket, only to have them disappear just as his finger tightened on the trigger. The sound of his remaining three men raising their weapons to their shoulders turned him about. He jerked the end of his bayoneted musket toward the threatening fog.

Brady groaned, twisted, and squirmed on the ground. His body burned with pain from blows and stabbs all about his person. Quick, but small thuds to his head made him wipe the blood from his eyes for a heartbeat. His eyes widened at the small boy wielding a tomahawk and striking at his head, all under the direction of an elderly chief by his side.

Brady's eyes glared at the brazen chief who laughed at the child's efforts. The chief ignored the white demon's look and took the boy's hand. Drawing it back high in the air, he directed him on how to deliever a proper blow.

The lesson rang true to the boy.

The tomahawk cracked Brady's skull. Bright blue and black flashes along with hundreds of small specks of light filled his vision, for a moment blinding him to all the pain. He rolled away with all his might to the laughs and scorn of his antogonists. Blackness quickly blanketed his sight. Gasping, he slipped into unconsciousness.

All the soldiers suddenly stopped and turned about to confront a rush to their rear. The four cradlers stumbled to a stop and stared into the fog behind the soldiers. The wide-eyed corporal also caught their eye.

"What?" one of them said on a whisper, "you ain't thinking on heading in there is ye? Ye will be murdered if ye do!"

A series of cries sounded in the air. The three soldiers looked to the corporal. All stopped and turned toward the cradlers.

"We best get back to Wallis's and spread the alarm!" one of the cradlers said, turning and dashing up the hill, "afor we all lose our scalps!"

"He's right corporal," one of the remaining cradlers said. "The others have skedaddled, won't no one blame you. But if you head in that fog, you've only your fool self to blame! We're off to Wallis's if we can make it!"

The corporal looked down and slowly into the fog. "It would be most imprudent," he said. "We shall make our way back to the fort by the road, until we meet a relief party."

With that the soldiers slowly backed out of the field and made their way carefully to the road. Their firelocks leveled at the all encompanassing fog, ready to greet whatever demon erupted out of its folds with their fury. Nothing could be done for the poor souls left in that field without joining their number each reasoned to themselves.

A dead soldier did no one good but the enemy.

Chapter Eleven

He rolled along the grass. His mind numb, he drifted in between the nightmare and conscious thought, trying to convince himself none of the dream actually happen. Nothing of those visions could be true.

A sudden, stark, pain forced his eyes open. Open to the horror. His scalp burned. His arm ached. Cuts all over his skin screamed for attention. His brain throbbed with each pulse of blood to it. Dried blood stuck to his face and clouded his eyes. Strands of matted hair from the fringes of his head clumped into the dried blood about his face. It happened! An empty horror flooded his thoughts. His mother! His father! His brothers! Oh, dear God, what has become of me? Never to see any of their faces again. Never to breathe the fresh air of the morning tinged with dew. Never again to see a sunset. Never to feel. He felt empty and cheated. He felt cheated and robbed of the very gift of life itself.

But he still breathed, he realized with his face in the gritty ground. He exhaled. Dust blew from around his face. It burned atop of his head, but strangely, he welcomed the pain. One had to live to feel pain.

A slight glimmer of hope made him turn his head from the dust. He raised his right arm, but, oh, how it throbbed in resistance. He pulled his left hand from under his body and wiped his eyes. The sun shone through lingering wisps of fog. It shone brightly, with the promise of the day. He lived-in terrible pain-but he lived!

He lay perfectly still and listened. None of the horrible devils of the forest moved about. No feet shuffled through the stubble of the wheat. None of their tired guttoral tones crept through the air. They had gone! The devils had retreated to hell, leaving their victim for dead, no doubt. But no! Others had been with him! They must still be about! He groaned and yelled as loud as his pain-filled lungs would allow. No one answered. He must find them! He must at least gain the shelter of the cabin. They would return, either the devils or his comrades. He had to be ready for either.

He raised his hand to his scalp and it tingled with an awful burning pain. He slowly lowered his fingers to his eyes and stared at the red dripping from them. He felt a fresh gush of liquid drip from the spot he had foolishly touched. "No!" he scolded himself. "No more touching!" He suddenly noticed a brown stock sticking under some matted wheat. His eyes lit up. His rifle! It had somehow missed the eyes of his tormentors! He crawled to it and clutched it to his chest with his good arm. The cold steel of the barrel felt good. He wiped his eyes free of the blood tricking down into them and stared up to the ridge. The cabin lay just beyond it!

Stumbling to his feet, he dragged his rifle by the barrel through the field. He gritted his teeth and struggled to force one foot over the other, falling once, but quickly regaining his footing and continuing his life march to the cabin.

He staggered past the sheaths of wheat, some smoldering from half-hearted attempts to set them aflame. "No, oh, no! Good Lord, don't let them to have burned the cabin!" he muttered, stumbling past the last tree on the ridge. He fell against its rough bark and brushed his face again. There, through the last hints of fog, it stood. Smoke still curled in the air from its chimney.

"Halloo!" he screamed. "Halloo! Hallo in the cabin!" He watched for a long moment but no one appeared in the door. He cocked his head and listened, trying to mutter another halloo but falling to the ground in exhaustion.

"James!" a voice slid from the shadows inside the cabin door. "Is that you?"

"Old man," Brady said, lifting his head. "Old man!"

The old man edged to the door, peering out cautiously before scappering out to the tree. He dropped the poker and knife he held in his hands and bent down to the blood-soaked and suffering soul below him.

"Oh my dear God, it is you," he said. He cradled Brady's head in his palms and stared into the blood shot and swollen eyes before him. He pulled a rag from his pouch and wiped the blood from around his face. He raised it to the festering red wound on top of Brady's head but pulled it back, fearing only to increase the poor man's pain by touching the tender wound. "Can you get up?" he asked. "Best get you in the cabin."

A mournful groan answered him.

Old man Van Ness lifted him up by the arms and helped the huge man through the door. He led him to the bed, gently easing him down onto it. He immediately ripped his shirt into long strips and bandaged the suffering man's wounds. After wiping away more blood from Brady's face he let out a sigh of relief to see the flow stop from the top of his head. He winced at the thought of the pain. To have one's hair literally ripped from one's skull while still alive must be most painful. More than a ball, he mused, lifting the hasty bandage to check the hole in Brady's right shoulder. It too stopped bleeding. He let a slight smile creep across his face that instantly disappeared at the sight of a brown mass oozing from Brady's belly. He regonized his own stew when he saw it, even if half-digested. He looked at the sprear wound and could not hide the horror in his eyes. How could this man still live? He wondered to himself. "You're agonna need some stitchin', you are," he said.

"I'm going to need more than that."

"Man, the stuff you Bradys is made of, the heart of the earth you is."

"You know it old man, and I don't want to be in it none too soon."

The gobble of a turkey gave both men a start. A turkey? None would be about after all the ruckus this morning. It could be only one thing! A savage!

"My rifle!" Brady called, trying vainly to lift himself from the bed. "My rifle! Old man! Fetch my rifle!"

The unmistakable boom of a turkey's wing taking to flight gave them another start but also a great sense of relief. "T'was a turkey after all, daggunit!" the old man said. "Why I'll be dipped in dung!"

Brady's eyes still glowed with fear. He eased back down on the bed and looked soulfully at the old man. "You best get out of here," he said. "They'll be back to finish their dreadful work. Ain't no sense in both of us getting killed."

"Now you cut out that fool talk right this second, damn it," the old man said. "Ain't no one leavin' you in such a state!" He rolled his eyes, thinking of the precipitous retreat of the others of their party.

Brady's glassy eyes stared up at him. "I thirst," he said. "I thirst something terrible."

Van Ness searched about the cabin, finally finding the small rum barrel. "Its dry," he said. "damn fools drank it all."

Brady's eyes rolled from right to left. He listened very carefully and locked eyes on the old man again. "The river," he said. "Get me to the river!"

Van Ness helped him up with no protest, not wishing to go against his will. A strong will it proved to be, strong as any he had ever known.

They stumbled the few rods behind the cabin and to the canoe landing. Brady flung himself down onto the gravely beach and sank his lips into the water. He gulped and drank copiously for several moments before raising his head to gasp, "my rifle, old man, fetch my rifle!" He immediately sank his face back into the cool water and began drinking again.

The old man soon appeared with a musket along with Brady's rifle. He slung a cartridge box over his shoulder. "Got this from one of them soldiers, seeing how he won't be needing it again, poor soul, took a ball right between the eyes."

Brady jerked his head up from the water and stared at the old man. He blinked once, twice, before collapsing to the ground. "Load it old man," he said through his pain. "Load it!" He twisted the pouch around his neck to his front, fumbling to raise it over his head.

"Now be careful," Van Ness said. "Mind your wounds!" He slowed Brady's flailing arms and gingerly slid the pouch and its powder horn over his shoulder and neck. He quickly loaded the rifle under Brady's intense eye. "There," he said, clicking the rifle's pan closed. "It's all loaded and primed."

Brady snatched the weapon with his good arm and clutched it to his chest. He promptly collapsed to the ground, immediately falling into a deep sleep.

The old man quietly loaded his musket, his ears alert for any noise and his eyes keen for any flash of movement. After loading he sat down next to his wounded friend. He thought for a moment stared up to the sky. "Lord, I's knows I ain't been much on praying, but I'm calling on you now. If not for my sake," he added, looking down at Brady writhing in pain even in sleep, "for others. Shouldn't no one die that professes such a will to live. Be a shame, is all. Amen."

A rushing noise sounded in his rear. He froze, listening to the creeping footsteps inch closer to him. "This is it," he muttered under his breath, cocking his musket.

The click woke Brady instantly. He rose to his feet, raising his weapon to his shoulder in a flash. He pushed the frail old man aside. Staring down the sights on the barrel of his rifle, he glared into stunned eyes. He lowered the rifle in relief and collapsed in a clump onto the ground. Looking up to the men standing with their mouths' agape over him he said, "Sunbury! My ma! I need to see her! Can you take me to Sunbury?"

"Yes, certainly," Captain Walker said, kneeling down next to the man. He looked him over and nodded his head to the teary-eyed old man next to him. "Yes, certainly, we can."

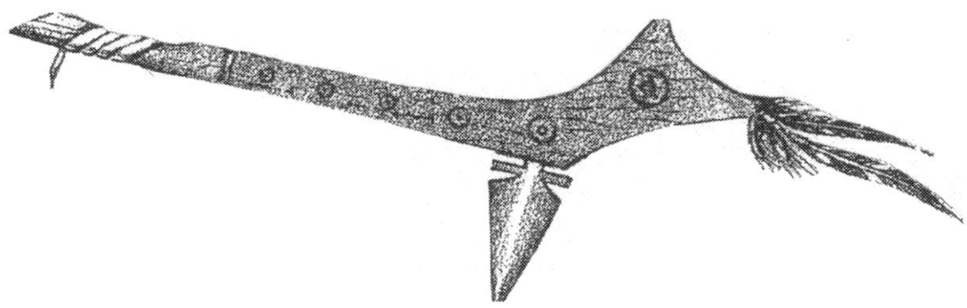

Chapter Twelve

"Lieutenant Gore, sir, what is all this about?" Colonel Butler asked, peering into the officer's makeshift pine bough hut along the stockade.

The officer rolled over the hard ground, slowly lifting the blanket up from his body. He wiped his eyes and looked at the man standing in the entrance. A irritated grunt rose from the other officers sharing the hut. One smacked his lips and cracked an eye toward the man standing in the entrance. His cold stare had little effect on him. He lifted his blanket over his head and rolled over, thankful he heard no protest from the stern-eyed officer.

"Colonel Butler?" Gore asked. He stretched and stood up, fumbling for his hat in the early morning light. "Assembly has not been sounded, has it sir?"

Butler folded his arms and took a few steps backward. His eyes rolled along the row of huts. "Are not you, sir, the officer of the day?"

"Yes sir," Gore said. He walked up to the colonel and followed his eye. The mess about the men's huts caught his own eye immediately. He sighed and rubbed his brow. Now all hell would be to pay.

"Orders," Butler said through gritted teeth, "are that subaltern officers visit the guards by day and by night inspect the soldiers' huts." He pushed the toe of his boot into a pile of noggins and trenchers strewn about the front of the hut. He kicked at a small iron pot, sending it clanging into one of the other huts. Cocking his hands on his waist he strutted over to the hut. Pushing back its blanket door he peered into it, reeling back initially from the pudgent smell from within it. "Huts and cooking utensils are to be kept clean and clothing is to be aired on a daily basis," he said on a gasp.

"Yes sir, but the men are beat from finishing these walls and what with scouting and all."

"You are a proper officer carrying a commision, are you not, sir?"

Gore said nothing but just nodded his head.

"I am sure Colonel Wisner kept proper bearing and all, especially in front of the troops," Butler said. "Your fine service to him proves you to be a good officer. Just because we are about our own makes no difference, disipline is all the more crucial. As you well know, men such as ours so unused to resistance must be led, they will not be drove."

"I know fair well, Colonel, I myself being of the same stock," Gore said.

"Yes, as I. But I will have no more of it. That battlefield over yonder across the river attests to what happens under popular rule, it has no place in these times. We must sacrifice to survive and we shall survive I assure you." He jerked his hand and gestured to the gate. Three settlers stood there, appearing all weary and worn from their trek through the wilderness. He cast a cold eye at the sentry standing near them.

Gore recognized one of the men, Abel Yarington, who kept the ferry across the river. He raised his hand and gave a quick wave to the sentry. The sentry gladly resumed his post.

Gore cast an eye to the rigid colonel next to him and nodded at Abel.

Yarington nodded back, raising an eyebrow at Butler. War brought the devil out in men, he thought. He rubbed his chin and motioned toward one of the packhorses behind him. "Well here are ye things, Zebulon, on this horse," he said, turning away and leading the other three horses and two men away. "I am to see about my house, if ye do not mind."

"If you wait just a moment I can provide an escort," Butler said.

Yarington grunted and raised the rifle he held in his hands up to his chest. "This is all the guard I need, no need to make a fuss 'bout it all."

Butler shook his head and turned back to Gore. "You have in your charge three sergeants and five rank and file, as of your report?" he asked.

"Yes sir."

"Well gather that horse, among the other things on it you shall find a marquee, fashion some poles and erect it with all due haste."

"Due haste?"

"Yes," Butler said, "you have your orders. I shall expect it to be up before assembly is called for we shall find adequate use for it. Set it up next to the great tree. *Courts-martial* shall be conducted within it. I fear we shall find great use for it until disicpline is restorted."

The loud grunt of a hog sounded just on the other side of the stockade, seeming to answer the colonel. He stopped and listened to the rutting beast for a moment. Scrunching his nose he said, "as for the number of hogs present, seeing their owners are not present, it is best they be killed for the use of the soldiers. Order that all such be brought to the Commissary and have their description and weight taken, and the Commissary to pay the money, at usual price, for use of the owners when called for by proper owner or owners."

"Yes sir," Gore said. He looked to the untidy pine bough huts soon to be inspected daily and kept tight, in more ways than one. That itself would probably fill the marquee with numerous *courts-martial* alone.

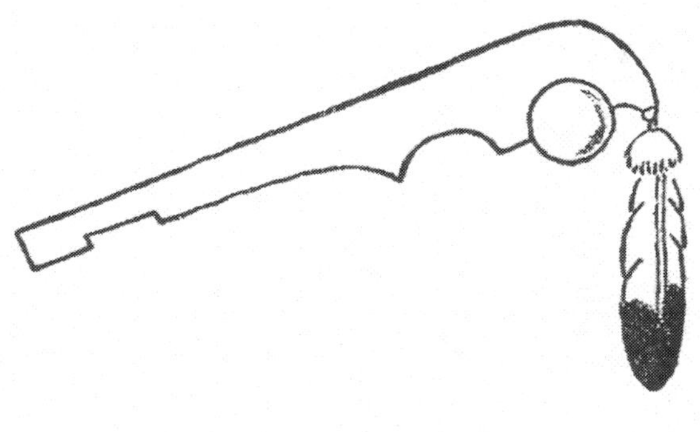

Chapter Thirteen

Great huzzas roared along the river and mountains of Wyoming. The cannon boomed in salute along with muskets. Hats waved in the air and relieved faces greeted the column of the Continental Line smartly marching into the green grass of the river common. Hands reached out and patted the backs of the worn and ragged men of the column. The frowns on some of the haggard faces in the column melted away to great grins. Equally enthusiastic huzzas erupted from their throats.

A lone officer wearing a torn red shash about his waist reined his horse to a stop in front of the officer standing in front of the fort.

The officer in front of the fort, clearly of high rank, stood with his hands cocked on his waist. His face beamed with a smile so grand his face threatened to burst. He extended his hand to the officer.

Another round of huzzas filled the air.

The mounted officer removed his hat in salute and handed down a copy of his orders to the waiting hand of the officer; a colonel no less.

The colonel immediately stuffed the papers in his pocket and extended his hand again. "No, not that," he said, "give me your hand man! We are overwhelmed at your presense!"

A smile immediately stretched across the officer's face. He donned his hat and gladly took the colonel's welcoming hand. "Captain George Bush," he said, nodding his head, suddenly forgetting the tiresome march, his torn clothes, and countless aches, "of Hartley's Regiment, with this fine detachment of the same, awaiting your orders, sir."

A thunderous roar erupted among all the men. Both officers eagerly shook the other's hand, only lessening their grip when the Captain Bush dismounted.

Bush graciously released his grip on the colonel's hand, straightened his clothes and slightly bowed before all the congratulatory waves and heartfelt greetings surrounding him.

"Fine sir, I am Colonel Butler, commanding, Camp Westmoreland," the officer introduced himself. Nodding his head, he waved his hand toward the gate and led the captain into the fort. Eying the captain over, he noticed the fine cuts of cloth making up his uniform. Even though it appeared torn and ragged he still wore it with pride and it seemed to fit him perfectly. The captain appeared to be of fine stock and with his manners and bearing seemed to only compliment his own style of dicipline, or, Butler feared, he had welcomed a dandy into his ranks.

"What do you think of dance?" Butler asked, opening the cabin door.

Captain Bush raised an eyebrow hearing the question, totally unprepared for such an inquirery. He smiled and thought for a moment, gauging the colonel's bearing before taking the seat offered to him by a table. Knowing these to be

New England troops, mostly of puritan stock, he carefully chose his answer. "I find the art of dance indispensable to the character of a gentleman and an officer, sir," he said, watching a sour expression overwhelm and vanguish the smile from Butler's face. "Just as His Excellency General Washington," he added for good measure.

Butler raised his own eyebrow. "We are about the very fringes of the frontier and the necessities of survival necessitate the exclusion of such frivolous distractions, such as dance, the playing of cards and such," he said. "I am sure His Excellency would gather the same conclusion in such circumstances. Discipline must be maintained, for our very lives and future depend upon each man rising above his faults and doing his duty."

"Yes sir," Bush said. He removed his hat and sat straight in the chair, as he had done before his old school marm in his youth.

"I am sure you noticed the marquee on the green under the tree," Butler said.

Bush nodded, faintly remembering the water stained, torn, somewhat patched, and frayed large tent. No doubt his headquaters, he mused, suddenly becoming flush with the thought of just how desperate this post appeared to be.

"I have had it brought here for the express purpose of holding *courts-martial* within it," Butler said. "And it has been quite busy as of late. I hope your men, being of proper sort, do not aggiate matters here at the present."

"No sir, I assure you, Colonel Hartley would have none of it."

"Yes," Butler said, suddenly eying the door to make sure it closed properly. He walked over to it and raised the latch string. "Privacy, is another reason I called you within these walls lest the marquee. Eager ears about and all. Some matters require the utmost secrecy, as per instructions from Colonel Hartley." He lifted a paper to the light of the lone tallow candle on the table. "He has deemed it necessary to march against the enemy at my and others' behest, seeing the full range of the frontier impossible to defend with the forces at his disposal. He has picked Wyalusing as the lauching point for such an expedition. Upon your arrival I am to inform him and prepare for the march to begin with an express from him at Wallis's near Fort Muncy. He is assembling a clever body of men about Wallis's. From Wyalusing we are to advance upriver to Tioga and meet Lieutenant Colonel Butler of the Fourth Pennsylvania Regiment. Thence we are to advance against Chemung and sweep the river clean of all Indians and Tories between there and here. Quite ambitious, but sheer necessity demands such an action, I durst say. You will consider the matter most accordingly. Secrecy is of the utmost importance. I am afraid Indian Butler, the Johnson's, and Brant do have ears about yet." He handed the paper to Bush.

Captain Bush read it most carefully in the pale light. After reading it he sat it down upon the table and rubbed his chin. "My men are threadbare," he said. "Sir, I shall have to inform Colonel Hartley of their most haggard state from their trek through the wilderness to reach this place." He reflected on the equally ragged state of the troops greeting them. "The men are in the most dire need of new hunting shirts and leggings at least," he added.

"As we all are," Butler said, pulling upon his frazzled regimental coat. The sound of a seam ripping made him regret the action. "But none of us complain, for the war is such and our duty so grave it precludes such wants. But I have also written the Council on the matter. I, too, hope they will act with due haste."

"Indeed," Bush said, turning and eye toward the door. The clamor of the celibration outside crept into the cabin. "But I see neither company is in want of spirit."

"That is most certain," Butler said. "And if spirit is the true arrsenal of war we have nothing to fear. Our enemies shall quake in its presence."

"Huzza to that," Bush said, gracefully accepting a mug of rum placed in front of him by Butler. Both drank heartily from their mugs and slammed them down on the table.

"Huzza to that!" they both said, exiting the cabin to join in the celebration.

Chapter Fourteen

The cold stare of Colonel Butler still cut into Isaac Tripp's mind even though they left Camp Westmoreland hours ago. The colonel let his position go to his head, Tripp thought, musing over the colonel's protests about he seeing to his cabin along the Lackawanna. No one had been there in over a month. No word, save that of the cruel fate of St. John and Leech, had trickled down from the far upper reaches of the river. Butler, spouting the importance of the crops and the settlement's buildings as a whole, did little to ascertain just what ravages had befallen the settlements along the Lackawanna. If he would not see to it, he had protested to the headstrong colonel, then he would, along with his grandson and two other young volunteers of the militia. He still beamed with appreciation at the two young men who volunteered to escort them. They had shut the brash colonel up once and for all.

One of the young men noticed his look and smiled back at him. "No worries, Mr. Tripp," he said, patting the stock of his rifle. "Powder and ball doth settle all."

He smiled at the odd phrase said by one of Captain Bush's men repeatedly until the words crept from everyone's tongue about Camp Westmoreland. The men, though mostly Pennamites, seemed a good lot. They seemed to not to give a damn about the Penn's claims against the Connecticut settlers but only about doing their duty; to protect the frontier. They understood the further they stopped the Tory and Indian menace away from their homes, the better. They also shared the spirit. The *American spirit.*

Tripp and his party hurried past the burned out mill

and cabins just above the remnants of Pittston Fort. The haunting words of Mrs. Leech played at each of their imaginations as they passed the carcass of a lone oxen, its putrid flesh prickled with spears and lances. Here is where St. John and Leech had breathed their last, caught up in the struggle between three great powers. Here they payed the price for their declarations, treason, patriotism, and simple honor. They gazed at the two hastily made mounds of dirt marking their graves along the road, thankful that some, even in their haste to escape the valley after the battle, had the decency to stop and bury them.

None of the cabins ahead of them along the rough road still stood. One in particular caught old Tripp's eye. He stopped before it and stared. He knew the cabin. He knew the Hickmans had stopped there and refused to go any further, confident no harm would reach them this far up the river. He knew their remains, man, wife, and infant son, lay in these ashes. He let an anguished gasp slip out of his mouth.

"What is it Papa?" his grandson asked. He stopped and gazed toward the charred cabin, wondering what horrors shone through his grandfather's eyes.

"The Hickmans, son," he said. "You remember them, don't you?"

"Yes, Papa, I do."

"Well this is all that's left of them."

A call from up the trail broke his gaze. The two militiamen waved them up the trail, toward the crest of a ridge.

The old man nodded. Tearing his gaze from the cabin, he put his hand on his grandson's shoulder. "We must come back," he said, "and make sure they too receive a proper burial."

"Come, come," the two men urged them, seeming

excited by the sight of something below them. They nervously fidgeted with their rifles, raising them to their shoulders only to slowly lower them again.

"What is it?" Old Tripp asked, gazing down into the gap below. "It's just Leggett's creek."

"Jim here could've swore he saw one of 'em darting off into the trees!" one of them answered.

Both Tripps scanned the gap below, intently looking for any sign of movement. The sight of a turkey strutting along the bank eased their minds.

"Are they the feathers you saw, young Hocksey?" the elder Tripp asked.

Jim shook his head, almost laughing in relief. The other raised his rifle and aimed at the turkey.

"No! No! Timothy!" old man Tripp said. "If there aren't any about that shot will surely bring them in, for sure it will!"

The young man promptly lowered his rifle, suddenly embarrassed.

"It's alright," Tripp said. "No harm done." He looked back over his shoulder. "We're a good twenty miles from the post. We must keep a sharp eye. But I think we shall be fine, as long as we lay low."

"My land's just a few miles ahead," Timothy Keyes said, raising his head high again and regaining his composure. All saw the new gleam in his eye. His military mindset, he being the Ensign of the Pittston Company, took over his demeanor. "We'll stop there and then push on to Hocksey's, then your place, Mr. Tripp."

Both Hosksey and the Tripps nodded. They slowly made their way down the trail to the creek, each looking a little more warily at the trees and bushes around them. Keyes looked to the creek and searched for rocks to step across the creek, ignoring the eerie tingle at the nape of his neck. He just put a foot on a rock when they sprung onto them. In a heartbeat painted men surrounded them, each staring deathly into their eyes.

No one spoke. The white men froze perfectly still, watching the circling Indians. Some pointed rifles at them within a few feet of their faces while others brandished tomahawks and spears. They locked eyes with them and seemed to almost dare them to raise the rifles held in each of their anxious hands. Their dark eyes and fierce stares warned what would happen if any of them even twitched a muscle.

Finally a wild scream erupted from one of the painted faces, causing the warrior's head to reel backwards against the sheer force of it. The turkey's wings sounded with a sharp thud. Squirrels scampered madly up trees. Birds took to flight from the spine tingling wail. The apex predator laid claim to the forest and all its majesty.

Old man Tripp released his grip, letting his rifle fall helplessly to the ground. He locked eyes with the screaming warrior and motioned very slowly for his grandson to follow his lead. His grandson's rifle fell to his feet.

Hocksey stared in wide-eyed terror at the warriors. Each screamed more fiercely than the other. Soon the forest echoed with their jaunts and jeers. His rifle fell involuntarily from his shaking hands.

Keyes stood frozen in mid-stride over the rushing water below him. If he fired all of them would certainly go to Hell or Tioga, which proved worst seemed inconsequential. Lives hung by the grip of his finger on the trigger. One shot against at least a dozen. But still, he stood gripped by solid fear, mutely mouthing a prayer amidst the screaming demons.

A huge warrior splashed into the creek next to him.

He raised his tomahawk high in the air and brought it down next to him, merely slicing at air to warn him. He exposed his teeth in the most grizzly manner and thumped his huge barrel chest, leaving momentary indentations in the paint.

Keyes watched out of the corner of his eye. He wanted to move, to bring the rifle to bear on the demon, but his muscles froze. He stood perfectly still while the warrior slowly reached out and touched the barrel of his rifle.

Sensing no resistance, the warrior jerked the weapon free and splashed back toward the others. He raised the weapon above his head in triumph and screamed at the top of his lungs. Two warriors spurted toward Keyes and knocked him down into the water. He struggled against a few blows before a gruff hand reached down and pulled him from the water. In one great motion a huge warrior tossed him against the bank of the creek.

Leather thongs bound the younger men's hands in an instant. Looped hemp ropes slid down over their necks. The warriors bared their teeth and yelled them into sumbmission before the shocked eyes of old man Tripp. He stood in a daze, staring through tear-strewn eyes at the young men.

An equally old warrior stepped out from the trees and stood next to the old white man. He crossed his arms and stood defiantly between the younger warriors and the old white man.

The warriors ignored them both, busying themselves in searching through the young captives' haversacks and possible bags. The older warrior cocked his head and looked back at his elder counterpart out of the corner of his eye. He waved a hand toward one of the gallivanting young braves and reached into his pouch. He pulled a small clay pot from it and eagerly rubbed his fingers into it. He turned toward the old white man and smeared his face red with the vermillion paint on his fingers.

"Jogo!" he said, waving his hand back down the trail. "Jogo!"

Old man Tripp stood in shock for a moment, cursing himself for insisting on the expedition in the first place. Colonel Butler did not seem such a fool now. His mouth dropped open and his eyes darted among the young men, trying to lock a reassuring but apologetic eye with his grandson. A gruff push into his chest sent him reeling backwards, sending a stream of tears down his cheeks.

"Jogo!" the old warrior said again, this time with a cutting motion by his neck. His eyes bulged. He looked back at the yelling warriors and to the seemingly stunned old white man. "Jogo!" he said again, scratching his head, "you die too if no jogo!" He threw his arms up in frustration.

The old man stumbled to his feet, trying in anguish to turn his head from the sight before him. Words of a prayer, which one he did not know, but any would do, rolled across his lips. He turned his teary eyes from his grandson and rambled madly back down the trail. He let his feet pull him away from the horror, feeling such deep remorse great tears clouded his vision. He collapsed just over crest of the ridge and openly wept. The screams echoed through his mind from one ear to the other. "Why?" he cried, "oh, why, dear God? Why?"

A terrible scream answered his plea. His wide eyes darted back toward it. He plodded down the trail, letting his heavy feet carry him out of earshot of the terrible sounds. Stumbling, he grabbed onto any tree or shrub along the way to escape the blind vision of death haunting his soul. "Oh dear Lord," he sobbed. "Hell hath return to Wyoming! Dear Lord help us all!"

Chapter Fifteen

Young Isaac Tripp watched his grandfather's back stumble over the top of the crest. A hollow feeling swept over his soul. He had never really felt so alone before, he realized. Alone and stripped of all dignity and integrity in one foul swoop. He closed his eyes and let a lone tear fall down his crimson cheek. A slap immediately forced his eyes open.

Hocksey stood, barely, in the face of one of the painted demons. His knees noticeably shook. A heathen breathed down on him in his full glory, his eyes beaming with the power of life or death. He spat full in his face and shoved the shaking young white man to the ground.

Hocksey rolled over and stared pleadingly at young Tripp.

Tripp shook his head. No words came to his quivering throat.

"Leave him be!" Keyes' voice demanded through the yells.

The warriors looked at him with pure contempt, each shaking their heads at the young upstart. One of them flung his knife from its sheath and put it to his mouth, mockingly acting like he cut his tongue from it. He nodded to the young white man with a gleaming eye.

Keyes took the hint. He bowed his head in silence. A rough yank at the rope around his neck forced his head up again. The rope grew mercilessly tight around his neck, making a red burn mark.

Despite the pain he said nothing. His Adam's apple

rose and fell hard in his throat, quelling his urge to cry out in agony and fear. But that is what they wanted. They would not get it, not from him anyways.

The old warrior stepped full into the melee, raising his hands and cursing at the younger braves. He shook his head angrily and pointed up the creek. “Jogo!” he yelled. “Jogo!”

The warriors grunted a few half-hearted protests and took up the tethers tied around their captives’ necks. They ran straight up the opposite bank, not waiting for the bound captives to catch their balance. They dragged them along, yanking at the tethers.

The old warrior, bringing up the rear, promptly scolded them in their native tongue. One of them spat back at him, but all stopped, allowing the captives to regain their footing on the leaf-strewn bank. After a momentary pause they skirted the edge of the gully along a tight trail. Branches snapped back in the young white men’s faces. Not having hands to block the limbs, they closed their eyes and braced for each new blow. They endured silently, praising God when the branches abruptly stopped stinging their faces.

After hurriedly passing through Leggett’s Gap, they all spilled out into a clearing on a slight plateau. Scrambling to the far edge of the clearing the lead warrior slowly raised his hand, motioning the others to halt, much to the young white men’s relief. They all stood gasping for air against the tight tethers around their necks.

The huge warrior in the lead stood tall, gazing carefully around the clearing. His hard eye locked on the gasping and beleaguered prisoners. Rolling his eyes from them, he called his fellow warriors to assemble around him. They parleyed for a few moments, glancing back at the captives and laughing every now and then, and suddenly stopped.

Seemingly not invited, the old warrior stood off to the side of the clearing, muttering to himself and pacing to and fro. A loud complaint crept from his throat to no avail. The younger warriors ignored him.

They slowly circled the grief-stricken boys without saying a word. One of them, then another, advanced to the boys and ran locks of the boys' disheveled hair through their fingers.

Young Tripp stood silently, oddly realizing his hat somehow still remained on his head. He looked up at it while the braves examined Hocksey's and Keyes' locks. They soon sauntered over to him and removed his hat, grabbing at his locks and shoving the hat back onto his head with gruff motions.

The old warrior, seeming infuriated, plowed into them and pushed them away from the frightened lad. He waved his hands at the other two captives and took young Tripp by the arm, leading him over to the edge of the clearing. He removed the boy's hat and gently lifted a few wisps of his hair, all the while waving his other hand and scolding the warriors. He put the hat back on the boy's head and played at the lone feather in his own hair. A tear cut through the red and black paint on his old cheeks, revealing the hint of a long faded tattoo. He again waved at the other white boys and to the gully below. He grabbed at a small medicine pouch dangling about his neck and raised it up to the sky, beseeching some unknown power to intercede.

The ruse worked, especially when a clap of distant thunder boomed seeming to answer the old man's prayers. The warriors' bulging eyes stared up into the sky. The huge warrior shrugged his shoulder and pointed at a lesser brave. The brave shook his spear in anger but quickly ceased under his companion's threatening dark eyes.

He laughed and walked over to young Tripp, squatting in front of him he pulled him down by the lead attached to his neck. He turned his back on his friends leading Keyes and Hocksey off into the gully. He watched Tripp's eyes mirror a deep concern and yanked the lead until his eyes locked with his.

Tripp lost all color in his face staring at the breech-clothed warrior in front of him. He noticed dozens of different tattoos covering his entire body. A long snake covered the entire width of his forehead. Along his upper torso and arms stretched a long line with triangles protruding from under its whole length. Small circles and dots covered almost every other spot of his skin. A silver nosepiece dangled beneath his grinning mouth, exposing yellow teeth stained by tabacco. About the great loops of cartlige cut wide from his ears dangled many smaller silver and brass oranments. Silver arm bands graced each of his arms about his biceps. The tuff of hair about the crown of his head glistened with bear fat grease around the lone and erect feather sticking in it. He appeared all the more horrid face to face than he had ever imagined. Even his breath smelled foreign and strange, bland, but somehow sweet with the smell of the herbs of the forest. And the dark eyes shinning from those bulging white pits, no eyebrows, no hair, save the lone tuff, about his entire body, no doubt painstakingly plucked as to make a smoother base for the paint covering spots of his body. All of him, designed by thousands of years on this land to insight terror in the hearts of his enemies, sat face to face with him. The depth of the war they waged showed starkly in the warrior's eyes. Look as he may not even the slightest glint of mercy shone in those eyes.

Here, sitting but a breath away from one another,

both recognized the vast and immeasurable gap formed buy a thousand different life experiences of they and their ancestors forged by two totally different lands. The gap seemed so insurmountable it could only be forged by a thousand more generations. They both paled at the realization of it. No, this war, this clash of cultures, could not be averted.

A grunt from the old man tore both their gazes from one another. The old man edged his way to the gully, all the while keeping a careful eye on the warrior squatting in front of the white boy. He cocked his head and peered ahead, cupping his hand to his ear. His eyes shone in terror for just a second and disappeared under his tired eyelids. He shook his head and slowly paced back to the clearing. He folded his legs and sat down next to both of them. He stared at Tripp with apologetic eyes but found no words to match the sorrow in his eyes.

The other braves spilled into the clearing from the gully below. They laughed and nodded at one another, mimicking their victims with little regard for young Tripp and the old Indian.

Tripp felt his stomach go sour. A wide grin stretched across the face of the brave squatting in front of him. He rose and jaunted over to the others, gesturing for the inestimable prizes he knew they possessed. With a loud gasp he held up the trophies passed to him by his fellows high in the air, examining them with a certain gleam in his eye. Full of pride, he sauntered over to Tripp and displayed the scalps. First he held the blond one under his nose, twirling it, before switching hands to the red one. A ribbon still tied the hair. A ribbon young Tripp had watched bob up and down in front of him on the trail all day. His jaw slackened and fell.

The huge warrior marched over to Tripp and slapped the hat from his head. He took a rough grab at his hair, pulling it taunt by its roots.

A tear slid down the frightened young white boy's face. He lowered his eyes and watched the warrior's hands plung to his belt. He closed his eyes, bracing himself for the blow from a tomahawk. He felt a fast movement of air about his cheek and stood tall. Do your worst, savage, he thought. I shall not give you the satisfaction of my fear. If my eyes betray me, I shall close them and open them in providence. He took a deep breath, certain it to be his last. A slap rang across his cheek. He felt a wet sensation. In another instant he felt a tug at the leather thongs binding his wrists. Suddenly his hands fell free to his side.

Instinctively he touched his face, feeling the wet sensation on his cheek. He opened his hands wide before him and stared in awe at the red substance on his hands. It felt sticky but too thick to be blood. He neverously smelled it to the roars of laughter erupting from the warriors. Paint, he realized, it's just paint!

The old man rose to his feet in one smooth motion. Overcome with relief he touched the paint on the stunned boy's cheeks. He too started laughing, but in a much less sinister way. "You live!" he said in English. "You live!" He nodded his head profusely. "You live!" He pointed his long bony finger at Tripp and up to the sky. "Hawenneegar! Great spirit! He with you this day!"

Tripp stared in disbelief and took a deep breath, relishing it. Life, even as a captive, never felt so good. He smeared the life-giving paint on his fingers back onto his face. His eyes wide in wonder, he allowed a laugh to escape from his chest, quickly quelling it at the sight of his friend's hair about the belts of his captors. He suddenly wondered whom shared the worst fate.

Chapter Sixteen

Old man Tripp sat unmovable under the great tree in the river common. His head sagged down to his chest. Drips of tears tainted with red paint stained his shirt. He repeatedly mumbled the words he had said when he first appeared in front of the fort, "they've taken them, Leggett's creek, they've taken them."

His grandson Giles Slocum immediately took charge of him, sitting by his side all night since John Jenkins had departed with the rescue party. He listened to his grandfather's mumbles and tried to reassure him, though he knew the doubt he felt tinged his words. But he stood fast, all through this horrid day and watched the sun set with him.

"Here, Grandpa," Giles said, handing him a canteen of rum and a piece of bread, "take this, it's good for what ailes you. You must eat something for when Jenkins brings 'em back you'll need your strength."

The tired eyes that looked up at him said it all. The old man politely refused the bread but took a deep gulp from the canteen.

"Well at least you're feeding your spirit," Slocum said, eating the bread himself. He leaned back against the tree and stared across the great fire in a pit between the tree and fort. He scratched his head and nodded at the two men standing with their arms folded and gazing at them. The two men shook their heads back at him.

"He's taking it hard," Nathan Denison said. "Poor soul."

"Yes," Colonel Butler said, "poor soul indeed. What with what's happen with Luke Swetland and Blanchard, these are trying times indeed. They are either in Hell or Tioga, who knows which, I personally hope heaven for the both, as well as for Keyes, Hocksey, and young Tripp. I fear what tortures those poor souls might have to endure."

Both of the men turned to the odd sound of music in the grim mood of the moment. They stared at the figure silhouetted by fire light against the wall of the fort. They watched his fine and careful movements to the beat of the liviley music and sighed.

"I fear Captain Bush is a bit of a dandy," Denison said. "Southern people are surely a strange lot."

"Yes they are," Butler said, raising his hand to his chin. "But they are his muscians and it is apparently their way."

"Nonsense, especially in these times, in this place," Denison said looking over to a group of women whom had dared return to Wyoming. He felt a relief from their age, certain these stout-hearted frontier women shared his aversion to the young dandy's acts. But they watched with a strange fascination, one of them almost dancing while the other stood coldly staring at the odd sight.

"It seems Mrs. York wants to join the good Captain Bush," Butler said.

The thought of the hard New England woman joining the dignified captain made a chuckle escape from Denison's mouth. He quickly quelled it at the sullen sight of the woman next to Mrs. York. The death of Mrs. Durkee's son but yesterday lay heavily about her face. A nosebleed of all things, he thought, thinking of his own son of equal age. All of Hooker Smith's efforts as well many others simply failed to stop the flow of blood and the boy bled out in front of all their eyes. A tragedy indeed, he being the eldest son of the brave Captain of the First Westmoreland Indepenent Company who fell on the field of the late battle defending their home.

That day still haunted his mind and the vision of the stubborn Mrs. York demanding to be let out of the fort before its surrender flashed through his mind again. The demands for surrender had been delivered by the man who had captured her husband and made them homeless, Parshall Terry. She refused to have anything to do with that rascal, as she called him, and would risk her life and the children's to get away for she felt certain he would slaughter the whole lot in the fort after its surrender. Time had proved her wrong, but such feelings died hard, nonetheless as hard as her stare back at him. He turned his eyes away but she locked eyes with him and marched around the fire to him. He raised a hand to shield his eyes in frustration.

"Oh, my dear Colonels," Lucrietia York said, positioning herself boldly in front of them. She brushed back her hair and cocked her head toward them. She looked out of the corner of her eye to the grieving man by the tree. "No doubt that rascal Terry is about this mischief!" she said.

"My dear Mrs. York it is good to see you," Denison said. Butler just looked down his nose at her without saying a word.

"My Amos died in Connecticut, heart broken and thinking we had all been killed in the massacre," she said. She looked over to the fire. Tears glistened in her eyes. "No doubt from the rigors of his, Fitch's, and Jenkins' cruel imprisonment in that hellish hole in Niagara. Fitch passed too, you know, soon after his exchange." She shook her head and stared up at Colonel Butler. "But you, fine sir, have picked the right man for this bussiness. Damn 'em if John Jenkins crosses paths with that rascal Terry or any of 'em. The only thing he'll bring back is the thieving rascals' scalps! And I pray his shot be true and his knife's sharp, for he's the man for the job, he is!"

"Well," Butler said, "I am glad some approve of my decisions."

"Mrs. York, Terry is but a lowly lieutenant in their ranks, you give him much too much credit," Denison said.

"Ya think, do ya?" Mrs. York said. "Well I tell you, and all my children shall, that no greater devil exists in these parts, man or savage! I bet if you get him, Tom Green, and that Tory dog Thomas Hill a lot of this mischief will cease, I grant ye that bit of wisdom!"

"We will deal with traitors, I assure you," Butler said.

Lucrietia York turned with a gleam in her eye toward Butler. "I durst say ye will, fine sir. I durst say ye will." With that she turned and sauntered back to the fire and sat by the grieving Mrs. Durkee.

"That woman does not lack spirit," Butler said.

"No," Denison said, "but spirit is not everything."

"To her it may be," Butler said.

A call from the other side of the moldy president's marquee gave both of them a start. They looked at the men sitting by the tree next to it. Old Tripp suddenly rose to his feet and took a few steps toward the road.

"Could it be?" Denison asked.

"We can only hope," Butler said, joining the others spilling from the fort to greet the party marching down the road.

All the eyes of Wyoming watched the tired party trudge down the road toward them. Captain Bush's musicians stopped playing. A few cried out to the party, only to have a few muffled grunts sound back to them. The glum mood of the party dampened their spirits, nonetheless more than Old Isaac Tripp. He stumbled toward a crestfallen Lieutenant Jenkins, who shook his head at him.

The old man grasp him by both his shoulders and gazed down to mother earth.

"No," he gasped. He swallowed hard and looked up to the lieutenant.

"No," Jenkins said, stepping off to the side of the road. He shook his head and waited until the two colonels approached within earshot. "We found nothing of them but two hats and a ribbon," he said. "The hats belong to Keyes and Hocksey, there was no sign of young Isaac, which is good, means they've adopted him." He looked sternly into the old man's eyes. "It's good, he'll be fine, I of all should know, and I assure you they'll treat him right. After all this horrid war is over he'll return for sure."

"Yes, young Jenkins," Tripp said, wiping his tears. "You would know if any would. I'll take your word on it."

"You have it," Jenkins said. "Only wish I could have caught up with them and relieved them of their charge and their scalps." He spat on the ground in frustration. "But we done all we could do."

"That you have," Tripp said, "and I, as well as the others, appreciate it."

Jenkins nodded and turned his gaze to the two colonels. They nodded back at him and stood aside, letting the exhausted man stumble to the fort with his men.

"Things are getting a bit hot in more ways than one," Denison said, wiping the sweat from his brow.

"I know," Butler said. "But Hartley and I are of the same mind. The only way to protect the frontier is to strike at them in their own haunts. They sit about Tioga and Chemung convinced they can strike with impudence at us. We must strike and convince them otherwise."

"That we must," Denison said. "That we must."

Chapter Seventeen

A slight mist in the early morning haunted the trees surrounding Fort Muncy. Men slowly rose from sleep and prepared to meet the duties of a new day. Fires crackled to life. Horses neighed and oxen bellowed. Besides the beasts of burden, all seemed quiet and serene to the lone sentries posted about the half-finished fort, so much so they paid little heed to the three men nonchalantly walking out the gate and into the early morning fog.

One of them, fearing the corporal of the guard, called behind them in German to halt. They turned and muttered something back to the man and waved off his protest.

Nothing stirred in the still of the dawn and the wild potatoes growing just beyond the fort offered a tempting addition to their bland rations. Some people worry too much, they said in German to each other before continuing their trek. They took but three more steps before stopping.

One of them pointed to the scrub brush immediately in front of them and cocked his head to gaze into it. A half dozen rifles instantly barked in the still fog. The man stood erect, gasped, and fell in a clump to the ground much to the dismay of his unarmed bretheren. Yells sounded from the spectors in the fog.

"Mien Goot! Das wildens!" one of them screamed, dropping his bundle. His fellow turned and ran pell-mell for the fort, leaving his stunned friend standing alone.

Out of the fog stepped a bold white man, dressed in a green coat with a leather cap. Several painted men sprang from the bushes behind him. The white man ignored the German in front of him and knelt down, leveling his rifle on the back of the running man. He fired, sending a clump of dirt flying just between the man's legs.

"Alarm! Alarm!" sounded from inside the fort. A drum immediately beat assembly. Several sentries fired at the men emerging from the misty fog. Groggy voices barked out urgent orders inside the fort.

"Damn!" the green coated white man said, quickly reloading his rifle. He glared at the Rebel militiaman standing before him.

"Tory dog!" the German yelled. He threw down his bundle and darted toward the green-coated miscreant, his eyes bulging with anger. A stout Indian checked his advance, swinging his tomahawk wildly at the infuriated German.

The mad German grabbed the Indian's hand and twisted the weapon from his grasp, sending him tumbling to the ground. He locked eyes on the other Indians milling around the body of his fallen comrade, becoming more enraged. One of them lifted his friend's bloody scalp into the air. He let out a agonizing groan and advanced steadily toward them, seeming oblivious of their number.

"He's a right smart one," the Tory said, carefully aiming his rifle at him. Before he could squeeze the trigger his target fell to the ground in a mass of arms and legs. The stout Indian had risen, full of anger himself, and tackled him from behind.

The Tory lifted his rifle and watched the struggle before him with a certain glee. Several whizzes about his ears quickly broke his gaze. He aimed at one of the advancing sentries and fired, watching the ball thud into the stockade behind them and send splinters flying in the air. He slowly backed into the shielding fog and scrub brush, yelling along with his Indian allies at the top of his lungs.

The militiaman and Indian rolled about the ground, grunting and groaning. Finding one another's throat, their hands locked around them. Blood trickled from each of their fingertips from their death grips. They stumbled to their feet, both stubbornly refusing to release their death hold on one another. Shots rang in the air around them. Spurts of dirt erupted in the air about their feet. With one great burst of strength the German picked the Indian up and threw him toward the brush. Branches cracked and a loud groan sounded in the air. In another instant the sound of feet madly scampering away in the brush filled the air.

The lone white man let out a loud groan and collapsed to his knees, staring with blank eyes at his fallen friend. He gripped great handfuls of earth in his clenched fists and flung it into the brush. He ignored the troops pouring around him and firing into the folds of the forest. Overcome with grief, he leaned over his friend's body and openly wept.

Colonel Hartley trudged through the field toward the disturbance. He waved and nodded for the men scampering around him to surge ahead, all the while holding a pistol in one hand while clenching a blanket tight around him with the other. He hacked and coughed to a stop by the grieving man.

The man turned his head toward the sick colonel. "Mien God, Herr Colonel, mien God, look what das wildens has done to poor Hans!" he said. "I'se knew him well, he was mien friend, poor soul!" He pounded his hands into the earth with a terrific thud. "All's we wanted was der bit of potatoes, that's all. Something must be done about these wildens!"

The colonel bowed his head, cursing his feverish

body. He turned to hear the thud of hard hooves racing toward them. He watched Captain Carberry crash his horsemen in the forest, yelling and screaming a warning to any of the enemy within earshot.

"Too late," Hartley said, shaking his aching head, "too late."

"Sir, a Tory was with 'em for sure, all dessed in green he was," an excited corporal reported to Hartley. He looked down at the body and to the fort not two rods away from them. "They're brazen devils, they are, bold as all hell, and getting more bolder each day." He scratched his head and turned to greet Captain Walker emerging from the brush.

"No sign of them," Walker said, doffing his hat. "They've disappeared."

"Yes," Hartley said, "something must be done, and now!" He moved one of his mocassins against the slight frost on the ground. It crunched. The hint of crimson shone on some of the trees. "The season is getting late and there is no sign of the Indians and Tories letting up," he said. He wiped at his nose in frustration. "Curse this damn fever, without it we should have been off against them weeks ago! Damn it all to hell!"

"The rains shall start soon," Walker said.

Hartley cocked a cold eye toward him. "Give this poor soul a proper burial and assemble everyone back in the fort. I am to write a dispatch to Butler, Hunter, and Bush. We will strike soon! Woe be to those savage devils when we do!"

"Yes sir," Walker said.

"But keep it under your hat, lest prying eyes shall see and hear," Hartley said, gazing down at the German. "No one is to say a word, no one!"

The sorrowful German let out a great sob and stood.

"No worries, sir," Walker said, taking the man by the shoulder and guiding him to the fort, "I don't think he's heard a word through his grief. We'll get the men ready on some pretense, no one shall suspect a thing."

"I hope so," Hartley said, staring into the forest. "I hope so, for surprise may be all we have against these devils."

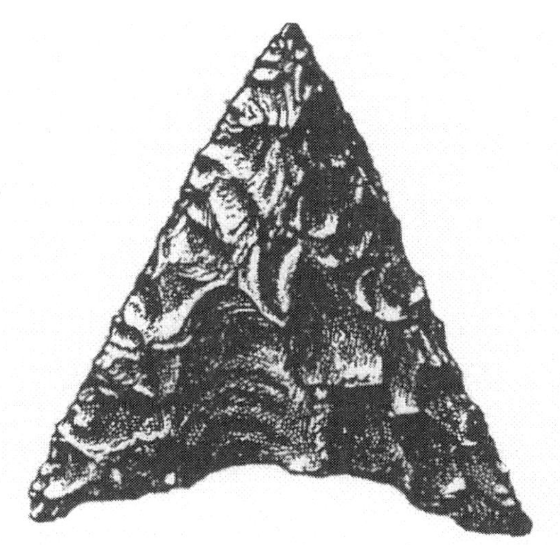

Chapter Eighteen

Robert Covenhoven moved with all the grace and stealth he possessed. He scampered over rocks when he could, knowing it would leave the least sign of his passing. The forest had eyes and he knew them. He had traded with them, scouted, and hunted all the far reaches of the West Branch before all these difficulties. He knew the trails, the white men, and the haunts of their enemies. This, perhaps, he reasoned, is why the good colonel trusted only he and his fellow scout William Stewart, sent to Wyoming while he went to Sunbury, with the dispatches sewn into their hunting shirts. He thought of the bogus dispatches in his pouch and felt the full wieght of his mission.

Apparently Hartley's faith in him knew some bounds, but he would try his best to keep faith in himself-and therefore his scalp.

He wound along the edge of the trail, ready to dart behind a tree at the first sight of anyone. This war produced many a traitor in patriot's clothing and he knew his mission to be too grave to trust anyone but his senior commanders. Still, the loneliness crept through his soul. With each caw of a crow or rustle of a deer his heart burst against his chest. Two rifles proved best in some tight spots, as well as two minds. But Hartley demanded strict secrecy, wipsing he and Stewart off in the dead of the night with dispatches to his other commanders. But at the last moment Hartley had sent an officer with Stewart, thus increasing the odds of he making his trek. He felt somehow cheated and it all felt errie but duty called and he would meet it or die, alone or not.

A slight movement of red in the trees ahead caused

him to freeze in his tracks. His eyes locked on the movement while he shifted his body ever so slightly around a huge tree. He listened. A few song birds whistled their tunes in the still air. The slight rush of a stream below mixed with the sounds-all normal, no sounds of alarm from man nor beast.

He crept along through great ferns carpeting the forest's floor, careful not to disturb any of the creatures, for he knew his enemy's ears depended upon their warning. Some slight rustling noises sounded ahead along with gutoral words. He stopped and listened to them, trying in vain to hear the gist of the conversation. Distance clouded the words. He had to move closer. He lowered himself fully to the soft earth, slowly easing his rifle along under the ferns. With each breath he moved a hand, then a knee, forward. His eyes darted all around while he moved. His neck tingled. All his senses poured into one. He focused on a great moss-covered rock just above his prey and moved ever so slightly toward it.

The voices grew from two to three to finally four. He stopped and listened just before the rock, contemplating a detour around the trail. The trail grew tight here, funneling down into a great gorge too steep to bypass without losing much time. No, this is the way he had to go. He crept to the rock and eased his back into the soft moss. Raising his rifle up to his chest he waited, hoping the enemy would move on before nightfall.

Moments ticked away with each beat of his heart. He sat without moving a muscle, listening intently to the sounds below him. A fire crackled. Feet shuffled now and then but always away from him, much to his relief. He listened to the voices, one bragging, while another belittled everything the braggard said. Another laughed and yet another pleaded that they head back up the trail to menace the *white-eyes* while they sat in their forts. More scalps needed to be taken to Tioga, he pleaded. More *white-eyes* needed to see no more until they finally left this land-their land.

Finally the argument grew in nature. A loud voice boomed in protest, only to be rebuked. Even the *white-eyes* could hear such loud boasts. One must lower their voice to be one with the forest and speak in harmony with it-not against it, as the *white-eyes* did until only their rants could be heard.

Covenhoven listened, fearful that if he retreated he would be detected. He felt down to the pistol in his sash and to his tomahawk. One shot, rifle, one gone. One shot, pistol, two gone. One throw of the tomahawk, three gone, but that still left one. One armed just as well as he. One just as fierce as he. He pushed himself flat against the moss and mouthed a prayer.

One after another the voices grew fainter with distance until finally only one remained, taunting the others in their retreat. After the retreating taunts faded only the sound of a slight rustle through the leaves of the forest slid over the moss-strewn rock.

He lift his head slowly around the edge of the rock. A lone back faced him but a rod away from his hiding place. Wisps of smoke rose from the dying fire off to his side. He watched the muscles in the tawny back flex while the hands diligently worked on something. Something he could not see, but prayed the task would soon be completed so both could be on their way. One his way and one the other, with only the former knowing that they passed. But that is the way he preferred it. A rifle shot would raise the alarm. Who knows just how far his fellows were up the trail? Perhaps they would soon return.

He watched the back work. The muscles rose and

fell. A grunt of frustration accompanied some exaggerated movements. One hand lowered a knife to the ground and another raised a small sapling to his front.

He noted the postion of the brave's rifle on the ground to his left by his pouch and tomahawk. Very little other possessions showed around the brave. He must be traveling light or part of a greater war party camped somewhere near.

He eased his rifle up to his chest and watched the trail off to his right. He reasoned he might make it past the preoccupied brave if he moved slowly to the right side of the trail. The day grew long. He had to move soon for he could not waste much more time.

A gasp, followed quickly by a grunt, and finally a cheer of triumph, rose from the brave before him. The Indian stood up and extended his arms fully, gazing with pride at the trophy in his hands.

Covenhoven's jaw dropped at the sight. Long flowing hair reached down from the sapling hoop in front of the brave. Hair of a woman. A helpless woman. His rifle slid over the top of the rock.

The brave moved his head in his direction and suddenly stopped. The whites of his eyes shone against the pale light of dusk. Eyes shining with surprise and terror.

A flash erupted into the whites of his eyes. The brave fell, all his life drained from him except for the slight twitching of his hand still cradling the prize on the hoop.

Covenhoven darted out from behind the rock, sprinting past the twitching Indian. He ran, his heart brimming with the satisfaction of exacting revenge for some poor unfortunate while pulsating with a fear for his own life. The others heard the shot, no doubt. The others would find the body. The hunt may have just begun.

Chapter Nineteen

Abel Yarington stood with his arms folded tightly across his chest and glared at the intruders sitting around his table. His fingers clenched his slouch hat in his hands. His grip tightened and scrunched the hat into an awful shape the more he thought about the invasion of his home by this *court-martial*.

He had worked diligently repairing his charred home while also standing picket duty and other activities impressed upon the local populace by Colonel Butler. Butler! There he sat at the head of the table, shuffling some papers and looking all the part of a regal lord. Had the colonel not heard of the Quartering Act? This revolution? No one fought it to replace a haughty aristocracy, but to eliminate it! And what of that damned marquee he had him drag over the mountains to him? Did the mold covering it get the best of him and cloud his common sense?

Abel bit his lip and noticed the uncomfortable looks from most of the officers assembled. They nervously fidgeted and gazed toward the window; paying more attention to it than they did to the poor souls paraded before them. And what for? This one had a bit too much to drink, for shame! This one did not show up for picket duty promptly enough to suit the colonel. These brazen souls played cards! Oh what sins! It seemed to him the good officers' attention should be placed on defending the settlement, not harassing their own men! And the punishments! Fifty lashes for this one! This man to stand five minutes on a sharp picket with his bare feet for simply discharging his weapon! This one to be confined for looking contemptuously at an officer! The enemy lay out there, my good gentlemen, do not make new ones among your own men! But he knew no protest would do him any good but would only bring scorn and accusations of he being a Tory. What nonsense! The only time they made the least bit of sense is when they rebuked their men for killing swine, sheep, or poultry, and for burning fence rails instead of firewood.

Finally the proceedings dragged to a close, much to Abel's relief.

Butler stood and his officers immediately followed his lead. He bowed his head slightly and looked to his adjuant who handed him more papers. "It seems our docket is full for the morrow as well," he said, casting a gaze at Abel.

Abel rolled his eyes.

"I am sure our fine host has no objection for the use of his fine and spacious home on the morrow, being the fine citizen he is," Butler said.

A few coughs sounded from his officers, no doubt masking chuckles.

Butler slammed his boot down on the floor. "Now see here!" he said. "All these proceedings are following the Articles of War and sundry General Orders which have been published throughout the American army! I myself am surprised to find that disciplined Continental troops should be so lost to good order as to be found violating those rules and orders. And if it continues, so shall these courts! Nowhere does it state that distance from the main army annuls all discipline! We are part of the American army and damn it and we are going to act like it! Do I make myself clear!"

"Yes sir," the officers answered in unison. Even Abel Yarington looked away in shame.

Butler glared at each eye that dared to look at him. He gritted his teeth against his anger. Wyoming will stand, he thought, if I have to give fifty lashes to every one of them!

A rush from outside the door broke the tense air. Everyone looked to William Stewart, scout from Colonel Hartley. A staunch officer stood silently beside him in a blue regimental. He stood rigid without saying a word or recognizing anyone's nod to him. The scout stepped up to Butler and handed him a dispatch. "It is most urgent, sir," he said, "orders are to have you read it immediately!"

Butler rolled his tongue against his cheek. "Very well," he said, "these proceedings are closed but none of you go far." He motioned with the paper to the door. The officers donned their hats and filed out the door quietly, only mumbling to one another when the door closed behind the last one.

Butler raised his palm toward Yarington.

Abel shook his head at the request he vacate his own home but nonetheless complied. He stepped into his kitchen and plopped down into a chair. The legs scratched angrily against the floor. Stewart stepped just inside the door and stood there, not wishing to tempt the already agitated man. He cleared his throat and leaned against the door jam, giving Yarington most of the room. The officer accompanying him strode across the room and sat at the table opposite the disgruntled civilian. He stared blankly at the man.

Butler sat down at the great table and gently broke the wax seal on the dispatch. He looked carefully about the windows before finally unfolding it. He drew it close to his face and began to read:

September 10, 1778, Colonel Butler,
commanding, Camp Westmoreland.

"Upon a full consideration concerning the Indian country, and a view of the circumstances of our affairs, I have come to these determinations. That it is absolutely necessary that the troops at Wyoming, those on the west branch, and in this department, should effect a junction before they proceed against Chemung, where, I understand, a great part of the plunder taken from our unhappy brethren at Wyoming, and a body of Indians and Tories, are collected. I mean that this town should be approached by the Lycoming path to the mouth of the Towanda, and that the troops should sweep the country down river to Wyoming. This will give relief to our frontiers, and intimidate our enemies. I have mentioned some of the particulars to Lieutenant Lemon, which he can inform you.

"I am informed many of your people have the highest inclination to go against some of the Indian towns, they may revenge the murders of fathers, brothers and friends, besides serving their country. You will detain Captain Kenney with a Sergeant and ten men of my regiment, a subaltern and twenty of Spalding's and Howe's men, of those who are the yeast able to march; of which Captain Kenney is to take charge, under your immediate direction, in your garrison. That Captain Bush, with the residue of my regiment and the other troops at Wyoming, do march from thence on Monday next by the route of Freeland's Mills to Muncy Fort, near Wallis'. They are to bring all the pack-horses, saddles, &c., with them. It is expected they will arrive at Fort Muncy the third night of their march, or the fourth day.

"It will be impossible to tell the troops or people where they are to march to. You must induce the militia to go-say they are marching against some Indian town. After they are marched, the garrison are to be informed that the men are gone to the West Branch to support the people there, who have been attacked by the Indians.

The route to Muncy will justify the last; the Tories will be deceived. You will act in the best manner you can doing the absence of the troops. I shall not, perhaps, go to Chemung (this is between you and I), and you shall be supported with all the troops in this quarter in case of emergency. A garrison will be continued near Nescopeck. You may communicate this letter to Captains Bush and Kenney ; and also to Colonel Dennison and Mr. Stewart-under the strictest injuction of secrecy. Mr. Howe and Murray have had some intimations, but I dare say they will keep them secret. The inhabitants who go on this expedition will be back time enough to put in some Fall grain.

Your most obedient and humble servant,

Colonel Thomas Hartley."

Well it has started, Butler thought. He suddenly felt a numbing preminition, not sure if it came from he being uninvited on the expedition or if it bore forewarning of some future disaster. Either way, orders had to be followed, as he so sternly reminded his troops, by he as well as by them.

He leaned back and rubbed his chin. The surrender terms of the valley flashed in his mind for a moment, but they, he assured himself, had already been violated by both parties. What a surprise lay ahead for the Indians. A surprise and a lesson. This time they would learn it well. He felt certain of it.

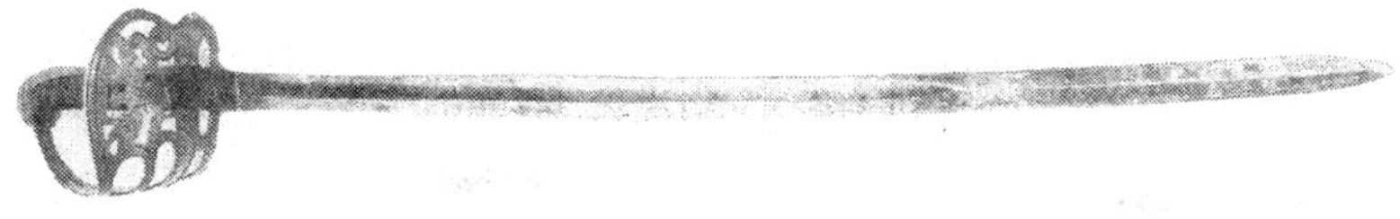

Chapter Twenty

Colonel Hartley watched the troops trickle into Fort Muncy with a hollow feeling nagging at his soul. Expecting a flood-Pennsylavania itself promised five hundred troops-the sparse numbers milling about the fort did not bade well for him, nor his plans.

He stood alone and by a great tree between the new fort and Wallis' stone house. He paced around once in a while and let his mind flood his thoughts with reassurances. They will come, he thought, they must. Surely men of such wisdom and resolve as to be elected to defend the nation could see their vulnerable back door. From the Iroquois Nation's southern door at Tioga Point a flood could sweep down right to Philadelphia. It already had, once. Thank God for some reason it halted at Wyoming. Do not leave the door open! It must be shut, or at least a foot put against it.

He rubbed his aching head and cursed the lingering ague pestering him. He pulled his regimental coat snuggly around his stout frame and drew a deep breath. Out of the corner of his eye he spied a pair of men approaching. Standing tall, he turned toward them.

"Colonel," the taller of the two said, doffing his hat. "This here is Hawkins Boone, Captain, as I, but he is of the Twelfth Pennsylvania, detached here to assist in any way possible, as I."

"Yes Captain Brady," Hartley said, extending his hand to Boone. "All are welcome, fine sir. A clever body of men are assembling here, are they not?"

"Clever," Brady said, "but not great in number."

"Numbers don't mean a thing where we're heading," Boone said. "Guts is what matters up there!"

"Yes, and thank God courage does not seem to be lacking," Hartley said.

"Each man carrying a rifle here is a crack shot," Boone said, raising his extraordinarily long rifle. It stood clearly a foot over his head. "Can't vouch for those carrying fowling pieces and muskets, though."

Hartley winced at the reference to Captain Murray's six month men and his own regiment. "I have ordered all not carrying rifles to load with swan shot and have supplied ample cartridges."

"Swan shot you say," Boone said. "That is fine, all one's to do is point and crack off a shot, anything near will catch the lead. It's great for bush fighting, it is."

"Well, I am glad you agree."

"It is time we taught the savage a proper lesson," Brady said. His eye turned to the sky in reflection of some haunting thought. "Young James needs to be avenged. A finer son no man ever had than James. He is sorely missed, he is."

"Much needs to be avenged," Boone added.

"We shall do what we can, I assure you both," Hartley said.

"Then it is true that this force is to march upon the Indians?" Brady asked.

"We shall do what we can, gentlemen," Hartley answered, putting a finger to his nose, "but we must remain tight lipped. Surprise is of the essence. These are dangerous times, one day a man is loyal to Congress, the next to the Crown."

Brady's hand fell to the long knife in his belt. He flashed the long blade up to his neck. "If I know of any such, they shall breathe their last by this blade!" he said, his eyes alive with purpose.

Hartley's eyes widened at the gesture. These grim men of the frontier meant business. Woe to the savage or Tory they encountered. He suddenly felt less worried about numbers; perhaps spirit accounted for more, making one of his men worth thrice the enemy.

A call from the fort caught all their attention. Captain Walker waved at Hartley and motioned to a stout little man standing next to him. Hartley raised his hand in reply. The man nodded to Walker and immediately started for Hartley.

"Well, we'll be about our business," Boone said, cocking his head to Brady. Both touched the brims of their hats before turning and walking toward the fort. The little man paid them no heed and marched past them, seeming hell-bent to reach the colonel.

"Herr Colonel," the man said, shifting his rifle to his left hand. He reached into his pouch and produced a neatly folded paper. He carefully unfolded it and presented it to the colonel.

Hartley took the paper and read it, slightly relieved it not to be another dispatch from a militia commander regretting his inability to answer his call at the present time.

"Ensign Fox," he said, reading the commission, "of the Ninth Company of the Twenty-Fourth Connecticut Militia. It is well to see you. Do you bring word of your regiment?"

"Nien, ich here on mien own account," Fox said. "Krieg has taken them all. Der wildens, der Tories! I hears they march to this place, to join you. Ich come to fight!"

"It is good to have you," Hartley said. "As of yet your regiment has not arrived but I do most earnestly hope they shall produce themselves soon."

"Ja, Colonel, they will, I'se knows it to be true," Fox

said. He lifted his rifle and rubbed its stock. "Fine shot I is, der wildens has taken me twice, they will not again!"

"This man has great knowledge of the up river country," Walker said, appearing as if from nowhere.

Hartley nodded to him and handed the paper back to the proud German.

He took it ever so gently. Lowering his rifle to the ground he painstakingly folded the prized paper and placed it carefully back in its coveted place in his pouch.

"He has property about the Towanda Creek," Walker said. "He knows Ester's village, as well as the Queen herself, Sheshecunnunk, and Tioga, as he knows the back of his hand. Such knowledge may prove indispensable."

Hartley glared at Walker for a moment. "Yes it may," he said through gritted teeth, "and it may not, also."

Walker stayed mute, taking the hint. He wondered why the colonel stuck to such measures when rumors flew all over the valley. It did not take much to figure out what this rendezvous could be all about, anyhow. But he minded his tongue, though he doubted whether the grinning Dutchman knew the importance of the matter. The man had proved himself no friend of the Crown but a staunch patriot, plus he held a patriot's commission.

"I'se see about mien interests," Fox said. The smile poured from his face. "Das burned, I bet it is. Barn, cabin and all."

"This war is hell on us all," Walker said.

"Yes, and hell has ears perked for just such information," Hartley said.

Walker shifted his lips and rubbed his chin.

"Anyway, Ensign Fox, we welcome you, find a place to settle and await orders," Hartley said, gazing up at the yellow and crimson leaves already dotting some trees around them. "I assure you shall not have to wait long, my good fellow."

Walker waited until the German walked well out of earshot before speaking again. "We have but eighty four assembled here as of yet. We have good powder, the best I've ever seen, and most of these men are fine shots. We have ample barrels of flour and whiskey for a two week march, I durst say."

Eighty four, Hartley mused, from the five hundred promised or even the four hundred he felt he needed for a proper expedition. One had to make due, but this seemed ridiculous. He clenched his fist and gritted his teeth against the doubts plaguing him. Those damn politicians. It is well to have good commanders in the field but of what use is it when he is ordered and regulated by hands far from the work; hands not stained by the blood, sweat, and earth. General Wayne had told him men of his vision could be just as valuable on the floor of congress as in the field. He considered the thought once more and reflected on the insight of the General. Congress needed men of good horse sense.

He glanced at Walker and strode around the great tree. It took a full twenty steps to manage the circumference of the thing. Each branch reminded him of many a tree about Philadelphia. He carefully looked around before approaching Walker again. "Look at it man," he said, sweeping his arms high against the sheer girth of the mighty elm. "It alone could build a fine house with many board feet to spare! Look about the land! It is rich beyond belief, and virgin, untouched by the hand of those without the foresight to develop it for the good of all mankind." He shook his head and looked down to the ground. He kicked it with his feet, scratching a patch in its fertile face.

"It is a rich land sir," Walker said.

"Yes, rich and in contention between three great powers," Hartley said. "Much more is at play here than a simple foray against some brazen savages. Empires are to be settled and won. Do not think Wyoming is forgotten! I tell you great minds are at work about this problem. If this war is settled now we risk the lost of great stretches of land. Our borders with Canada shall be the Hudson and as far down as Sunbury, perhaps even Carlisle! No, this land is much too important for America. We must subdue the great enemy to the north, the Six Nations, if we are ever to have any hope for peace. It is paramount to any expansion of our fledgling nation to the north or west!"

Walker stayed silent, letting the colonel vent his frustrations.

"Colonel Butler of the Fourth Pennsylvania is poised to march at this very moment along with Morgan's riflemen. We are to meet at some northern point, possibly Tioga, and from there teach Brant, Butler, and the Johnsons a lesson they shall not soon forget. What of Brant? Is he about Tioga, just waiting for us to step into an ambuscade of his design? Eighty four is not enough. My God where are Captains Bush and Spalding? Perhaps with their number we shall have a chance, without them it shall be sheer folly. I cannot risk such good men. And Wallis, along with that man Smith, I have my doubts of both of them, but Wallis holds the high command's confidence, and Smith holds his." He stopped and considered his words, embarrassed about exposing his deepest thoughts to the captain.

"I think," Walker finally said, "that the good men, this clever body of men, shall be wondering where the devil their colonel has gotten off to."

"Yes, I suppose they shall." With that Hartley stood

tall and threw back his head, regaining his composure. "Thank you for your ear, Captain."

Walker let a slight smile spread across his face. "Come sir, there is the matter of whom shall reign over this great land to be settled. I assure you it shall be by Americans before all is said and done. I feel the hand of God in this."

"What is it Doctor Franklin has said? God helps those whom help themselves? Why, by jingo, it is time we took stock of the great man's insight," Hartley said.

Walker gave a courtly bow of his head.

The two men stepped out into the great clearing of five hundred yards all around the palisides of the fort. They both spiritedly marched toward the bustling fort, hastening their steps on hearing the sound of cheering and martial music by the gate.

A column marched smartly into the clearing. Two mounted men sat in its van, one in a smart blue regimental coat with white facings and the other in a double-breasted short brown coat with red cuffs and collar. Both sat high in the saddle, doffing their hats to the many cheers and salutes greeting them. Four musicians marched briskly immediately in their rear, beating and playing lively airs. A wide assortment of men marched in step behind them, though some ragged and threadbare, they appeared nonetheless smart.

Every face they encountered beamed with joy at them. Rifles fired straight into the air. Cannon boomed a salute. The wave of apprehension in the air lifted in the faces of the jovial men.

"They bring a great spirit with them," Walker said, stopping with Hartley just to the front of the column.

"To say the least, my good Captain, to say the least," Hartley said. He looked up to the two captains reining their horses to a stop and ordering their column of men to halt.

"Colonel Hartley!" Captain Spalding said, removing his hat and sweeping it in a great arc to the column of men behind him. "Wyoming has arrived, sir!"

"Indeed it has, Captain," Hartley said. "Indeed it has!"

Chapter Twenty One

Colonel Hartley shifted neverously in his bed. The hoots and calls of the forest plagued his mind. Were they the real creatures of the forest or the pretenders, corrupting the creatures' calls for their own means? And at whom and or what would they strike? Another poor soldier far from home? A soldier in his charge? And what of the civilians they all swore to protect? Another eerie yell sounded in the still of the night, sending a shiver clear down his backbone. He threw his blanket aside, looking around for his boots. The report of the sentry announcing all is well eased him back down onto his bed. "Will it never end?" he asked himself aloud. How could it? How is one to fight the night and those cloaked in its folds?

The war cries in the dead of the night had become more frequent in the past few days. Could it be just the braggadocio of a warrior in a passing war party or an affirmation that they watched and saw all about the fort? These thoughts kept him awake and tossing and turning in his bed. Just when he managed to drift off to sleep the war cries would start as if on cue. He wondered of it. Could it be an omen or just chance?

He pulled the blanket up to his neck and stared out of the window. He waited as he did every night for the gentle glow of the sun to rise. How would he greet this day? Two days ago the remainder of his regiment and the Wyoming troops arrived. No one else had answered the call. A decision had to made soon. March or cancel?

A slimmer of light crept through the window and

shone on the stone walls. He threw the blanket aside and reached for his boots. Today he reviewed the troops. Today he decided, he told himself. The season grew too late with each passing day. Soon what few troops he had assembled would need to return to their fields. The grain needed to be harvested, but first the mighty pests must be dwelt with or there would be no peace. He had half the troops he felt he needed to proceed on a proper expedition. Half the troops, half the chance. Could the frontier stand against another great defeat? But on the other hand an equally great victory would certainly raise the spirits of the settlers, thus hastening their return to the Susquehanna frontier.

A noise at the door cast his eyes toward it. Wallis' servant called to him, as if waiting outside the door all night. Could he be watching or just an overanxious servant? "Yes, I am up," he answered.

"Fine, sir," the servant said from the other side of the door. "I've already fetched some fresh milk. I'll be waiting for you."

"I'm sure you will," he said under his breath. "I'm sure you will."

He quickly washed and shaved in a basin. Donning and straightening his regimental coat he lifted the latch on the door, half expecting the servant to be there to greet him. He sighed at the sight of the empty hallway and made his way downstairs. A bowl of fresh milk sat on a table in the kitchen, along with a loaf of bread beside it. He sat, passing his hat to the ever-waiting hands of the servant.

White teeth shone from the great smile stretching across the black man's face. He bowed and courtly retreated to the stairway. "Master Wallis wants to know when his guests rise," he said. "I'll fetch him."

"No bother," Hartley said.

"No sir," the servant said. "He's a want'n to know and the master gets what he's a want'n, he do for sure!"

"Very well," Hartley said, crumbling a chunk of bread into the milk in the bowl. He took up his spoon but then lowered it, suddenly losing his appetite. A drum roll sounded from the fort, followed by grumbling complaints from Wallis down the hallway. A bit of his true colors showing in the grogginess of being awakened too soon? Hartley thought. One's true colors did shine in the first light of the day, before they became shaded with the complications of the day.

He ate a few heaping spoonfuls of milk and bread before his host rose, wishing to be about his business without Wallis' influence. Wallis seemed to become more and more interested in the workings of the high command as of late.

If Wallis did not hold the confidence of Benjamin Rush, John Dickinson, and General Washington, Hartley would have retired long ago to the walls of the fort and observed the cunning land owner from the safety of arms length. But to do that now would be an insult not only to Wallis, but to those whom confidence he held. Perhaps they knew more of the man than he, he surmised. For now he would be polite and except his advice with a smile, along with his thinly veiled compliments.

"I have business to attend," he called up the hallway, not waiting for a response before donning his hat and walking out the door. "I apoligize for any inconvienince."

The bright sun greeted him. He raised his hand to shield his eyes and carefully surveyed the surrounding area. After nodding to the saluting sentry he marched toward the fort.

Captains Walker, Bush, and Spalding greeted him at the gate of the fort. They all turned after cordual salutations and gazed about the troops. Fires crackled all along the parade ground. Men rose and stretched from the frames of the few logs placed as a beginning of barracks and other buildings. All seemed antimated and eager to rise. No grumbles or complaints filled the air, as they had in every other camp Hartley had ever known. A pleasant surprise. He smiled at each of the officers, conveying his compliments to their troops.

"A fine lot they are," Bush said, straightening his fine uniform. He looked out of place among the ragged and threadbare men surrounding him, but he always did, Hartley mused. Somehow the man had repaired his uniform and maintained it immaculately though he participated in all the activities of his fellow officers. A bit of a dandy, but a fine commander of troops all the same. He would not trade the man for any other officer of equal rank.

All three of the other officers eyed Bush, each seeming to silently share Hartley's thoughts of the man.

Bush raised a questioning eyebrow to them in return.

"None the more finer than the officers which lead them," Hartley said, breaking the uneasy air. "I have assembled a clever body of men, have I not?"

"Each man-jack of them is equal to three of the enemy, I durst say," Spalding said.

"Yes, no doubt," Hartley said.

"Are we to march soon?" Bush asked.

"I am considering the matter," Hartley said, gazing at Walker.

Walker nodded.

"I pity any savage this lot encounters, sir," Bush said, "be he blue-eyed or what! Yes sir! I do!"

"Yes," Hartley said. "Let the men eat and then assemble them for review."

"Yes sir," all of the captains said at once. They smartly

turned and marched toward their awaiting troops, all wearing cocksure and reassuring smiles.

Hartley acknowledged a few of the many nods and stares at him while he walked around the fort. He climbed to the platform along the wall, politely nodding to the men, but anxious to escape their questioning eyes. He clasp his hands behind his back and stared blankly over the walls, becoming lost in his thoughts.

He only turned when the drum beat assembly. He unclasp his hands and gazed down at the well assembled ranks. The line of men stood rigid and stern, each eye to the front and each firelock sitting straight on a shoulder. Pausing in a moment of admiration, he slowly climbed down the ladder. He turned at its bottom and smartly faced the straight ranks.

Bush drew his sword, raised it to his face and lowered it to his side in salute. The other officers quickly followed suit in order of rank.

Hartley marched along the ranks immediately, stopping now and then to face a few of the men. One in particular caught his eye. The character in the man's eyes shone above the rags covering his body. His beaver skin hat sat mishappen on his head. Disheveled clumps of hair flowed every which way from under its brim. Bits of red, soiled and faded, sat on the collar and cuffs of his well worn short brown coat. A frayed shouder strap dangled from his right shoulder. A soiled white strap intersected a brown one across his chest, which jutted out full of pride. One strap ended with a cartridge box while the other held a cutlass in a sheath. Both appeared well worn from use; the brown strap mended with a knot tied half way up it. Torn and frayed and once white breeches clothed his thighs, barely, below them bare legs, scratched and cut with many thorns, led down to buckless shoes. A tied rag bound the right shoe while toes protruded from the front of the left shoe.

Hartley fought to hold the shock from his face, but he knew it shone through by the curious look in the soldier's eyes. "Don't fret, Colonel," the soldier said, forsaking military disipline for the sake of the moment. He stared directly into the colonel's eyes. "We're all ready for the march, if'n you're ready to lead us all. We'll make you proud."

"You already have," Hartley said, casting a gaze down the entire line. "You all have."

He locked eyes with the soldier again, but this time only a soldier's eyes shone back at him, full of bravery and a call to duty. Where do we get such men? Hartley thought to himself. Emaciated and in rags, these men clamored for the march and a meeting with the enemy. Rags may clothe them, but the spirit of patriotism fed their souls. All doubt drained from his thoughts while staring into those eyes. March we must! Conquer we must!

"Captain Bush!" he said, taking a few careful steps back from the Wyoming soldier. "Prepare for the march! We shall depart at first light on the morrow! Cook four days rations and damn the Tory and Indian rats to hell!"

A roar of huzzas immediately erupted from the troops as well as from the officers. He turned and lifted his head high, marching back toward that devil Wallis' house to prepare he and his troops for the rigors of the march and certain battle that lay ahead.

Come hell or high water Wyoming would be avenged!

Chapter Twenty Two

Great fires illuminated the night. Many shadows danced to and fro against the tall stockade of Fort Muncy. Nary anyone had slept but a few winks since Colonel Hartley's decision to march yesterday morning. But no one complained. No one dragged their feet. They had waited too long for this opportunity. They would fight this war on the frontier with all the rigor of those fighting the regulars; for they knew not only their country depended upon it but also their very lives and prosperity.

Colonel Hartley walked up and down the line of pack-horses, inspecting each one by the light of a burning pine knot held by a private. He stopped now and then and tugged at the straps holding the barrels and packs snug to the horses' backs. "Very fine," he said, gently patting a horse on the rump. "Good job to all." He looked over to the officer watch-ing him. "All is well, Captain Sweeney, is it not?"

"Oh, yes sir," Sweeney answered. "We've whiskey and flour for a good twelve days!"

Hartley strode past him and to one of the many smaller cooking fires dotting the ground. He looked down at the flat hots rocks sizzling with flour cakes. "Plenty of boiled beef and ash cake for all," he said, walking over to another group preparing for the march. A great huzza met him.

"We are ready, Colonel," an officer said, doffing his hat in salute. He raised his rifle in the air and slapped its butt. "Any savage fallin' under these sights shall breathe his last!"

Another huzza erupted in wake of the boast.

"I do indeed have the best powder and marksmen I

ever saw!" Hartley said. Many a noggin raised in salute to his words.

"But take it a bit easy on the whiskey, lads," Hartley said. "For it does have to last the whole of our trip. Be smart about it. We shall march soon, so if any wish to catch a wink do it now, for once we lay our feet down it shall be with blankets on the thump and at the long trot!"

Another huzza from a spirited group of men answered him. He looked to their captain, Simon Spalding, and smiled in the firelight. Spalding lifted his head high and nodded back at him, removing his hat in salute.

Hartley raised his hand and hurried off to other parts of the camp, becoming more invigored by the growing spirit of the men the more he talked among them.

"There's a fine man," Spalding said to the lieutenant standing next to him. "On the Canadian campaign, he was, and performed admirably, he did. He has General Washington's ear at that, too."

"Yes, I feel Congress has made the proper decision placing him here," Lieutenant Jenkins said.

Spalding could see the hint of concern in Jenkins' eyes despite his words. "Is a hell of a war, it is, not for land or for some far away soveriegn, but for an ideal," he said. "An ideal that a man has the right to be treated as he is fit to be treated, not as his father was. Such a war, such a brave new step forward, takes a special breed of man, one whom steps up when needed, but fades into the background when not. I believe Mr. Hartley is of such a breed, as Captains Ransom and Durkee were."

"That is for sure," Jenkins said.

"This country, this new land founded on ideals, treads on shaky ground, ground which has not been trod but a few times in the whole history of man," Spalding said. "Beginning on such shaky ground we have but few resources, we must make due with what we have, and trust providence shall shine upon us in our great endevour."

Jenkins looked in awe at him. "You've been thinking on this," he said. "Have you not?"

"Aye, through many a march on the cool summer grass and upon the hard and frozen ground. One must not take it all upon one's shoulders, but trust that others shall take up the staff as well as ye. God is with us, despite what happened on that field at Wyoming, one must suffer to grow, and we have certainly have had our fair share of that. Now comes a new turn, and we are at the head of it."

Jenkins looked down at the back of his right hand. He rubbed it as he had done when he had been taken captive last year to Niagara. He rubbed it on the spot where his dear Beth had last held it to her cheek upon their parting. He still felt the warmth of her tears. He still felt the warmth of her heart when he touched his hand. It had substained him through that dark and awful hole at Niagara and on his trek through the forest after his escape. It would sustain him now, also.

Spalding noticed his odd habit as soon as he had met him after the late battle. He did not blame him. The beauty of Bethiah Jenkins had touched and inspired all in Wyoming. If love could not substain us, what else could? He looked away from him, pretending not to notice his actions.

"For Beth it is that I fight," Jenkins said under his breath. "And for everyone's Beth."

Spalding raised an eyebrow at the comment, remembering his own wife and children. "You are to keep an eye on the country through which we pass, noting all you can," he said. "I, as you know, am here in more than just the capacity of Captain of the Wyoming Rangers, as His Excellency has been known to call us, but as military advisor."

Jenkins stopped rubbing his hand. A man of Colonel Hartley's experience needed little advice, but would be more apt to give it.

"More is at play," Spalding said, squinting out of the corner of his eye at his young lieutenant. "After this expedition either you or I shall be called to headquarters. There we are to brief His Excellency on all we witnessed on this expedition, as I am sure Colonel Hartley will, also. But His Excellency wants a frontierman's eye about things. One who knows the land. One who walks it in war and in peace. One who knows the enemy in ways others could only imagine." He looked down to the fire in front of them. "That is why it shall probably be you who reports to General Washington. A great part of the country lies teetering in the balance when this war is finally settled. We want to make sure it remains part of our nation, not the bloody Crown's. I have told you all you need to know, at present, consider it an order. In all of it remember. Remember how they fight, where they are apt to fight, and how we beat them, or they us."

Jenkins looked over to him and nodded. "I shall, sir," he said.

"I know you shall," Spalding said, "you are a good man." He waved a hand toward the bustling troops around them. "Now, let us prepare these men for the march, for they are in our charge and their mothers, sons, and daughters trust us to return them safe and sound. Now let us be about our duty and trust in the hand of providence to deliver us safely through this valley of death."

Chapter Twenty Three

Colonel Hartley took from his waitscoat pocket an estimable and rare prize on the frontier-his watch. Squinting his eyes in the fire light he read its hands, painfully aware of the sea of eager faces watching him. It read four o'clock in the morning. The sun still teased the hozizon, but the ardor of his men demanded they march now. Taking it as a good omen, he raised his hand and shouted "forward!"

The men took the first step in perfect cadence. An off the cuff song with a chorus of '*Nothing like Grog*', filled the air. The men tramped proudly behind their officers. Nary an eye turned to gaze back at the fort. All eyes stared ahead, into the mountains and its shielding forest, hoping with their stern ardor to teach those dwelling in its shadows a lesson they would never forget. It simply had to be done.

The sun rose to their front gracing the mountains in a heavenly light. Lively footsteps splashed across a ford in the Loyalsock Creek with no problem. Spirited eyes looked to one another and to the drops of rain falling from the darkening sky.

"Close up," Hartley called back. "Flankers tighten up! Be mindful of anything in the bush!" He rode back along the line to spirited huzzas. He nodded at each of the yells and ordered the men to look smart and close up the ranks. But to his apprehension the line slowed rather than accelerating at his word.

He immediately turned and rode to the front.

Robert Covenhoven, along with an eager few of the Wyoming scouts, met him. "No worries," Covenhoven said.

"It's just here where the trail cuts north it gets a bit rough, is all, but we'll manage."

Hartley looked ahead and down into the gully which the trail led. Cattails swirled in the threatening wind, revealing intermittent spots of water. He looked back at Covenhoven. "A swamp?" he asked.

"Just a bit of a wade is all, Colonel," Covenhoven said. "These men will get through it fine enough. Besides, it's nothing to what lies ahead. The Sheshequin Path can be a right proper devil in some places, but it's the best we have at this time."

Hartley raised his spyglass to his eye and gazed through the rain to the other side of the swamp. The trail rose steeply into dense trees, once it passed a great defile of rocks. "What is that?" he asked. "Rocks?"

"It's the wilderness, Colonel, all that God's hand has made," Covenhoven said. "We'll get through, with his help, we will."

Only seven miles from the fort and already his scouts beseeched the help of the Lord. But the season grew late. After a report from his scouts on the possible difficulties of using the Wyalusing Path, he wondered what ground could possibly be worse than what he eyed through his glass. He bit his lip. "Very well," he said. "Let us continue until dark."

"We'll be fine, sir, for with this lot one's just as hardy as the next," one of the men assured him.

He dismounted and led his horse down into the swamp. Already men tugged against the mud. Sucking sounds filled the air with each footstep through the bog. Even his horse stumbled and neighed in frustration in a few spots. He finally led his mount to solid ground among the rocks and stood watching the men struggle past. To his surprise not one complaint, only encouraging words, drifted through the ranks. When a groan did rise, a quick scold silenced it. A sense of pride swelled in his heart at the sight of his rain-soaked, struggling, men bearing the difficulties without a whisper of scorn. These men wanted at their enemies badly, he thought, but so did he.

They trudged through the swamp and into dense hemlocks, but found little relief from the drenching rain. Few voices sounded along the trail, for with all the difficulties everyone knew to keep silent now, without word from their officers. The dense shadows spoke to them a warning far deeper than any of their officers. The rut filling the trail became muddier. A few tumbled and slipped, but quickly regained their footing.

The day slowly dragged into night. Drenched branches added to the deluge from the heavens. Finally the wet column dragged to a halt atop a carefully scouted hill.

"This'll be fine, sir," Walker said, reporting to his soaked colonel. "It's best to be high so as we can keep a better eye out below, besides, they won't expect us to camp up here."

"Very well, Captain," Hartley said, plopping down from the saddle. Touching the ground, his boots squeaked and a flood of water surged over the top of them.

"You best remove them for the night," Walker said.

Hartley shook his head and almost chuckled. "Yes, perhaps I should take them down to the creek to dry out, seeing how wet it is up here."

Walker shook his head at the colonel's attempt at humor. "We'll break down a few boughs to get you as dry a spot as possible, sir."

"Talk about the impossible, it would be this expedition and want of a dry spot within it," Hartley said. He slapped his horse's rump. Water splattered his face. "Do the

Iroquois have a navy?" he asked.

Walker raised his head from below his wide slouch hat. A smile stretched across his face.

Hartley walked over to him and placed his hand on his shoulder. "Come my good man, we shall partake in the whiskey, no chill can stand against it," he said.

"Boiled beef, fire cake, and whiskey," Walker said, following his commander into a particularly dense grove of hemlock boughs. "It is a proper campaign, after all, is it not?"

Chapter Twenty Four

The dull thud of axes echoed in the wet forest. Torrents of rain drenched the hardy men yielding the axes, but they ignored it and kept swinging their axes with all their fury. The path had to be cleared.

"The axe seems as important as the rifle on this campaign," Hartley said under his breath, watching the men furiously hack at the fallen trees and underbrush blocking the trail. He reached down in his haversack and pulled out a piece of ash cake, hurriedly putting it into his mouth before it disintegrated from the rain. Munching on it, he glanced back at the huddled men patiently waiting for the path to be cleared. A failing moment of frustration poured over him like the pouring rain. "Fate ordained that I am to go make war on the savages of America instead of the British," he said to an officer walking to his side.

"Yes, but it is a war which must be fought," the officer said.

"Ah, it's true, Captain Stoddert," Hartley said. He dipped his head, letting a steady stream of water pour from his hat. "You, being fond of the sea, must feel quite at home."

"I've never seen such rain," Stoddert said. He turned and looked at the silent men, each clutching their weapons tightly to them to keep them from the rain. Some wrapped bits of leather around the locks. Others covered them with bits of their own ragged clothes, ripped from their very backs. Not a murmur or a complaint rose from any of them.

"But with men such as these," Hartley said, noticing Stoddert's gaze, "it is a pleasure to command. If properly led

I think them capable of anything. Ester and Brant beware."

"They well should at that," Spalding said, approaching from the rear. "This is a different kind of war, Colonel, but nonetheless more brutal than any action between so-called civilized men. Do not take any heed to old stories of British humanity, for out here, it seems to be banished. The lads I lead expect none and will give none. Is there not some chosen curse, some hidden thunder in the stories of hell, red with uncommon wrath, to destroy the monsters who make use of such instruments to establish tyranny?"

Hartley blanched at the reference to the British officials who held the leash of their native allies. Hatred of them ran deep in these Wyoming people, even more than others who had suffered at their hand. Woe be to them, he thought. He only wished he had the power to curb their wrath when they finally encountered the enemy, for with wrath ran injustice, which corrupted the avenger as well as the aggressor.

"They are good men to the last," Spalding said, seeming to sense Hartley's concern, "and shall follow the orders of those placed above them."

"As will we all," Stoddert said.

A call from the front raised all eyes toward it. Several of the axmen waved back to the ranks, motioning them forward while they themselves eagerly advanced to the next cluster on the trail. They promptly assaulted the next tangled mass of brush.

"Will this never end?" Hartley asked.

"At Tioga Point it will," Spalding said, urging the men passing to close up and advance.

Covenhoven suddenly appeared from the brush by the side of the trail. Popping up from nowhere, he appeared like an apparition. All of them shuddered for a heartbeat.

Spalding's rifle swung to him but quickly lowered. "I'd watch that if I were you, scout," he said.

Covenhoven nodded and approached Hartley.

Hartley nervously wiped his brow and stood to the side of the trail, heartily reminding himself just how fast anyone could appear from the dense forest around them. A different war, indeed, he thought.

"No worries," Covenhoven said, "I have scouts out three thick on each flank. Nothing will get past their eyes, I assure you, Colonel." He led the officers up the trail.

"That is good," Hartley said. "But what of this trail?"

"The Lycoming is just a mile or so up, from there we'll follow it up to the Towanda, and then it's Indian country," Covenhoven said, taking a snapped branch in the face. A welt immediately showed across his cheek. "It's rough going, I grant ye, but this path hasn't been used but infrequently in the past years. They won't be expecting us."

"I can see why," Stoddert said. A slippery root sent him tumbling to the muddy earth. He gasped and grabbed at a moss covered and saturated log to his front. The moss slipped off in his grasp, sending him to the ground again. Both Hartley and the scout helped him to his feet.

Frustrated neighs tore their eyes to Carberry's horse filing past them.

"I pity the horse," Stoddert said, rising to his feet.

"I pity the Iroquois they encounter," Covenhoven said, "I feel there will be no quarter given."

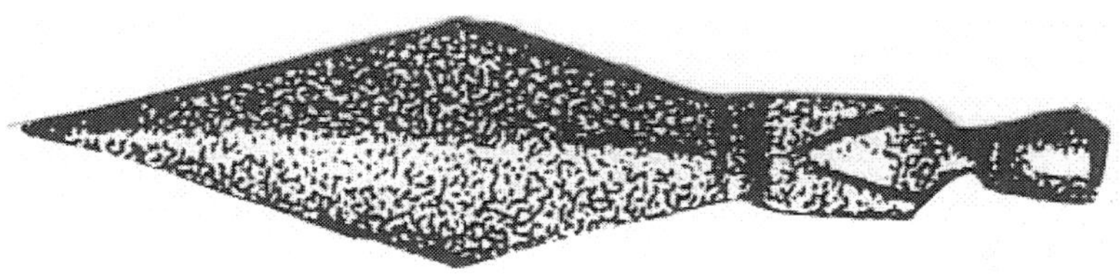

Chapter Twenty Five

The sound of rushing water reached their ears long before they caught sight of the creek below them. One by one they filed down the narrow trail to the slight clearing on the bank by the raging waters. No one spoke, all remained silent in the face of the torrent. Their vision hampered by the heavy rains, they fell back to the use of their other senses to warn them of threats-Indian threats.

A movement to the back of their line made them part and make way for their colonel. Hartley walked up to the bank and looked down one side of the stream and then the other. "The Lycoming Creek?" he asked. "What you people call a creek would prove to be a small river where I come from."

"None of this land's cleared," Covenhoven said, slapping the wet buckskin clinging to his mud-caked body. "Moss, dead leaves, old rotten logs, they all hold the water, like this accursed buckskin. Makes it run higher than it does on cleared farm land as about York and Lancaster." He eyed the stream and shook his head. "With these rains it'll play hell on our adavnce. Was afraid of it. But the trail is tight and this is where it leads."

"Yes," Hartley said, rubbing his hand under the brim of his soaked hat. "This is where it leads. Are there any better fording places about?"

"I am afraid what you see is what you get, sir," Covenhoven said.

"Well blast it, it shall not stop us," Hartley said. "If the savage and Tory can manage this trail, so can we!" He raised his hand and pointed at the horsemen still on top of the ridge behind him. "Captain Carberry, set your horsemen downstream to catch any carried away by these mad waters! The rest of you keep your horns and cartridge boxes as high as you can! Tallest men to the front to lock arms and form a chain across the river. The others shall advance along it! Now let's get to it! Straight away!"

The horsemen immediately reacted, charging down the trail. Men parted and made way for them, all the while fixing their powder horns and cartridge boxes to the ends of their bayoneted muskets. Some of those with rifles hastily hacked down saplings and small tree limbs to hoist their powder horns above their heads.

Without any hesitation Carberry plowed his horse into the brown water. It stumbled at first, almost rolling over before regaining its foothold and rising again. Carberry fought with the reins in one hand while balancing his short-barreled rifle in the other. White water foamed and splashed against his horse's flanks. A fine animal, it stood with a zeal and an air of courage equal to its master.

"Come now!" Carberry called to his horsemen on the bank. "Let's go, the water's fine!"

They dutifully followed their leader into the raging torrent. In no time they placed themselves downstream a few feet apart from one another.

Carberry whistled to those waiting on the bank and waved his hand in the air. "Come, let's get a move on!"

Taller men plunged into the rushing waters. At first they stumbled against the bottom but soon a brusque line of men stretched from one bank to another. Water crashed against the strongest men in the center, splashing against their chests and into their mouths. With mighty oaths against the Tories and Indians they spat out the brown water and stood fast, interlocking arms with one another.

Hartley, gazing at the wide eyes watching him, stepped down into the water first. He slowly plodded along the line of men, struggling against the current. The water drew high to his neck in the middle of the line but he trudged onward, ever mindful of the eyes of the rank and file behind him; much of whom stood a full half foot below his average height. Nonetheless, he gasped a sigh of relief upon reaching the safety of the far bank.

"You shouldn't have done that," Covenhoven coughed behind him. "We haven't scouted the bank yet, you're lucky to have your hair! Blast it!"

"I," Hartley said, turning to offer his hand down the bank to the scout, "intend to keep my hair well into old age, thank you." He lifted the man out of the water and lowered his hand to help the next in line. "Don't worry about me," he said, turning briefly to the scout. "Now be about your business!"

"Woe to any Iroquois than run up against that obstinate devil," one of the scouts following Covenhoven up the trail said.

"Just the type we need for this business," Covenhoven answered.

Both men folded back the brims of their soaked slouch hats and scanned the trees. "Damn the luckless fool that would be out and about in this weather, anyhow," Covenhoven said. "Be he friend or foe."

The other scout nodded his drenched head and took a great gulp of whiskey from his canteen.

"Amen to that," he said, passing the canteen to Covenhoven. "Amen to that."

Chapter Twenty Six

At first light they rose, drank copious amounts of whiskey, and trudged up the tight trail through the narrow valley. Negotiating the hairpin turns of the Lycoming proved frustrating enough to try the most patient man's fortitude. Tangled wild vines hung from every tree in some places. Tomahawks, long knives, and axes in the tough calloused hands of grim and determined men cut against them, only to have their feet sink in a new morass when they emerged on the other side of the underbrush. And all the while the Lycoming Creek hissed and raged within earshot, heightening the sense of dread of having to ford it again.

Colonel Hartley, pulling a long sticky vine from his foot, finally ordered a stop. Sitting on a huge moss covered and soaked boulder he waited for his scouts and officers to make their way to him.

They tramped up and circled the rock, some kneeling at its foot while others paced around it. Nary a soul spoke through their frustrating thoughts. Each silently surveyed the trail ahead, which to their dismay they noticed crossed over the raging waters again. It would be the seventh time in this day if they forded it! Others looked up to the strange conical-shaped hills that surrounded them. Their steep faces brimmed with slippery rocks and half-rotten logs. They waited for the colonel to speak, for the foreboding terrain spoke for them.

"Look at that damn water," Hartley said, removing his hat and slapping it against his thigh. The rain immediately poured down his face, making him squint against it. "Damn it," he said, madly forcing his drenched hat on his head again. "What of these damn mountains! They resemble anthills more than any mountains I've ever seen! I say we try to scale their steep face instead of fighting those damn waters again."

No one argued with his logic. They looked back to the exhausted men lying about in the mud, on boulders, fallen logs, or anywhere that offered a respite from their impossible trek.

"The closer we get to the head of that damn creek the better," Hartley said. "It has lessened some in force, but I'll be damned if I want to ford it again, not this day at least."

His officers and scouts remained silent in their exhausted state.

"Then it's up the damn anthills," Hartley said. His mind flashed back to that awful trek to Canada he had made but two years ago. No, he thought, not even the rigors of that horrid march compared to this hellish trail. But plod on they must, he reasoned. He slid down from the boulder and waved a frustrated hand to the side of the nearest hill facing them. "Let's get to it," he said. He looked up to the miserable sky above them. "Daylight's burning, I think, if the sun has not abandoned us too."

A few chuckles answered his attempt at humor.

"Ester's warriors are waiting if the sun's rays are not, though," he added with a stern look. "So let's look smart and keep alert. More threats may be afoot than one of those accursed rattlesnakes that seem to infest this land behind every rock. Personnally, I'd take one of those vile serpents to any savage, at least the rattle gives you some warning before they strike!"

In single file and in order, the men responded to the waves of their exhausted officers' hands. No words needed to direct them up the side of the mountain, no matter how steep. Every man thought the same about it since their last crossing of the furious waters. The waters seemed to boil with nature's wrath.

"This had better be quite a surprise to our enemies," Hartley said, watching his men slip against the muddy black soil and wet rocks on the side of the mountain. "For it has been somewhat of one for me, to say the least."

"Nothing ventured, nothing gained," an anonymous voice commented from the ranks.

"Oh the gain shall be quite substantial, I guarantee that," Covenhoven answered the voice. "Just keep your powder dry and your flints sharp, never know when the savage may supply us with some sport."

"Remember Lycoming!" came another call from along the ranks.

"Remember Wyoming!" quickly answered it.

Both calls crept from everyone's tired lungs. The words faded with the last man disappearing around the steep mountain. Silence now prevailed. Silence in their dark enemy's land. Silence tinged with despair. Despair quickly fading in light of their thirst for revenge.

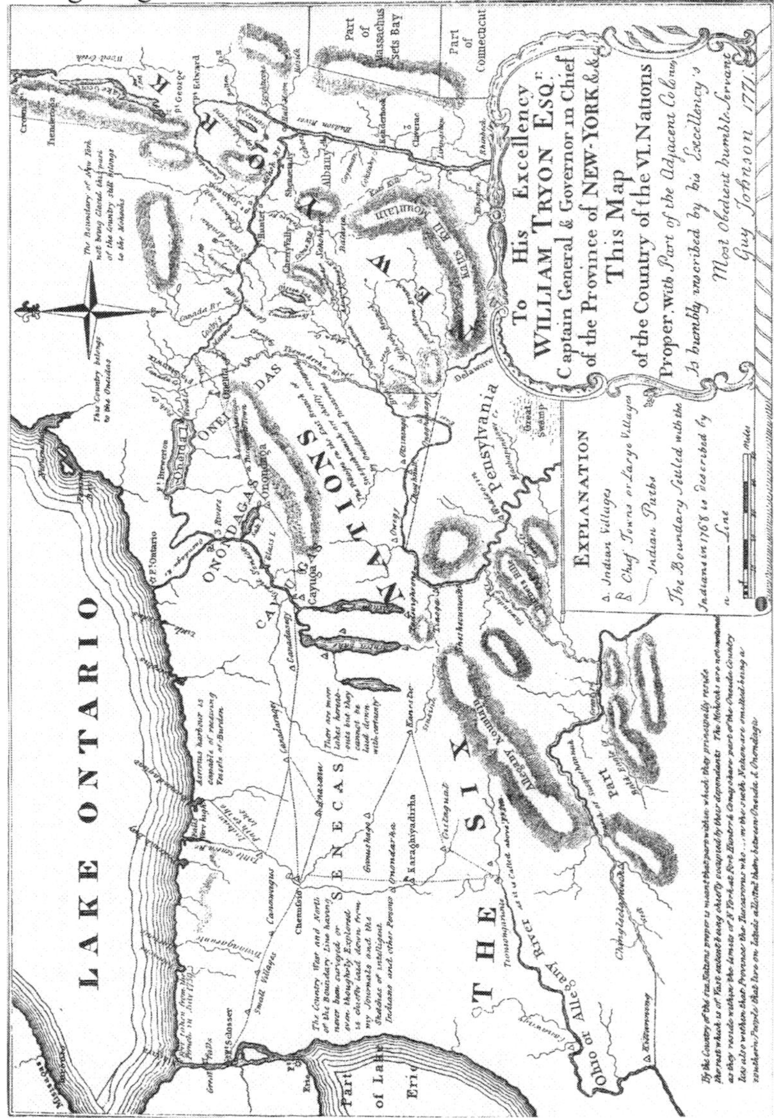

Chapter Twenty Seven

Ester's village sat cloaked in the early morning rays of the sun. A few captured sheep from Wyoming bleated in the still air. Bellowing cows answered from the plain they shared just to the west of the village. Beyond the sun's rays crept into the deep shadows of the lofty trees blanketing the mountains all around the village and gleamed across the face of the mighty Susquehanna River. Great overshadowing trees crept all along the river, bending far down as if to drink from its waters. Only a few sparse bare spots interposed between the trees, they being some round fields just lately harvested of their corn, and canoe landings. A few lone pine bough huts graced the riverbank by one of the landings.

Some ragged and threadbare children emerged from one of the huts. Their light skin drank in the early morning rays of the sun. They knelt by the embers of a smoldering fire, one of the boys carefully placing logs onto it. Two other boys sat and watched while a third child, dressed in a torn and filthy dress, slowly edged her away from the others and trudged toward the village.

None of her brothers protested through the gnawing feeling in the pits of their empty stomachs. But they did look to the blanket hanging over the hut's door with a certain apprehension. They watched the sun creep through the holes in the blanket and waited.

The bright rays intensified and shone on the face of the woman curled up in a deep sleep among the boughs on the floor. She lay half-asleep, drifting back in her memory to her cabin at the mouth of the Wysox Creek. For a moment all seemed well. She slowly stretched her arm out across her imagined feather bed to touch Sebastian, her husband. The sun shines, Sebastian, we must rise, there's stock that needs tending. Her hand felt the rough and cold ground. She stretched it out frantically, searching for her husband's firm touch. She feared to open her eyes. No, it can't be, she thought in her stupor. No! Her hand finally grasped something round and the width of her husband's forearm. But it felt cold! It felt dead!

She opened her eyes to the horror of captivity again. Staring at the pine branch she held in her hand she dropped it like a hot piece of iron. She scurried back and away from the light, finding sanctuary in a dark corner. Sounds crept into the hut from the outside. The heavy and monoutious thud of a pestle pounding corn in a hollow wooden stump-mortar invaded her thoughts. The strange guttoral sounds of a foreign language echoed through the air. The howl of Indian dogs added to her apprehension. No! It must not be!

"Ma?" a voice called from outside the hut. "You alright in there?"

The familiar tone of her child's voice brought her back to reality. The children! They must be watched. Still, after all these months in captivity, they did not understand. Their sense of innocence prevented it. She must tend to them! Sebastian would never forgive her if some evil befell them. Oh, Father, she mouthed to herself, fumbling under the pine boughs for the one treasure, besides the children themselves, she still held of her past life. Her hands felt the pages and the leather binding them. She gripped the huge bible closely to her chest. Father saved you from the flames the savges had thrown you into to keep the family alive. This, the family bible, must never be compromised. It must be preserved. Find the strength within it! Rise! Face the day and its horrors with the resolve and faith that this too shall pass. It must! Have faith!

She slid the bible carefully under the boughs and ran her fingers through her disheveled hair. She tied it back with a piece of old cloth and scampered through the ragged blanket door.

"Boys," she said to the wide-eyed children watching her from around their small fire. Her eyes darted all around the camp. She stood over the hut and looked down to the river. "Jane!" she called. "Jane!"

She stood still and listened. No one answered her call. "Boys! Where's your sister?"

All three boys strugged their shoulders and looked curiously at one another. "Don't know," the elder of the three finally said.

"Oh, she'll be the death of me yet!" she said. She took a few anxious steps forward and shielded her eyes from the rising sun. She looked all around the village facing them, but saw no sign of her daughter.

"She's just hungry, Ma," one of the boys said, kneeling down and poking at the fire with a stick. "We're all hungry."

"Well you just be the men your Pa would want you to be and get about fishin'," she said.

"But Ma, they ain't bitin' no how," the boy said. "Ain't been in two days. Berries are about played out, too." The boy turned a curious eye toward the bustling Indian village. Corn lay across dozens of racks in the sun. Dozens of cattle grazed about the plain on the far side of the village. "Why don't they share with us, Ma?" he asked. "They's got plenty. You and Pa always shared with them when they visited." He looked to an old man slowly walking by their hut. "Why that there is Old Nicholas. We shared plenty of food with him at our cabin. Why don't he with us now, seein' we's in such a bad way?"

"War makes enemies of friends," she said. "It's just the way of it. You just mind or you'll get the switch likin' your sister's fixin' to get! I told her to stay away from the village! That goes for all of you!"

"Yes, Ma," the younger boy said. "Do you want us to help fetch her?"

"No!" she said. "I want you to get fishin' likin' I'se told you! Now get to it if'n you want anything to eat this day."

"Yes, Ma," the three boys answered simultaneously. One of them slowly picked up the line lying by the fire and all three trudged to the riverbank behind the hut.

"And you mind the Indians!" she called behind them. "And stear clear of the blue-eyed ones, too, they're just as mean, maybe a bit more! You hear Henry, Isaac, and John?"

"Yes, Ma," crept up the riverbank.

She gritted her teeth and slowly walked toward the village, trying to remain as inconspicuous as possible. She avoided eye contact with any in her way, bowing her head so as not to offend any of the Indians. Most ignored her. A few old women waved a wooden spoon at her from the pots they tended by their fires, but to her relief none threw anything at her or chased her back to her hut. Perhaps the early hour had something to do with it. She noticed none of them seemed energetic at all in the morning. Most of the men preferred sleeping in the huts until midday, unless some festival, hunting, or war party called them out in the early morning hours. A life of no worries indeed, she thought. They lived day to day, with little regard for the next, except the women. They prepared for the winter. They hoed the corn and planted the fields. They remained the heart of their civilization, much as their couterparts in western society.

Nothing really changed in the way of things, except Indian women seemed to hold far greater sway over matters in their society than the white women did in their society.

She darted around in the early morning light, keeping to the shadows. She slid through the deep shadows by Ester's castle and stood and listened. No one moved about inside it.

She breathed a sigh of relief, for the betraying Indian Queen drew the most hatred from her heart. She saw the ring of scalps she proudly displayed after she returned from the Battle of Wyoming. She heard her boasts of lifting the hair of those she once called friend. She witnessed the darkness of the savage's heart. She would never forget it.

A dog scampered up to her and sniffed her leg. It let out a yip and started to howl. She immediately ran away from the castle, not wishing to be the cause of disturbing the haughty queen. She rounded the corner and stopped with a gasp, staring at her daughter standing in rags by an Indian fire with one finger playng about her bottom lip.

She watched the two Indians standing by the fire. One, a wrinkled old man, stood pounding a huge wooden pestle down methodically into a hollowed-out stump. Corn spilled over the edge of it now and then, catching the eye of the little white girl. She stood mesmerized by it, gauging her time for the moment to swoop down and scoop up some of the disregarded corn kernals.

Her mother recognized her stare and noticed the old woman by the fire had also. The Indian woman eyed the nervous white woman and the child, letting the wooden spoon she held fall into the iron kettle she tended. She rose and wiped her hands on her buckskin dress, seeming to dare the white woman to move. She nonchalantly picked up a long twig.

The white woman slowly backed away, bowing her head. In another instant she darted forward, scooping up the child before turning her back to shield her from the old woman's wrath.

The old woman's switch immediately fell heavily upon her back. She ignored the pain and scooted her child along, flexing her arms against the blows intended for the child.

A laugh sounded from the old man. He pushed the long braid on the side of his head back and watched the flight before him with a certain glee. The scolding voice of the old woman placed his hands on the pestle again. It soon thumped out its tired rhythm again.

The old woman ceased beating the white woman and pointed the switch threatenly toward the old man. Before she turned back the white woman and child gained a hundred yards on her. She threw the switch in the air toward them and warned them with her fast paced tongue. After finishing her rant she turned back to her pot as if nothing had happen.

Lydia Strope did not stop until she gained the sanctuary of their little hut. She stopped by the fire and pushed the child from under her. She stretched her back against the welts and grimaced. "I told you to stay clear of the Injuns!" she said to the sad-faced child.

Jane put a finger innocently to her mouth and said, "but I hunger so, Mother."

Lydia bent her arm around to try and ease the burning pain and looked down at the emaciated child. "Oh, it's all right," she said.

"Ya mean I ain't gonna get the switch?" Jane asked.

"No," Lydia said, "I think there's been enough switchin' for this day." She arched her back against the pain. "See what it'll get ya if'n you mess with the Injuns? Just think what that old witch would have down if you did scoop up some of that corn."

"I'm sorry Mother," Jane said, plopping down next to

the empty clay pot by the fire. She looked soulfully toward it. “When’s it going to end? When’s Papa going to fetch us out of here? He went down to fetch the soldiers to get us. Where are they?”

“I’m afraid the Indians and Tories got all the soldiers months ago,” Lydia said, taking her up in her arms.

“And Pa, too?” Jane asked.

“Well they said they has,” Lydia said, remembering how the braves teased her with each new scalp they brought into the village saying it belonged to ‘Boss’ Strope. But after careful examination-much to the Indians’ amusement-she reasoned none of the hair belonged to her husband. “But I don’t put much stock in what they say,” she added.

Chapter Twenty Eight

Rays of sunlight cut through the early morning fog. They reflected off the many rocks and glistened from the leaves burdening the drenched branches arching over the rocks. Gruff men slept huddled under the branches on and around multiple sized rocks. Some sat against the rocks, their heads bowed down to their chests. Others lay directly on top of some of the moss-strewn rocks. Others lay upon the cold and wet earth. All wraped and draped themselves the best they could with their threadbare blankets and overcoats.

One pair of half-opened eyes watched them all. Boss Strope tightened his wet blanket tightly to his chest and arched his back away from the rough bark of the tree he sat against. His feet dug into the black and soggy earth. He looked down to his torn moccasins and thought of the last two pair in his pouch. He had started this expedition with five new pair. He wiggled his toes against the leather of the moccasins and swore to wear them until they fell from his feet. He let his heavy eyelids fall only to have some loud lip smacks and gasps force his eyes open again. Nothing moved, save a few men struggling for a better position in which to sleep.

He looked through the white foggy mist all around the camp. The silhouettes of sentries shone like shadows in it. He watched the slow and careful movement of their heads; their eyes forever searching the perimeter. He felt comfort from their vigilance and swore he would do the same when his turn came to stand guard. A slight drip falling on his nose gave him a start. He wiped it and realized it had ceased raining. Only the drops from the leaves overhead fell onto the camp. This, he thought, squirming in his soaked clothes, is a good thing.

He finally found a somewhat comfortable position and stopped squirming. He knew in a few moments the officers would come to rouse them for the march through this dreadful wilderness. But that did not bother him, for he had greater reasons than the rest to gain Ester's village-his family.

He lay back and let his eyes follow a leaf dancing on a gentle breeze above his head. In his mind's eye he drifted back to his homestead at the mouth of the Wysox Creek. He had always liked these quite moments just before the dawn and would sometimes rise and stroll down to the river before anyone else awoke. There he would watch the swirling waters and the life slowly awakening around them. A fish would jump, leaving only an expanding ring and a splash in his wake. A blue heron would fly gently along the face of the waters. Ducks, hidden in some cove just out of sight, would quack and flap their wings. Occasionally deer or elk would swim the waters. It brought him closer to God; thus closer to the things which really mattered.

Usually the sound of the axe would echo soon in the early day. His brother John always rose and chopped wood first thing. He said it brought him peace. Anyway, with him around, they never lacked firewood.

He would then stretch and rise from the Indian grass along the bank and stroll back to the cabin, there to see his Lydia already hard at work around the hearth preparing the day's victuals. Her smile never failed in the early morning. It always greeted him and the thought of it now made a warm feeling surge through his tired bones. "Oh, my dear Lydia. My dear children. Old Father Van Valkenburg, Isaac, Hermonos, and all," he whispered. "I pray for you all to return safe. Amen."

His eyes felt wet at the thought of it all. On that late

May evening last, an Indian had stayed overnight with them. Overcome with their kindness to him, he threw out hints of a pending attack on Wyoming, and they being but twenty miles from the lauching point of the attach, Tioga Point, knew they must act. As soon as the Indian departed he had taken up his rifle and started for Wyoming, there to gain the promised assitance in evacuating his family, while bringing word of the invasion. Colonel Denison immediately dispatched some scouts to escort his family down river but to their dred they only found the smoldering remains of his cabins, barns, and outbuildings. Making haste to depart the scout separated to throw off any pursuers. He and three others returned to participate in the battle. Three others, taking the river, did not. He wondered of their fate, and feared their hair probably ended up on some Indian buck's pole. He shuddered at the fate of his family.

Not everyone slept around him, he being in the company of Franklin and other Wyoming scouts and rangers. "I'se knows the feelings, I'se do," a husky and deep voice called in the air.

He lowered his eyes to see Rudolf Fox staring at him. "Mein Goot, don't you worry," he said. "You know the wildens took me twice, they's did at that, der second time along with yours." The stout little Dutchman raised his lower lip and nodded his head. "Ester will see they's well tended too," he said.

Ester! The thought of the back-stabbing Indian Queen boiled in his mind. Oh, to just get his hands around her neck. He had seen her ride triumphantly on a captured horse-side saddle facing backwards-into the fort displaying a ring of still bloody scalps to Colonel Denison and mocking him and all the people of Wyoming with them. She wore so many captured petticoats she appeared fat and found it difficult to move on the horse. An equally high stack of bonnets-all facing backwards-adorned her head. She appeared almost as a joke, a mean joke, the cruelest of all time. She yielded the war club on that bloody rock at Wyoming, cracking the heads of many a captured patriot, all of them his friends. She incited the Indians. She held sway over all along the Susquehanna. If she opposed the invasion it certainly would never had happen, not even with all the persuasion and trinkets Indian Butler could muster.

"The rain has stopped," Boss Strope said.

Rudolf would not let him change the subject. "We's all rebuild when das war is over. Lydia, you, mein, and all's our childs."

Boss looked back up to the leaf. "If a hair is harmed on any of their heads or is on some buck's post, all hell and Brant himself cannot save Ester from my wrath!" he said.

"Amen to that," a voice sounded from those huddled around the tree.

"And if I find no satisfaction with this lot, I'm heading back to the Hudson among my own," Boss said. "We have a certain way of settling things with the savage!"

"Mein shoe," Rudolf said, raising his foot up from the ferns. He wiggled his toes through the top of the remains of a once fine shoe. "I'se don't know if it take another crossing."

"Relax," Boss said, thinking of his own worn moccasins. "We're nearing the head of the creek, rain's stopped, the water will be down, not like yesterday." The thought of negotiating the steep anthill-like mountains only to end up fording the creek half a dozen more times yesterday made him wince.

"Yes," Captain Franklin said, slowly rising from some ferns not far from the tree. His tall frame seemed to sprout from the ground itself as if he were born of it. He knelt down and emerged with a rifle nearly as tall as him. "We're gettin' close." He turned his head to and fro and sniffed the air. "I can taste 'em. Everyone is to look smart this day, for we may have some sport!" With that he nodded and walked toward the group of officers meeting by a huge boulder.

"That man scares me sometimes," someone said from around the tree.

"That's good," Boss said, "means he scares the enemy all the more. Just the kind of devil we need about this work."

"Oh, he's a devil, I'll vouch for that," the voice answered. "A devil indeed."

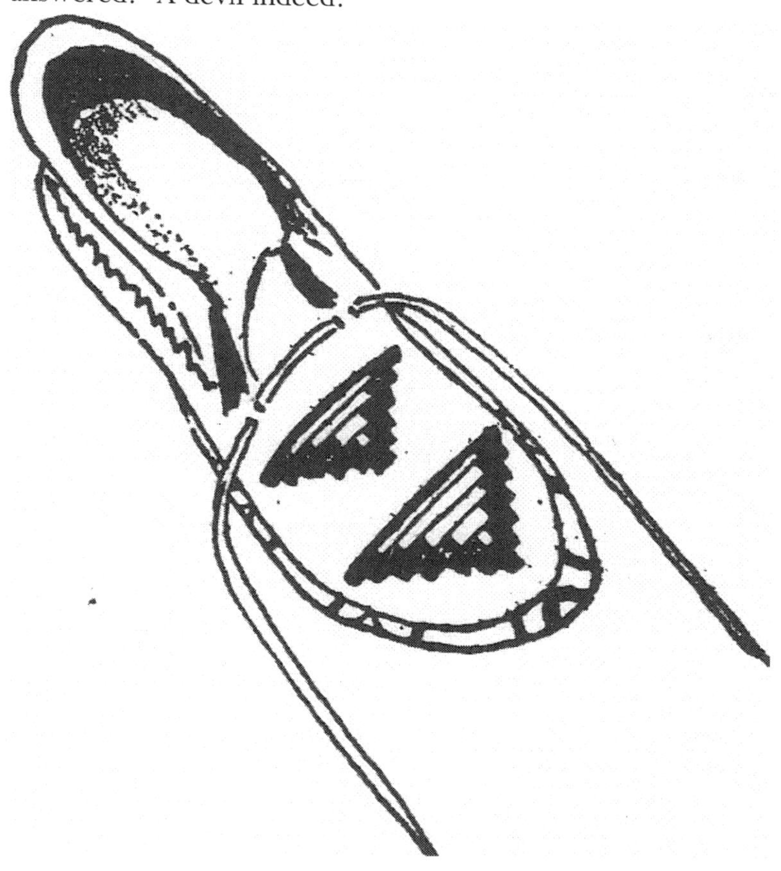

Chapter Twenty Nine

The Indian village nestled along the banks of the Susquehanna bustled with activity. Warriors yelled and screeched war whoops. Muskets fired into the air. All the Indians and their white Tory brethren formed to the south of Ester's village, anxiously watching the path.

Canoes plowed up the river and beached themselves just below the pine bough huts sheltering the captives of the village. Braves hurriedly beached the craft and darted by the huts, some of them screeching loud war whoops.

Lydia Strope jumped up from the floor of her hut. Tired from lack of food and their dismal efforts to procure any drained her spirit, but not her curiosity. Besides, the wide-eyed stares of her four children looked up to her in anticipation. Perhaps in this celebration or what not they could gain a morsel of food.

Lydia moved the ragged blanket door a sliver and gazed at the village. "Now, you children mind your places," she said, glancing back over her shoulder. "Don't draw no attention to us, but just behave and mind and we'll go out there and see what all the ruckus is about."

All four nodded their heads.

She pushed the blanket aside and crawled from the hut. The children spilled out behind her. She raised a hand to shield her eyes from the sun, already bright despite the early hour, and gazed at the gathering and hooting Indians. She looked back at her children and motioned them toward the village, careful to keep them all within her arms' length.

Several shots fired in the air from the trail, followed by more exhilarating hoots and calls. An equally estatic series of hoots and yelps answered them. Queen Ester suddenly appeared by the edge of her castle, her regal eye bearing down upon the spectacle.

Five painted braves, covered from head to foot in black and vermillion paint, strutted from the trail and into the clearing on the south side of the village. Their fierce eyes stared straight ahead. Attached to a long leather strap between them struggled a terrified white man. He cocked his head from side to side to scan the faces surrounding him, searching for any sympathetic eye. Only a careworn woman with four emaciated children held closely to her side on the fringes of the crowd gazed back at him. But her look of concern tinged with dread did little to sooth his soul.

He twisted his head against the leather strap and raised his voice over the clattter. "I am of Virginia! I have no quarrel with you northern people! Why do you do this?"

One of the scattering of white men wearing green coats and hunting shirts in the sea of brown and painted faces stepped next to the terrified man. "A rebel is a rebel, no matter from which colony he hails!" he said, grinning at the man straight in the face. "Now be a sport! Don't ruin the fun!" he added, laughing in a sinister way.

A brave bluntly pushed the gloating Tory to the side and stepped full in the face of the prisoner. He distorted his face to the utmost of his muscles, snapping his teeth. His bulging eyeballs darted about his head and suddenly locked dead on the man. He slowly turned an eye toward the Queen's castle. All other eyes, including the prisoner's, followed his gaze.

The Queen, her form erect and commanding, raised her head high. She stared across the distance at the ragged and terrified white man and slowly lowered her heavy eyes to the ground. She raised her hand in a slow motion and dropped it.

With that she turned and disappeared into the door of her cabin.

An instantaneous tumult broke out amongst the Indians. The Queen's indifference meant sport. All, from young to old, man, woman, and child alike, formed a twin line parallel to one another. In the intervening slot they swung war clubs, tomahawks, clubs, and bare fists. Several braves jumped in frantic leaps of anticipation. Yelps and war whoops filled the air. The Tories raised their hands and hooted all the more and stood just behind the Indians' line for a front row seat of the action soon to unfold. The captive white woman cautiously eased her way up to the line, but carefully kept her distance. She herded her children along with her hands, not letting them drift from her easy grasp.

The Virginian stared down the line before him, cocking his head back to wisp back his matted and disheveled hair falling down onto his face. "What mischief is this?" he gasped. A chorus of whoops answered him. "I am just a simple farmer! I have done nothing to warrant this! Oh my dear God! Oh my dear wife and children! Shall she be a widow this day?"

"You'll soon have your warrant served in full!" one of the Tories screamed above the wails. "You Rebel scum!"

Lydia Strope watched as she had many of the tortures about Tioga, with deep shock and awe. Still, for some strange reason she could not find it within herself to pull away from the gruesome rituals. She wondered of it and glanced down at her children, wanting to shield them from it but knowing she could never shield them from the horrible screams and bedlam about to erupt. It just happened to be the way of the Indians. She gazed with empty eyes at the terrified man. He looked back, the hint of a tear showing in his glassy eyes. In his eyes she saw her husband. In his eyes she saw every

American husband on the frontier.

A gruff kick and shove from behind sent the man spiraling head over foot into the slot between the lines. Before his first step a war club cracked against his skull, twisting his head in a peculiar motion. He instantly fell, moaning piteously. He moaned for his mother. He moaned past the ages for every man's mother, one from whom all descended. In that he wished to find pity or mercy but only whips, war clubs, tomahawks, fists, and sticks answered his pleas. He rose, blood pouring down his face, and pleaded for his life. His head twisted again in a strange motion, his neck seeming only a thread holding his head upright. His bones cracked. He stumbled, one, two, three steps more against the merciless onslaught before collapsing in a writhing heap onto the ground.

The Indians shouted and cheered. The line of Indians closed in a circle all around the lifeless body and continued their assault on the body. Woman and men peeled away after they blungened the corpse to make way for others to have their turn. It lasted until all had kicked, spat upon, or stabbed the corpse. Finally a brave emerged from the sea of hands waylaying the corpse with a bloody trophy held tight in his grasp. He screamed and held the scalp high in the air before spitting on the corpse one last time. With that, all peeled away from the scene of horror, congratulating one another and patting each other on the back.

Lydia fought to hold down the contents of her stomach from the bloody and gruesome sight before her. She released her hold on the children and raised her hands to her cheeks. Jane ran off toward the hut. The boys stared ahead, seeming mesmerized by the macabre sight. She stumbled toward the clump of flesh that just a few heartbeats before had been a human being. Bits of the matted hair lay strewn around the blood soaked corpse. Twisted arms and legs wrapped in an unnatural way around the flesh. A purplish mass of flesh, once his face, gleamed up at her with one eye, alive with the shock and horror of the last sight communicated to the brain from it. No hint of the other eye shone through the glob of flesh. Such anger, she thought, such pure hatred. In her mind's eye she saw the figure of Ester, tall and regal, bright eyes shining, condemning any acts of barbarity against the men of the party which had been captured with her and the children. She insisted that they be taken to Fort Niagara at once. Though cruel fetters cut into their flesh, the men stumbled up the trail led by one of her staunchest warriors to watch the unscrupulous Tories escorting them, not to the guantlet as this poor soul, but to Fort Niagara, captives, but alive.

She lowered her hands and gasped. Looking all around she counted three children, not four. She ran over to the boys and felt each one, running her fingers through their hair, and hugging them while she scanned the area for her precious daughter. Her eyes locked on the corner of Ester's castle.

Jane stood perfectly still, staring up at the dark haired woman covered with silver trinkets and little brass bells from head to foot. A smile stretched across the woman's face. Her hand stretched out to the child.

Jane smiled and took a few careful steps forward, only to be stopped by a firm hand from behind.

Lydia pulled the child close and stared defiantly at the Indian Queen. She buried her child's face deep into her chest, cupping her close to shield her from the dark apparition before them.

Ester stared back at her with an understanding eye, seeming to sense the mother's need to protect her child.

With fresh tears forming in her eyes she thought of her own son, shot down by the Yankees just before the Battle of Wyoming. She understood. She knew the feeling. She could not condemn or admonish a mother's love and desire to protect her children, no matter how misguided. She scratched her head and smiled before turning and walking away.

"Oh Jane," Lydia said, holding the child tight. Both watched the Queen walk away, "I told you to stay clear of all Indians, most of all her, their Queen! Your father's flesh may stain her hands, child!"

"No Moma," Jane said, staring down to the ground. "Not Ester, remember, her and Pa is friends. She wouldn't let anyone harm him nor us. Oh, Moma, can't you see?"

Lydia gently pushed the child away her arms' length and stared at her in shock. Sometimes the wisdom of the innocent shined through the hatred of the times. She smiled and pulled the child close. "Perhaps so," she said, hugging the child and resting her cheek on her shoulder, "perhaps so."

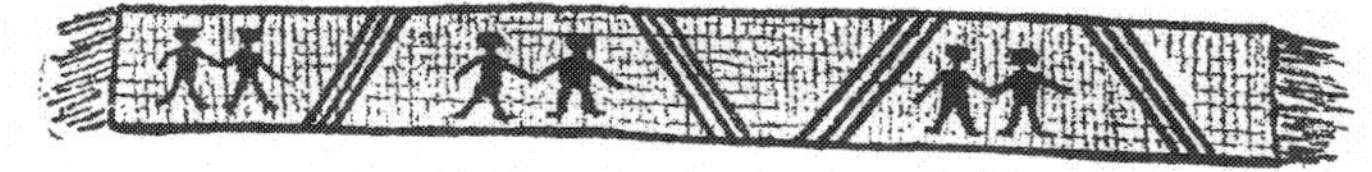

Chapter Thirty

Ira Stephens slipped through the cramped underbrush with his rifle held at the ready. He moved slowly, letting each branch grabbing on his clothing snap back silently. The air of silence around him bore witness that his fellow scouts did the same. He looked down to his hands gripping his rifle, imagining his fingers cocking the weapon in an instant should the mysterious foe they hunted appear to his front. Despite their orders for stealth, Colonel Hartley's top order to 'shoot on sight', rang in his ears. He knew the words also echoed in every other scout's mind advancing through this tangled mass of hell.

To his relief the underbrush faded and cleared just ahead, giving way to a grove of fine trees atop a high ridge. The beauty of the grove and the scrub brush free expanse beyond it made him gasp. Such land, such beauty, such prospects of wealth lay in these mountains! It staggered his mind. After the war, after all this hell, a man could do very well by this land, he thought. A heaven could be made where hell once dwelt. He liked the thought, and his heart rose in anti-cipation of the bright day to come, after the dark clouds of war faded.

A quick wave from a scout emerging from the under-brush to his side caught his alert eye. He watched twelve others slowly emerge behind him, spacing themselves in a wide-sweeping line to his right and left. The waving hand of Captain Franklin stopped them all dead in their tracks.

Franklin lifted his arm high in the air until all along the line nodded or waved back to him. He put two fingers to the front of his eyes and pointed for the two men next to him to ease forward.

Stephens just happened to occupy the position to Franklin's left. He glanced over to his opposite, Sergeant Baldwin, kneeling on the other side of Franklin. At Franklin's nod both men cocked their rifles and crept silently to the edge of the steep ridge.

A slight wisp of curling smoke immediately caught their attention. Baldwin looked anxiously over to Stephens. He turned and made a swirling gesture with his fingers to Captain Franklin. The distinctive click of many firelocks being cocked ran all along the ridge.

Franklin nodded in confirmation of the clicks and slowly crawled forward, motioning for Stephens and Baldwin to follow.

Franklin, Stephens, and Baldwin inched to the edge of the ridge and peered over it. They all let out a deep sigh at the sight laying before them. Smoke curled from a hole in the top of a bark hut nestled in a slight crook in the creek below them. All three men's eyes darted all around for the slightest hint of motion. Nothing moved, save a woodpecker beginning to peck a tree just above the hut. Its pecking began to echo throughout the grove, pounding through the nerves of the anxious men around it.

The three men eased back from the edge of the ridge. Franklin nodded and waved the palm of his right hand up and down to the men watching him. He pointed with his left hand to his eyes. Moving slowly he pointed with his forked fingers first to the right and then to the left of the grove.

The alert eyes watching him immediately responded. Men spread out to the left and right to surround the hut.

He waited for the men on the flanks to signal before he crawled forward again. Suddenly stopping, he pointed to his eyes again and gestured behind him back to the way from which they advanced. He pointed to a wide-eyed man on his far left.

The man nodded and slowly turned, quick to take back word to Colonel Hartley and alert the horsemen of their discovery.

Franklin let his hand fall to the tomahawk stuck in his belt and rubbed it along with the top of the handle of his long knife. He slowly grasp his rifle tightly and stood. With a slow wave of his arm the entire line of rangers stealthly moved forward. Their movements seemed so natural the woodpecker kept about his work, his pounding masking whatever slight noise the rangers' movements made.

They advanced but a few feet from the hut before Franklin motioned them to a stop. Every third man in the line turned, facing backwards to check their enemy's approach from the woods. The rest of the rangers leveled their weapons on the hut itself.

Leaving Stephens to cover their rear, Franklin and Baldwin crept to the entrance of the hut. Franklin knelt to the entrance and slowly eased his rifle to the ground. His hands slid his knife and tomahawk from his belt. Baldwin stood just to his side, his rifle pointing threateningly at the door.

Franklin gave him a quick glance and locked eyes with the door. Without warning he lept through the blanket door and rolled inside the hut. Baldwin quickly follwed, fanning his rifle all around the inside of the door.

All of the rangers watched the door of the hut, their ears alive to catch any telltale signs of struggle within it. They watched Baldwin slowly step back from the door and lower his rifle. He turned and looked all about the grove behind them.

Franklin popped out of the door behind him with his tomahawk stuck back in his belt and his knife in its sheath.

His face wore a sour expression and his hands held a series of small hoops. One of the hoops held a long wisp of hair strung tight by leather thongs about the center of the hoop.

He threw down the empty hoops at the feet of the gathering rangers and carefully examined the hoop holding the hair. He flipped it over to its back side and winced. He held the brightly colored backside up for all to see. "It's the way they identify it for proper sale to those Crown fiends at Niagara!" he announced. "One color for this poor soul and one color for another. What fiendish mind thought of this I'll never know, and if I ever find out and cross his evil path he'll breathe his last, I grant you that!"

The woodpecker suddenly beat a hasty wing out of the grove.

"Empty is it?" one of the rangers asked, motioning to the hut.

"Yes," Franklin said. "But the fire's still warm and they left the trinkets of their trade about." He lifted the scalp hoop again in disgust. "They can't be far, must've scattered just before we got here or be off on another hunt about." He waved his free hand all around in a great arc. "Be about finding them, but don't stray too far. If those cowardly heathen have caught our wind they'll be miles away in an instant. But look just the same."

A niegh from the top of the ridge tore everyone's eyes to it. Captain Carberry sat atop his mount glaring down at the hut. Several anxious horsemen surrounded him along with Franklin's footsore runner.

"They may still be lurking about!" Franklin called to the top of the ridge. "If you're quick you may just catch one of the rascals!"

With a quick nod Carberry waved his horsemen ahead. Hooves thudded over the top of the ridge and disappeared into the trees beyond. Anxious rangers hurriedly followed the horsemen, all thirsting to exact revenge from the gruesome trophies Captain Franklin had found.

Franklin watched them go and bid them all fair hunting. Watching the last disappear over the ridge he sat down and awaited Colonel Hartley and the rest of the rank and file. His exhausted body suddenly ached with a dull pain. He sat the scalp hoop to his front in plain view for all to see on their approach.

Looking down in disgust he harshly wiped his hands against his buckskin leggings, hoping to wipe them clean of the grimmy touch of death tainting them, but feared only the blood of the savages could wipe them as well as his heart free of it. Only when the savages breathed their last would the air be free of their tainted stench, he thought.

Mulling over the thought, he promised himself to do his damnest to clear the air.

Chapter Thirty One

Lydia Strope sat crestfallen by the smoldering fire in front of her pine bough hut. She lifted a half-shell gourd to her mouth and drank heartedly of its contents, hoping the water would quell the burning rage of her empty stomach. She offered the gourd down to Jane who lay across her lap.

The child looked at the gourd and pushed it away, rolling her head over on her mother's lap. Her empty eyes haunted her mother.

Still, Lydia looked down at the child without saying a word. No words could solace their hunger, anyway. She sat the empty gourd down and ran her fingers through the child's hair. Both perked up as Isaac, Henry, and John trudged over the riverbank behind the hut. Their spirits quickly sank, noticing the boys' empty hands. The boys shook their heads and plopped down around the fire.

"There ain't no fish bitin' no more Ma," John said. "The berries is all picked dry and I can't find anymore wild plums or potatoes nowhere."

"I know son," Lydia said, "but don't you fret none, you've done all ya could. Yer pa will be proud to hear about it, proud of all his boys."

"What's we's to eat?" Henry asked. He looked down to the empty half-gourd shell. "More water?"

"You just wait and pray on the Lord," Lydia said. "He'll see us through this."

John stood and looked down the river bank. "Ain't right," he said. "I can see why the Injuns don't share with us, but not why the other white people about don't. Provost's got a big place up yonder. Then there's Secord's apple trees about the point, and Moore with his ferry. Ain't none of them got any heart?"

"No, son, I don't believe they have," Lydia said.

Noticing the anger in her younger son's eyes she decided to voice another warning against any rash acts. The welts on her back still ached from saving Jane from the wrath of the old Indian witch from whom she had tried to steal a morsel of food. "And don't none of ye go about their places! No telling what they'd do to us if given a trumped up call to. Leave them be, cruel as they are."

"But Ma," John said, "they's got so much! It ain't Christian."

"No it's not," Lydia said. "But all people don't follow the word."

A sudden commotion in the village caught their attention. Their eyes followed the Indians and Tories clamoring to the north end of the village. Two men led a train of pack-horses fully laiden with food and other commodities into the awaiting village.

"There's Secord now," John said. "Looks as he's come to trade." He squinted and raised his hand to shield his eyes from the sun. "Don't know who that is with him, never seen him afore."

Lydia sat up and looked toward the commomtion again. Any change, be it in person or what, might welcome some consideration, and pity, to a starving christain woman and her children. She eased Jane from her lap and stared at the pack-horse train.

"Now, ye all stay put!" she said. She fingered back her hair and walked toward the pack train. "John!" she called behind her, "make sure the others stay put!"

She eased up to the train, trying to remain inconspicuous until the right moment. She walked carefully around the other whites engaged in trading with the sutler from Tioga Point. The sharp crack of an ox whip suddenly turned her head toward the noise.

Old man Secord stood cracking the whip presented to him in trade. A cruel smile crept across his face with each new crack of the fine whip. He seemed fascinated with it.

The other whites, not so enamored with his new toy, stepped away, preferring to trade with his partner while he admired his recent acquisition.

Lydia saw her moment. She carefully approached the whip-cracking man, waiting until he finally looped the whip up and tied it to his belt before taking the last steps toward him. Bowing her head in submission, she stood before him.

"Why, if it isn't Boss Strope's wife," he said, shaking his head. "You still about? Sometimes I wonder of Ester's judgement. The Indian's call him Boss, short for Bostionian, seeing how they think all the hubbub comes from Boston. They only call the most ardent Rebel dogs such names! For his treason he should suffer, as well as his family!"

His harsh words caught the attention of the others. They all turned toward his booming voice in anticipation of some sport. His trading partner watched the strange behavior with a curious, yet cautious, eye.

"Yes sir," Lydia said, bowing again. "Be that as it may, I have children who almost starve about this place." She looked to the bulging bags of flour on the pack-horses' backs. "A bit of flour from your grace would surely go a long ways to easing their suffering."

"What impudence you Rebels possess!" Secord yelled. "Let them starve! And you as well! Nits breed lice!" He let out a harsh laugh. "Where is your Congress now? Where is your Denison? Where is that upstart Zebulon Butler and that penny-pinching Hollenback? Growing fat and safe by their warm hearths no doubt! Now be gone! A damn Rebel's sufferings are no concern to me!"

"But sir!" Lydia said, collapsing to the ground and crawling up to the man. She tugged at his buckskin britches and cried "my children shall starve! Are you to have that play about your concience?"

"War has no conscience!" he said, gruffly kicking her aside.

Tears flowed down her careworn cheeks. She rose to her knees and peered at the man through tears of anguish.

"You wretched wench!" he said, yanking the whip from his belt, "be gone or feel the lash!" He snapped the whip angrily in the air, only checking the swing when his partner interposed between he and his target. "Stand clear, Cyrus! Son or not this lash shall swing!"

"No father!" Cyrus said, kneeling down and helping the distraught woman to her feet. "She is not to blame for her husband being a Rebel!"

Secord snapped the whip at his feet. He jumped, eyes glaring in disbelief at his father.

"Disobedient children do deserve the lash as well!" Secord said, his eyes bulging in his head. He brought his arm back wide, ready to bring the whip down on the woman and his son as well.

"No!" Lydia screamed. "Are you not the man whom once took his place on the Committee of Safety at Wyoming? Did we not trust you once with our very lives and property? Were not you once fast friends with Mathias Hollenback and Nathan Denison of whom you now scorn? Now you would have a woman and children starve because of others' failings? What has happen to the once good man?"

"War," Secord said through gritted teeth. "You Yankee rascals would not let a man be in peace upriver but insisted he take sides when he wished neither!" He checked his words, noticing the eyes watching him. "You hauled me off to the Simsbury Mines and but for leveler heads in Congress I would still be there in that hell! I did nothing to warrant such acts! You impudent rats!"

"I had nothing to do with that!" Lydia screamed.

"Then it'll be the innocent to pay for the sins of the guilty," Secord said, looking with glaring eyes up to the whip. "But someone shall pay!"

"Father!" Cyrus called, twisting Lydia behind him to shield her from the whip, "are you mad?"

"Secord!" an odd voice sounded from behind him. He turned to see the Indian Queen, standing erect and regal. She raised her arms against the blue blanket wrapped around her. Her dress, rich, showy and adorned with a profusion of gittering ornaments, shone beneath the blanket. The bells on her imported blue cloth skirt and moccasins jingled in the hushed air. She took one slow step forward. "No more!" she ordered.

Secord let out a huff and lowered the whip. He rolled it up tightly in his hands and strode away toward the Indian village, cursing all behind him.

Ester stood for a moment and looked to Lydia who cocked her head around Cyrus. She smiled at her and lowered her head. She slowly walked away.

"Thank you," Lydia mouthed behind her.

"Do not worry," Cyrus said, turning his eyes from the curious Indian Queen. "She liked you once, at least it seems."

Lydia nodded, wiping her tear-strewn cheeks.

Cyrus waited until most of the Tories melted away to their cabins before ushering Lydia behind a pack-horse. He grabbed a small bag of flour and motioned her to stick it into the ragged folds of her dress.

Lydia's thankful eyes beamed back at him.

"Take this flour for good use," Cyrus said. "This war

makes mad men of once sane men. I hope it shall soon pass so all shall be as it was." He looked down to the questioning woman's eyes. "Well, perhaps it shall never be the same, but I shall not have a woman's and her children's deaths on my conscience when this madness finally ends. Take the flour and be quiet of it. I shall try to sneek more down the river from Father's stores at night. I shall canoe them down. We must be careful, for father accounts for every ounce and every shilling, but we shall manage somehow. I shall think of some trifling excuse or whatnot."

"Oh, God has finally sent his angel," Lydia said. The tears flowed down her cheeks again.

"There are no angels in war," he said, waving the woman to go to her hut. "Only demons partake in its hell."

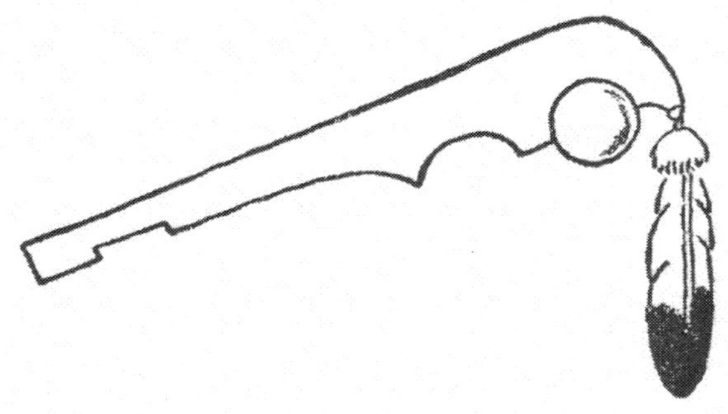

Chapter Thirty Two

Colonel Hartley slowly walked up to the ranger sitting cross-legged in front of the lone bark hut. He examined the area around the hut and gazed down at Franklin again, his eyes following the frontiersman's to the object of his seething anger.

"Who knows to what poor soul this hair belonged," Franklin said. He shifted his eyes to the pile of empty hoops and shoved them with his hand. He picked up a few of them and flung them in the air. "And who knows who's hair was meant for these," he said, fingering one of his locks with his free hand. "Perhaps your's! Perhaps mine!" He looked beyond the colonel to the sea of eyes straining to see over his shoulder. "Perhaps everyone's!" he added.

"Yes, but these will not be made for good use," Hartley said, bending down to pick up one of the hoops. He tossed it into the stream running a few yards away from them.

A shaking sound from the other side of the bark hut turned their eyes to it.

"Made sturdy," Robert Covenhoven said, leading a group of a half dozen other scouts. All of them shared the same look of contempt and disgust. "Made to last through the upcoming season," he added, circling the hut and coming to a stop squarely in front of Franklin. "Probably a Yank's hair," he said, noticing the scalp. "Matted so."

Franklin immediately rose, standing full and erect in front of the Pennamite scout. His taller frame dwarfed the man, even though Covenhoven stood higher than the average man of the times. "Matted, eh, that makes it for sure a damn Pennamite's hair!" he said through gritted teeth.

Covenhoven stood firm, slowly shaking his head and tonguing a cut of tobacco around in his cheek. He cocked his head to one side and spat a great glob of tobbacco juice onto the ground.

Franklin's hand fell to his tomahawk.

Covenhoven raised his rifle ever so slightly and spat again, but this time closer to Franklin.

"Now see here gentlemen," Hartley said, "one war at a time!" He placed himself squarely in front of the two men. He noticed all the eyes staring at him, Yankee and Pennamite. This is a time for a leader to unite and resolve the differences in his command threatening its cohesion, he thought. He rubbed his chin and raised his hands, separating the two men even further from one another. "We," he said, before they could utter any protest, "all of us, are here on a dangerous service! It gives us few opportunities for gaining laurels, but so be it! We have a dangerous and most vile enemy! Vigilant and strange as they shun danger when among us." He stopped and slowly looked around. "But they fight brave when we are near their own country! Well we are not just near, but definitely *in* their country! It is no time to let past differences tear us asunder, but to unite in the face of this potentially devastating foe! Let it give us pleasure to think that we serve our country and fight to protect the helpless and innocent!" He raised his arms in a sweeping motion. A series of huzzas soon answered his words. He stood firm, eying both the stubborn men.

Covenhoven moved first, slowly lowering his rifle and offering his hand to the huge Wyoming scout. He let a nervous smile creep across his face.

Franklin's stern look faded into a grin.

Both of the men laughed and broke toward the pack-horses, no doubt in search of the whiskey barrels.

"Dismantle this vile structure and throw it into the waters," Hartley ordered a few of the soldiers mingling about him.

"Put it to the torch, sir?" one of them asked.

"No, by heavens, do you wish to announce our advance to the entire Six Nations?" he quipped.

"No, sir," the man answered.

"Then be about it man," Hartley said. He took a few steps toward the officers approaching him.

"Them was some mightly fine words," Captain Spalding said, "mightly fine, indeed, they was."

"And I meant every syllable," Hartley said, looking to the other Wyoming and Pennsylvania officers. "One enemy at a time!"

"Shall we make camp here?" Sweeney asked, looking up to the fading glimmer of light through the treetops.

The thunder of some hooves answered his words. Captain Carberry reined up in front of them with a half dozen other Light Horse. He looked down and shook his head in disgust. "Sir! Didn't see hide nor hair of any of the devils!" he reported.

"You can make your camp here, Mr. Sweeney," Hartley said. "Make sure the men get plenty of rest for we may have sport on the morrow."

"Yes, sir," Sweeney said, already waving his arms and motioning for the men to set up camp.

"Lieutenant King," Hartley called to one of Coven-hoven's retreating scouts. The man stopped, turned, stood his rifle up and leaned on it. He gazed back at the colonel through his exhausted eyes. If the good colonel wanted to have words, he would have to come to him, he had his fill of everything for one day.

Hartley briskly stepped over to the man. He nodded his head and gave the man the once over, noticing his torn and ragged clothing. Spots of red shone through some places in his tattered clothes.

Hartley thought of his own sore knees from having to bend down and crawl on his hands and knees over some places on the impossible trail. His water logged feet reminded him of his own struggles wading knee deep through ooze and mire. And he traveled on the trail proper; he shuddered to think of what the scouts such as this hearty soul endured on the flanks.

"Yes sir," King finally said.

"Yes," Hartley said, "On the morrow we shall set out all the early. I suspect we shall have our first run-in with our wily foes. That is why I wish to have you, along with Captains Boone and Brady, Peter Grove, Covenhoven, Dougherty, and Van Campen, to join with Captain Franklin's scouts in the advance party. You are to travel fast and light and advance with all due haste to clear the trail all the way to Sheshequin."

King looked over to the pack-horses. Already Captain Franklin, the returning men from his party, Covenhoven, and the others gathered about a barrel of whiskey, heartily partaking of its contents. "I see no problem with that at all sir," King said. He lowered a hand from his rifle and swung around his grimy haversack. He opened it and showed it empty to the colonel. "There's plenty of boiled beef yet, but the ash cake's about all played out. Seein' how's we ain't had no time for fires, I bet mine's not the only empty haversack in this lot."

"Yes," Hartley said. "I guess we shall have to make fire this night, but we must make them low and only enough for each man to fill his stomach and haversack for the next day's march. Use only the hardest wood, heat the stones, but put the fires out after that."

King nodded. "Is that all Colonel?" he asked.

"Yes, my good man." He patted the scout on the back. "I've heard of your troubles, what with your family and all, and of your other narrow brush with the savages just before we marched. Your escape was most spectacular and I am glad of it. We shall see about putting an end to this nonsense, or at least troubling our foe as much as he does us. We'll show the Six Nations we can deliver a blow as well as take one."

"Oh," King said, patting the stock of his rifle, "I have trouble for them right here, I do."

"Of that I am sure," Hartley said. He saw the scout off and turned to the officer hovering behind him.

"I heard what you said to the scout, sir," Stoddert said. "Fire for all?"

"Yes, but keep it well in hand, we do not wish to announce our presence for all to see."

"Very well, sir," Stoddert said, turning smartly away, "the men's stomachs shall thank you."

Another officer passed by him before Hartley could sit down on a nearby boulder. "The stores, sir," Sweeney said. "Already three pack-horses are empty of their loads, two of them carried whiskey, one flour." He looked around at the men spreading around fires and heartedly drinking from their canteens and noggins. He looked back to Hartley.

"Look where we are," Hartley said. "Look at the hell we already have had to endure. What more to do it on an empty stomach? I think not. Not a mumur of discontent has escaped any of their lips on this whole march. I do not intend to give them reason to gripe. Let them eat and let them be merry, for who knows, it may be the last night they endure on this earth. And besides, we are on the crux of the enemy's land. He eats too, Sweeney, and of the plunder of Wyoming and the West Branch at that! No, everyone shall eat and drink his fill this night."

Sweeney would have none of it. "Whoever heard of fat men starting a revolution?" he said.

"Have you never seen General Knox?" Hartley asked, straight faced. He raised an eyebrow and motioned widely about his waist, trying to entice a response.

Sweeney tried in vain to keep a smile from corrupting his stern look. What a man, he thought, this colonel sitting atop a boulder in the middle of an untamed wilderness with one knee cocked under an arm while his other leg dangles freely over the edge of the boulder, drinking copiously from his canteen full of whiskey. "I have seen General Knox," Sweeney said. "And I have heard Colonel Glover's comments about the man."

"Well there you have it," Hartley said. A grin stretched from ear to ear across his plump little face. "Oh, Captain Sweeney, let them eat and be merry, for their spirit demands it, especially in this dismal place. The thread of leadership is never so thin than when faced with troubles and predicaments such as these."

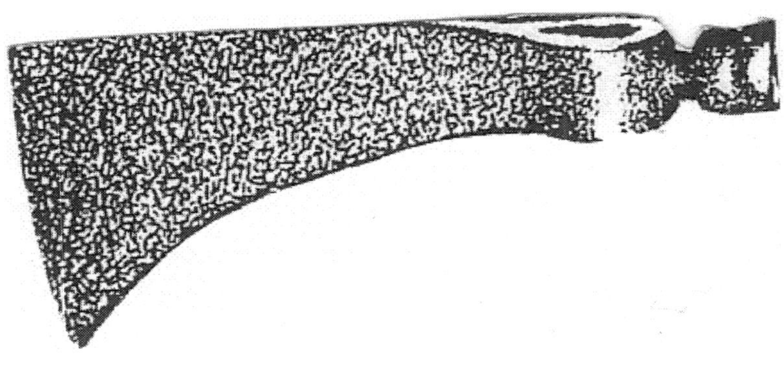

Chapter Thirty Three

The hollow thud of the water drum echoed all along the valley. Great fires illuminated Ester's village in the early dusk. Dogs howled and seemed to want to join the chants and war songs resounding in the air. Warriors danced in full war outfit, painted in gruesome swirls of red, black, and white. Their feathered heads circled around a lone pole. Atop the pole eight hoops hung, pulled tight with hair.

The muscians ceaselessly pounding the drums beat a quicker time and bellowed their war songs, answered by the braves with approving war whoops. The dancers moved with great care around the pole, flashing their teeth and bulging their eyes on a certain cue from the muscians. The firelight reflected off their painted skin and from their bulging eyes, giving them a perfectly terrifying apprearance. Young women stepped just to the side of the circling warriors, chanting and urging them on with great exuberance.

Lydia watched, as she always did, from the safety of her hut Queen Ester forbade anyone to approach; especially in times of celibration. She stood now and then, her hands on her hips, and mouthed a silent prayer in the face of the hethen rite. She heard from a bragging Tory of the eight scalps taken at German Flats. Now the eight deaths brought joy to their slayers and grief to the victims' families.

She shook her head to erase the horrible memories she witnessed in her months at Ester's Town. How many scalps she saw and poor souls meeting their demise in the gauntlet or at the torture pole proved too great for her to recount. She watched the Indians make bales of scalps, each one painted on the back with a certain color to show how it had been taken, to be delivered for payment at Niagara. It all made her shudder.

The drums suddenly stopped, making her heart thud in anticipation in her ears. She looked to the flickering light for any sign of trouble, but made nothing out for certain. The hooting braves, musicians, and young women all trotted toward Ester's Palace, leading the others with them.

"Stay put," Lydia said to her wide-eyed children sitting around their humble fire pit. The fear in their eyes told her she need not repeat herself. Every since the delivery of a steady supply of flour from Cyrus Secord the children seemed better in all respects. A full belly seduces all, she thought.

She edged up to the side of the crowd to see Ester's tall form towering above all the others, even the Tories in green. One of them, wearing a smart looking tri-cornered hat with a cockade cocked jauntily to one side, stood defiantly beside her. He seemed hesitant to defer any authority to the Queen. He seemed a prince himself; in his own mind, at least.

Ester raised her arms, revealing her brightly adorned clothing underneath her blanket. Her huge white necklace with a cross dangling from it shone in the reflecting firelight. Instantly, the crowd fell silent. She gestured with her hand toward the door of her palace. A man slowly emerged from the half-opened door, tugging his hunting shirt down. He cocked back his head and sauntered toward the gathering.

Ester spoke loudly in her native tongue before deferring to the advancing white man.

Lydia recognized the cocksure stride of the man, for they all had it, the Pawlings, the Wintermoots, Van Gorders, and this traitor-Van Alstyne. She glared at the man with a cutting stare, hoping to catch his eye for but moment to convey her disgust of him and his like. In that one blinking of an eye all of the hatred due a traitor would shine from her eyes. But the man, full of his own self-importance, ignored her, stopped, and stood tall in front of all.

"I have come at great peril from the *Wild Yankees* at Wyoming!" he said, pausing for effect. "There I pretended friendship only to discover their designs! Now I have found them! They marched not three days ago from Fort Muncy, nearly seven hundred strong! Perhaps many more!"

A wave of whispers crept through the crowd.

"And now they shall know we know of them!" the man in the fine tri-cornered hat said, swaggering in front of Van Alstyne. He played and pulled at a pair of fine gloves in his hands, eventually raising them high in a gesture of contempt. "They will figure to where you have disappeared," he added.

Van Alstyne would not be upstaged. "They know not where I have gone," he said. "For all they know I have gone on the wind!"

"Yes," the man scoffed. "A north wind, straight to Tioga! Rebel Butler and Denison are no fools. They know what you are all about and no doubt have surmised your intentions!"

"Denison?" Van Alstyne said, "why Captain Butler sir, he leads the Rebels along with Hartley!"

A gasp, then a hush, swept through the Indians. The white men looked curiously about the sea of brown and painted faces, wondering for the life of them what so upset their tawny neighbors.

Walter Butler did not wonder. He knew well and right what upset them. They had a solomn promise from the Yankees to stay out of this fight, especially their leaders.

"See!" he said. "See how the Yankee speaks with a

forked tongue?" He placed his thumbs in the large black belt around his waist and waited for the mumurs to die. "We must make ready to meet the lying Yankees! This time they shall feel our full wrath! My father's misplaced mercy shall not be found in his son's heart! In my heart!" He thumped at his chest with the gloves in his hand. "I have suffered too long in their prison at Albany!" he added, his eyes full of a deep pain upon reflecting on the place. He closed his eyes and lowered his head to his chest, slowly dropping his full hand of gloves to his thigh, seeming overcome with grief and purpose. A few of his fellow Tories quickly interpreted his words into various native tongues. War whoops, cheers, and huzzas followed his declaration.

Butler kept his head low, waiting for the full effect of his act to be conveyed by words to the anxious eyes watching him. Few noticed his eyes rolling from corner to corner under their half-closed lids watching to see if his ruse truly worked. To his great satisfaction the crowd quickly turned into a frenzy, only to be stopped by the haughty Indian Queen's voice. She raised her arms again and muttered something in her native tongue. As all eyes watched her slowly drop her hand into the folds of her blanket and produced a tomahawk. She raised it high above her head and let out her own terrifying yell.

Pondimionium reigned. Indians ran to and fro, hastily meeting one another and swearing oaths that the lying Yankee Denison would pay for his breach of promise. All Rebels would pay with their lives! Their boldness would cost them their lives! The Queen and other chiefs dispatched runners in every direction to spread word of the bold Yankees' and Rebels' advance into their country.

The Tories formed around their finely dressed captain. Raising his head in triumph he barked out orders to this one and that one. He finally mounted his horse, announcing he himself would carry the word to Chemung and Kanadasaga. From there he would mount a counterstrike against the Rebels all the way to Wyoming. He departed spouting how it would take another week for such a large body of men encumbered by such a huge supply train to reach Tioga, anyhow. By then they would be ready and strike the Rebels in their hearts until they ran clear of blood forever.

The Indians, including Ester, ignored the boastful white man. They would do what they could do, Ester announced, with or without the bragging white men.

A screech rising from the scalp pole tore everyone's gaze from Ester to it. A large chief stood next to the pole, pounding it mercilessly while urging others to join him in a strike against the invading forces. It did not take much urging. Braves scattered about, hurriedly gathering up their weapons and accoutrements for the red-hot war path. In no time the chief led a great party of no less than ninety braves down the southern approaches to the village. Their heart tingling wails faded in the distance under the pale light of the moon.

Lydia slowly slid away from the growing tumult, making her way through the growing shadows back to her sanctuary by the riverbank. She slid slowly into her dark bark hut, happy to see the faces of her children staring anxiously up at her.

"What's happening, Ma?" one of them asked.

"Your Pa's coming," she said with the first real smile to stretch across her face in months. "Your Pa's coming with the soldiers, finally, thank God!"

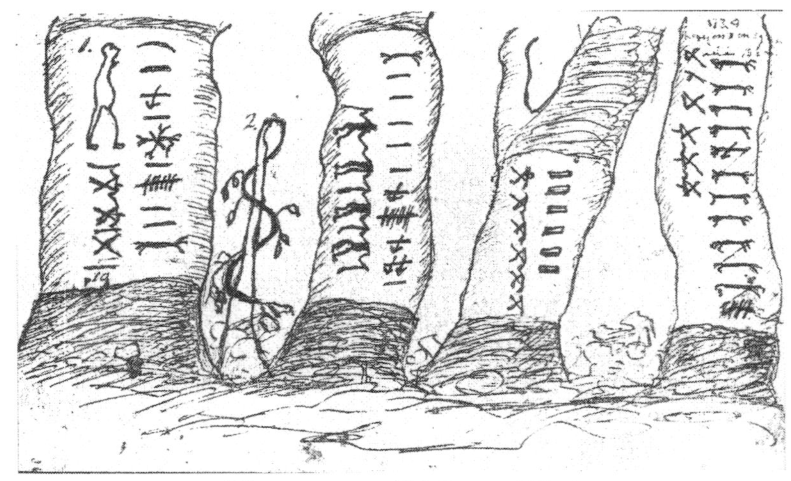

Chapter Thirty Four

The advance party hovered about three curious looking trees, stripped of their bark about their trunks and standing one after another along the trail. Figures and symbols painted in red dotted their bare trunks. Figures with arrows through them. Headless figures painted by the hand of their foes.

"What the hell is this all about?" one of them finally asked.

"Pay it no mind," another called. "The rest of the column is fast approaching, we must push forward!"

Despite the man's pleas no one stepped forward. They stalled, all looking at the figures and into the dark folds of the forest ahead. Several of them nervously checked the prime in the flash pans of their rifles. No one spoke, but just stood pondering their situation.

"These," one of them finally said, stepping forward and pointing at the signs in the early morning light, "show how many scalps they took, of men in arms." He shoved his rifle barrel toward a set of figures opposite the others. "These are those not in arms. Old men, women, and children, no doubt." He took his tomahawk from his belt and thudded into the painted marks. "These represent their losses, which I intend to increase until they can't find a tree big enough to paint all of them onto it!" He pulled the tomahawk from the tree and walked over to a sapling with its top bent and twisted around its trunk. "This means they are strong and united." he said, hacking down the sapling. "But not for long, if I can help it!"

"Here, how does he know all this?" a man asked.

"That's Jenkins," another answered. "The one taken by them and put in the hole at Niagara. Knows them inside and out, he does. They's all afeared of him, they is."

"For good reason," Jenkins said, hacking away at the remaining images. He finally contained his rage and regained his composure. Lifting his rifle, he pointed down the path. "Let's give them something more to draw their silly pictures about, shall we?"

All immediately followed him with rifles held at the ready. Fueled by the boastful signs on the trees, their steps became more hurried. Soon they darted down the path, their woodsmen's eyes scanning all around while they silently slid down the path. Over ravines and hollows they trotted, anxious to vent their fury. A huge outcropping of rocks jutting from a deep green veil of great and lofty cedars caught many of their eyes, slightly slowing their pace. Jenkins, Covenhoven, and Franklin slowed and raised a hand to halt the men, paying no attention to the sight, but paying deference to tingling sensation playing at the napes of their necks.

"We're getting' close, but twenty some miles I reckon," Franklin said. "We best slow up and await the column."

Jenkins and Covenhoven nodded, turning back to the men spilling from the trail behind them. They greeted each, ignoring their tingling necks. Eyes widening with terror at some sight beyond them brought the tingle back to their necks manifold. They instinctively turn around, especially when all the men raised their rifles.

A band of painted men stood stunned on the trail ahead. Men spilled out behind them also, so sudden did the two parties come upon one another. A huge warrior painted solid red from head to foot in their lead stared in disbelief at the white demons. His eyes widened with anger. He raised his rifle.

Both parties instantly fired at one another in the same moment. White smoke clouded the tight path. Angry balls whizzed through the air, cracking branches overhead and thudding into the ground. A mad cheer erupted from the Indians, but the whites stood fast in the clearing smoke, gathering around a bullet-riddled red painted mass of inert flesh on the trail. They advanced, giving their own yell.

Several sporadic shots whizzed through the air at the advancing and whooping whites. The whites ignored them, madly plowing forward and loading their weapons on the run. The thrill of the hunt took over their emotions. Nothing could stop them short of death now.

Covenhoven and Franklin both ran toward a crook in a tree along the path, each fumbling with their powder horns to get off one more shot at the retreating red men. Franklin reached the crook a half step ahead of Covenhoven and slid his weapon down into it to steady his shot. Undeterred, Covenhoven flung himself to the ground. Both fired at the same instant, twirling a brave around on the path. In another heartbeat the brave rose and ran madly away from the hornet's nest of angry white devils.

"Get up here! Get up here!" Franklin called behind him. "Lay fire into 'em before they melt into the forest!"

Several men scurried up and fired blindly down the trail to no effect.

"It's alright," Franklin said, taking heed their shots did nothing but terrify the surrounding wildlife scurrying for cover. "Ya put the fear in 'em! Nothing like a ball whizzing behind 'em to scare the be-Jesus out of 'em! It'll check 'em it will. They won't be so anxious next time."

Covenhoven rose and fired once more down the trail. "Rascals!" he said. "But I do think I winged one of them!"

Franklin smiled at his reference to the twirling brave. "I think I did too, by God, I do."

They both laughed and hurried back to the fallen brave in the path.

"He's a chief," Jenkins said, rising from the bullet-riddled body. The chief's face appeared nothing but a red glob of flesh. A fresh red spot atop the crown of his skull attested to the scalp one of the men proudly displayed before him.

"Can't tell who he is," Jenkins said, "account of his face being all shot up. But he's a chief, Muncy, I believe."

"Who the hell cares? Just so he's dead is all that matters," Moses Van Campen said. He walked over to the man displaying the scalp and said, "seeing how no one knows for sure who's ball dropped the painted devil, does anyone protest to this man claiming the scalp?"

"Hell no!" came a reply from the men hastily re-loading and checking their weapons. "There's more where that one come from anyhow!"

"Fine shots, for all," Franklin said, bending down and examining the Indian's face. "But next time spread your shots out a bit more, lads. Do more damage that way."

Captain Carberry and his Light Horse galloped madly up the path. "We heard gun play!" he said, reining his horse to a stop in front of the man with the scalp.

"Yes, met a party equal to our number and let 'em have it," Franklin said. "Got one for sure and winged another. They've high tailed it back to Tioga, the painted rascals!" He lifted his head and glanced at the scouts. "No one's hit, is they?" he asked.

"Hell no," came a quick reply. "Hell no!"

"Then get your rifles in good order," Covenhoven said. "For that hell you mention is just up the trail this day and is all anxious to meet us, it is for sure!"

Chapter Thirty Five

Hartley bent down and hastily examined the body of the slain Indian chief. He lifted the pouch, already torn free of the body and rifled through it. After a moment he threw it back down on the ground in disgust. "How was he provisioned?" he asked Captain Franklin at his side.

"He had plenty of powder and ball, some corn cake, jerked meat, and a gourd for a canteen, plus his tomahawk and knives," Franklin answered, looking down to the trophy knife stuck in his belt. "I got his belt knife," he added. "The rest is divided amongst us."

"Very well," Hartley said. "So they were well provisioned for war, means they've come out to meet us."

Franklin stood tall beside him. He shook his head. "Oh no sir," he said. "They weren't coming to parley, I assure you of that! They fired as soon as we did, the instant they saw us!"

"Then I take it you both stumbled onto one another," Hartley said.

Franklin rubbed his eyes and shook his head again. "But who came out the victor?" he asked.

"Be that as it may," Hartley said, slowly rising from the body, "they know of us for certain. You say an equal body of savages more or less met you?"

"Yes sir," Franklin said. "I winged one, too." Covenhoven's surprised look at him made him reconsider. "Well, one of us winged one for sure, don't know if'n any more balls found their mark. As you see, most aimed at this rascal."

"I see, and with deadly marksmanship," Hartley said, looking down to the unrecognizable face of the dead man.

"Be that as it may, now has come the time to move fast. The element of surprise has most definitely been compromised. Gentlemen it is time to forge ahead at the long trot! We must reach Tioga before they have time to gather their forces if we are to have any chance of success! Are you with me?"

A rousing chorus of huzzas answered him.

"Very well," he said, nodding his head in approval. "There is to be one change, though. Captain Carberry, you are to proceed ahead with the advance scouts and assist in any manner possible. Prisoners are what we want now, not scalps! We need to learn all we can of the enemy's disposition!"

The rank and file immediately formed and marched up the trail, scouts to the front with horsemen taking up the flanks when possible. One by one they marched past the body of their slain foe, some casting a sour eye down to it, while others simply ignored it, focused on what lie ahead more than what lay behind. A few obstinate individuals slowed enough to give the body a swift kick or poke it with their rifles or banoyneted muskets. One or two even spat on it.

The column of men moved with ease down the leveler terrain of this valley, compared to the impossible path a-long the Lycoming Creek. Anticipation of a promised fight fueled each of their tired steps beyond the endurance of ordinary men.

Sometimes quality outdoes quanity, Hartley thought, watching the spirited woodsmen trot along the trail mile after mile. Their example fueled the regulars of his own regiments' steps. All behaved admirably, and he swelled with pride witnessing the resolve of each man. A sudden slowing in the step gave him immediate alarm. He strode to the front of the column with haste, passing nervous eyes along the way.

"What?" he called to a horseman reining his horse in front of him. "What?" He walked up to the horse and placed his hands on its flanks, all the while looking up the trail.

"The scouts have discovered a spot ahead where they reckon close to seventy warriors bedded down the night before," the horseman finally reported. "It's an abandoned village, still some corn hills about and a few mounds, but no structures to speak of."

"Very well," Hartley said, nodding his head profusely. "Then we shall not bother with it. Tell the scouts and Captain Carberry to push on, we must make Tioga by this night!" He pushed himself back from the horse, having to admit the slight restpit fell good to his aching and sore legs. He fought through the pain and stiffened his back. "Push on!" he called to the column now moving in front of him again. "Push on, for God's sake, push on!"

After another few miles fatigue overcame them all. Men spilled from the ranks, only to rise from the swift kick and prodding of their sergeants and officers. Hartley watched it all with his own head bobbing down to his chest. "We must stop," he mumbled. Noticing no one obeying his orders, he plopped down to the ground and shouted "halt!"

He did not need to repeat the order.

Men sank down to the edge of the trail in pure exhaustion. Horses neighed in the relief they shared with their masters.

"We shall rest here for a few hours and then continue," Hartley said, lifting his tired torso from the ground just long enough to mutter the order clearly. "The men of the Light Horse shall stand guard, half on picket and half at rest." With that he let his tired body fall completely to the ground. In an instant he fell asleep.

Carberry ordered the six men next to him to file

around the exhausted men while he and the others fell from the saddle. "We'll spell you in an hour," he mumbled before he fell into his own desperate sleep.

The hours drifted by quickly, as most feared, and soon the men rose to their feet. The brief respite helped a little, but the bags under their eyes and aching muscles warned it not to be enough. But onward they must strive, they all knew; with no need for the officers to remind them.

Hartley stood back, watching the men trot in front of him, waiting for the pack-horse line. Supplies must be getting low, he mused, now regretting his decision to let all drink and eat to their fill. The sloshing of half empty canteens on the men passing added to his anxiety. The empty haversacks on their sides also caused concern. He raised his lip to the men passing him, though, wishing to blanket his worry with the confidence he had in his men. The feeling raised his spirits. "You'll be dancing at Tioga this night," he called to Captain Bush.

Bush nodded, and bowed his tired head gracefully.

Finally the lead pack-horse stumbled into view. He walked back to meet the lead drover, though a mere boy, and walked along side of him. He quickly noticed many of the horses behind the boy traveling with very light loads, some with nothing at all on their backs. "Provisions low?" he asked the boy.

"Yes, sir," the boy answered, "but we were directed to give the men all they wanted."

"Oh yes," Hartley said, "I know, don't fret about it. Soon we will gain Sheshequin and Tioga, from there possibly Chemung. There we will gain new provisions, I assure you."

"That's what we all figured," the boy said, suddenly becoming enamered with the colonel's spirit. "Rome and Carthage," he added.

The colonel raised an eyebrow.

"The Senate figured the best way to defend Rome was to carry the war into Africa, and put the Carthagenians on the defensive. From that day onward it has been considered good defensive tactics to carry an offensive campaign into the enemy's country." the boy said.

Hartley stood aghast by the boy's reference to military tactics. He would not expect such insight from the educated people of Philadelphia, let alone from a mere boy on the frontier. He wished some in Congress shared the boy's insight. "Yes, it has," he said in reference to the lad's approval and understanding of his tactics.

"War has never been easy, especially one of such great odds as this one," the boy continued, "but with true faith, courage, and a belief in God who drives and guides us we shall emerge victorious." He looked down and nodded his head. "My Pa has told me this time and time again."

"Your Pa," Hartley said, trying for the life of him to figure out to whom he preferred. "A man of great insight and high rank, I hope, for he sounds as a man we need in such times." A thought flashed in his mind. He had heard-no read-of a man speaking in such a manner. "Would your name be Butler, perhaps?" he asked with a sly eye.

"Why, yes sir," the boy answered. "Lord Butler, son of Colonel Zebulon Butler of Wyoming." The boy's eyes beamed with pride. "Pa likes me and my sister to read and keep up on things. Had them set up a route to deliver the *Courant* all the way from Connecticut, he did." He rolled his eyes. "Well, Pa among others," he added after a moment of reflection. His Pa also taught him the value of honesty.

"Well he certainly has done a good job with you, son," Hartley said. "How old are you?" He reflected back on Sweeney telling him of how a boy from Wyoming had taken over the commissary duties of the new regiment of regulars, frontiersmen, and militiamen he commanded. He excluded the boy's name though, and Butler himself had declined to tell him of his own son joining the expedition. Denison had not mentioned it neither.

"Seventeen," the boy answered. "But I'm just as fit and capable as the next!"

"Oh, no doubt, son, no doubt," Hartley said. He looked back to one of the empty horses, pondering whether he preferred its back to his feet.

"You're welcome to any of 'em," Lord said, noticing his gaze. "Most officers always ride, anyhow, that's what Pa says. Says those in command must be seen."

"Yes, but these are special circumstances," Hartley said. "If my men walk, I must walk. After all, in such a place as this and engaged in such a campaign it is crucial that the men feel as they are led by one of their own."

"That's a right smart way of putting it," Lord said. "I'm sure Pa would approve and say the same."

"I'm sure, also," Hartley said, promising himself to get to know his counterpart at Wyoming better when they actually met face to face. "I'm sure, also."

Chapter Thirty Six

Solemn faces greeted the crestfallen warriors creeping into Ester's Town from every direction. They emerged from the woods and trails in groups of threes and fours, none numbering more than a half dozen. They ranted and warned of hordes of Yankees coming up from the south and milled about, each looking for rhyme or reason in each others' eyes. Stark looks stared back at them, each somehow empty and void of a thought of what to do next. It all came too sudden. Somehow the Yankees swooped in through the backdoor, with none knowing how to close it in their faces. After a while they returned to their cabins, swearing oaths against the *white-eyes* and praying for deliverence from the Great Spirit. They found little relief in the green-coated forces spilling into the town from the north, despite their boasts to smite the Yankee scourge once and for all. They heard it all before. The rangers' plans seemed to multiply their troubles rather than solve them. Angry grunts greeted each of the white men's boasts.

Queen Ester walked among the agitated warriors, noticing the great chief *Big Man* missing from their number. His widow cried the most mournful wails. Feeling her grief, Ester stopped to comfort her while warriors gathered around them, becoming more enraged at the sight of the grieving widow.

Ester herself let out a wail and raised her hands up to the sky, beseeching the heavens to intercede on their behalf. With tear stained eyes she noticed the sun setting behind the mountains. She looked to the green mountains and wept. "Is this the last of her people?" she asked aloud.

Hearing their Queen's pleas to heaven, many warriors screamed in protest. They thudded their chests with spears gripped tightly in their clenched fists, swearing no *white-eyes* would enter the village while any of them still stood. Several of the warriors, overcome with sheer emotion, cut at their chests and arms with sharp knives.

Ester immediately scolded them. "Injure the *white-eyes*, not yourselves!" she said. She regained her dignity and rose tall, facing the last rays of the evening sun flooding the valley with its golden light. No! This would not be the last of her village-of her late husband Eghobund's posterity! He swore his kingdom would last as long as the waters flowed and his widow carried his determination from the grave. She barked orders for all to assemble and retreat to a deep glen up the trail along the Chemung River. With its high walls they could defend and fight off an enemy thrice their number.

Women and men quickly gathered together all they could carry, including the crestfallen prisoners from German Flats. Horses neighed in protest while braves hastily rounded them up, leaving the ones too far away to tend to themselves, as well as the other livestock. No time could be wasted! They must flee for their lives, for the fury of the Yankees would fuel an unquenchable rage. A rage that threatened all, even if they played no part in the late battle.

The leading officer of the white men shook his head and mounted his horse. He yelled down at his mingling troops to fall in and follow him to Chemung. A protest from one of his subalterns turned his eyes down to him. "What are you about Terry?" he asked the frustrated man.

"Captain Butler would stay and give them battle!" Lieutenant Terry said. "You should do the same in his stead,

Captain Caldwell!"

Caldwell glared down at the impudent man. He reined his horse next to him, enraged at being second-guessed in front of his men. "If you wish to stay do so," he said, nodding his head toward the mass of confused Indians. "But expect no help from this lot! There're all leaving, and so am I!"

"But what of Captain Butler?" Terry asked.

"Captain Butler is somewhere between here and Kanadasaga, fine sir, if you wish to fetch him do so, you have my leave! But at this moment here and now I am in charge and I say we retreat to Chemung, there to give battle in the defiles between here and there!" He turned his horse toward the trail leading north and galloped for it.

Terry glanced at the men hurriedly trailing behind Caldwell and suddenly found himself alone in a sea of terrified brown faces. He lifted his rifle in a huff and trotted up the trail, nervously looking behind him. His capture, from those in the ranks he once served, would mean the loose around his neck and he knew it. He fingered at the neck stock around his neck which suddenly felt tight and restricting. His feet moved all the faster because of the sensation.

Lydia Strope ignored the agitated Indians and fleeing white men. She looked to the south along the far riverbank, searching the horizon for any sign of her deliverers from hell. She thought of herding up her children and escaping to the south, there to certainly meet up with the army, but reconsidered as she turned to the thoughtful eyes of her children. This is the wilderness, she sullenly reminded herself. Panthers, wolves, bears, and rattlesnakes ranged freely along the trails. If they should somehow miss the fast moving army a hundred miles separated her from any form of civilization. No, the risk outweighed the chances of success.

She could risk her own life, but not her children's lives. Ester protected them so far, though they nearly starved, but at least they still drew the breath of life.

She turned her head sullenly toward the approaching braves, knowing their intentions. In a rush she gathered her children and precious bundle of fire cakes, passing the bundle down to the awaiting hands of her eldest son. At the same time she tore down the ragged blanket covering the hut's door. She hastily wrapped her huge family bible in its folds, urged along by anxious braves who screamed "Jogo! Jogo!"

Gathering her terrified children, she joined the ragged column of refugees filing from the Indian village.

The whole village headed north under the guidance of their Queen, trusting their lives to her care. The Queen knew the Yankees. She knew the rage within their souls. She would deliver them and shield them from its terrible wrath.

Trudging forward Lydia turned her head and looked back, clutching the bible tightly to her chest and hoping against all odds for the soldiers to burst upon them and free them. But alas, no one came. Her heart filled her eyes with tears and she bowed her head in grief. Would this never end?

Heartrending cries of wailing and moaning Indian women sounded all around her. She felt free to mouth a silent prayer without any resprisal and beseeched the heavens to deliver her and her children from the hand of the savage as loudly as Ester did to smite them.

The wails and prayers drifted into nothingness in the still night air. Only the bellows of the abandoned cattle and neighs from a few horses sounded among the howls of the dogs in the abandoned village. The dogs, suddenly delirious with the bounty left them, spilled every pot and bundle, feasting on the abandoned food.

A few fires still flickered among the lonely village,

but no human life shone about it.

Ester's Town sat alone in the night, drained of all its inhabitants without even a shot. The wrath of the Yankees proceeded them, conquering with just its threat alone.

Chapter Thirty Seven

A sharp chirp and rustle of leaves jolted rifles to their shoulders. Staring at the dozens of scampering little tails retreating up fallen logs and underbrush calmed the hearts of the scouts just as quickly as it had startled them. Any of them glancing about at one of their fellows would have been a liar if he did not claim a monumental amount of relief. Still, no one spoke for the longest moment from the awful feeling of their hearts thumping up their throats.

"Chipmunks," one of them finally scoffed under his tired breath, "chipmunks, of all the damn things."

"Don't worry about them," Covenhoven said, now passing to the front of the scouts down the steep trail, "worry about the varmints with painted faces and feathers."

The scouts slowly resumed the march behind the intrepid scout in their lead. Everyone of their bodies ached with each new step, but they knew their only chance for victory lay in moving fast. Thus, they quickly moved forward in the waning light of the day, tired, but alert to the ever present danger they feared lurked behind every turn of the tight trail. The Narrow Way, the Moravians called this last stretch of the trail descending down to Sheshequin. Aptly named, most of them agreed.

More small game, mostly squirrels and rabbits, scurried away from them the further they descended the steep mountain trail. Rifles rose and fell appropriately, and with the same overwhelming sense of relief each time they recognized the harmless culprits causing the noise.

"We're getting close," came down the line of scouts. "The Indians let these small varmints feast on the leftovers of their fields in the summer while they hunt further away, that ways when the cold weather strikes they got plenty to kill for food right around their village. Cunning rascals they are."

All of the advance scouts paused for a moment and watched an enormously fat raccoon swagger away from them up the side of the trail. "My God," one of them said on a whisper, "he's fat enough to make a coat for my whole family! Damn if'n these Indians don't live in a paridise!"

"A paradise soon to be lost," one of them said.

"Keep it down," Covenhoven called back down the line. He pointed down the trail and to the flatter plain beyond. Fire flecks showed between the trees. Silhouettes of cabins shone against their faint light. Covenhoven waved them all forward into a bunch around him. "I don't know how many are there or if'n they all ain't taken wing before us. Everyone check their firelocks and make ready, call the horse to the front," he said in hushed tones. To the curious eyes of those near him he dumped a little of the contents of his canteen onto the ground before him. He swirled it around in the dirt and smeared his face with the black earth.

Approving of his masking efforts, many of the others followed his lead. Soon white eyes shone from dark faces, giving them an unearthly appearance in the pale moonlight.

Trotting to the front Captain Carberry and his horsemen nearly collided with the huddled men, reining their mounts to a stop just behind them. "Good God you men appear as if you popped from the bowels of the earth itself!" he said. "We barley saw you."

Covenhoven and Franklin both put a finger to their lips and motioned for Carberry to look down the trail. The fires flickered all the brighter.

Carberry dismounted and knelt down next to the scouts. "We've done it," he said, beaming with pride. "We have swept down upon them unawares."

"The hen is the smartest of all of nature's creations," Franklin said, "for she only cackles when the egg has been layed."

"He's right," Covenhoven said. "We've a cunning foe who may wait in ambush anywhere to our front. We must move with due caution."

Carberry nodded his head and mounted his horse again. "You're right, Captains," he said. "Fine sirs, I await your orders."

"Well, first we need to send a runner back to Colonel Hartley," Covenhoven said. "In the mean time we shall push forward, I am sure we shall gain no protest from the good colonel, for all are tired and footsore and I am sure he wishes to gain the village as soon as possible."

Franklin and Carberry nodded in approval.

"Move swift and quite," Covenhoven said, staring into the darkening trail between them and the village. "If we take fire from the hills, the horse is to sweep around making all the noise possible to disrupt our foe. We shall attack from the front. They should bolt in the confusion." With that he slowly took the first step forward, anxious, but wary of what lay ahead. He hoped to set a good example. Their very lives depended on proper concert of action, from Pennamite, Yankee, and regular alike. In this light their petty squabbles and differences truly did seem frivolous.

The closer they crept to the village the more spirited their steps, especially those of the scouts from Wyoming. Visions of the terrible battle flashed in their minds, strengthening their resolve and their thirst for revenge. Soon all sense of their tired and aching bodies faded. Their fingers gripped their firelocks all the tighter. Their eyes all darted back and forth, taking in the slightest movement. The closer they gained the village, the more the shadows around the fires became clearer. Not only dogs, but people moved about the flames, though most of them sat deathly still, occasionally one rose to look down the south trail.

The scouts slid among the shadows and melted into the village, encircling the fire and those around it without their knowledge of them. At a signal from Covenhoven they sprang from the shadows, leveling their weapons on the frightened and shocked people.

To their astonishment great smiles welcomed them. People-white people-rose from their places around the fire and ran to them, overjoyed by their presence. "Glory to God! We have been delivered from the hands of the savages by the grace of God!" one of them exclaimed, wearing the hint of a white collar around his neck. "Rejoice children! Rejoice!" He ran to the nearest scout and openly embraced him. Many of the others followed his lead.

"Now just hold on a minute," Franklin said, waving one hand at the grateful white people while waving his men toward the cabins. "Where's the devils at?"

The thundering of hooves all around the perimeter of the village caused a start in the rescued people. They retreated into a huddled mass around the fire.

"You!" Franklin called to the preacher. "Answer me! Where's the devils at?"

"They've all fled," he said, trying to soothe and comfort his flock. "They left at dusk in such haste they just left us here by the fire. They knew of God's delivers! Knew they drew near with the terrible sword of his wrath! Praise be to the Lord!"

"Praise be to the Lord at that, preacher," Franklin said. Nonetheless, he motioned for his men to continue their examination of every cabin, ever mindful of their wily foe.

One of the scouts spurt forward and hastily examined all of the faces of the huddle masses. He rose in disgust when none of the faces proved familiar. “Are they still about Ester’s Town and Tioga Point?” he asked the preacher.

“I know not what lies upriver, my dear man, only that God has delivered this flock of deserving souls from the hands of the savages,” the precher answered, bowing his head in prayer.

“More deserving souls lay upriver, preacher,” he said. “I know that for sure!” He darted away from the fire and madly searched all the cabins. Letting out a disgusted groan he crept toward the fire and collapsed from complete exhaustion, emotionally as well as physically.

“It’ll be alright, Boss,” Franklin said. “We’ll head up there at first light.”

“First light hell,” Covenhoven said before Boss uttered a word. He knelt down next to the crestfallen man and patted his shoulder.

Carberry galloped up to the fire and reined back his horse on its haunches. “Who are these poor souls?” he asked.

“Just the faithful servants of the Lord delivered from Satan’s wrath,” the preacher answered the horseman.

Carberry quickly counted their heads. “Fifteen,” he said. He looked up the dark river. “How many more poor souls await deliverance up river?” he asked.

“Perhaps more,” a commanding voice broke the air.

Colonel Hartley emerged from the shadows full and stout. He smiled and stared with a comforting eye at the emancipated souls huddling around the fire. Troops filed into the village from behind him and helped search the cabins.

“Oh, an officer of high rank,” the preacher said. “Sent to deliver us from evil!”

“Well,” Hartley said, gazing up the trail to the north,

"I don't know about that, but delivered you are. I hope you are right about God's hand being with us, for I fear we may be in need of all the help we can get."

Boss Strope rose from his grief and plodded up the trail to the north. Anxious eyes looked to Hartley.

"Go on," he said to the scouts and Carberry, "if you feel up to it. Capture all you can and lay waste to all you cannot carry. We shall see to this place. There is livestock to be herded and plunder to be reclaimed. Send word back if you require assistance. But proceed no further than Ester's Town, for I fear Chemung too far off this night. We shall see on the morrow."

The majority of the scouts and Light Horse scampered up the trail and disappeared into the dark folds of the trail. No longer tired, they trotted lively along the trail into the night, invigorated by their thirst for the hunt.

"Gentlemen, I shall have a strong guard posted this night, the parole shall be 'victory'," Hartley called to the last scouts clamoring up the trail, "the countersign shall be 'or death!'"

Woe be to Ester if they found her this night, for no mercy lay in their hearts, only a thrist for revenge. It seemed the only elixir to quell their ravaged thirst for justice.

Chapter Thirty Eight

The Light Horse galloped ahead in the darkness, swooping down on Ester's village with a vengeance. Outdistancing the scouts afoot, they surrounded and galloped through the village, scattering the hordes of dogs in front of them. They raced up to the doors of the cabins, kicking them in with one foot from their mounts while brandishing pistols, carbines, and swords.

Fireflecks from still smoldering embers and flames in the firepits dotting the village cast eerie shadows against the cabins' walls. One of the horsemen grabbed a pine knot laying by one of the cabins and bent down to a firepit. The pine knot glared to life, illuminating the man's grim and determined face. He kicked his horse's flanks toward the nearest cabin.

"No!" Carberry called to him. "There's still plunder in them, let the foot soldiers take care of it! After they clear it all shall burn!" He galloped toward the north end of the village. All the Light Horse followed. A series of shots in the night hastened their trot.

Two horsemen sat astride their twirling mounts, trying to rein them steady while fumbling to load the pistols in their hands. "A half dozen of them scurried up the trail!" one of them reported. "got a couple of shots off but to little effect, I'm afraid!"

Carberry galloped up the trail a few rods and stared up it, raising his own pistol. Anxiously, he looked back to the village. Noticing the scouts spill into it from the south he turned his head toward the north trail again. "The foot's arrived!" he said. "It's a fine night for a fox hunt! Let's go!" With that they thundered up the path. Soon the sound of their thundering hooves disappeared into the foreboding darkness.

Boss Strope raced wildly through the Indian village, slamming doors open with his rifle butt and instantly twirling it about, ready to dispatch any savage lying in the shadows. No faces peered back at him. Visions of Lydia's smile flashed in his mind. He must find her! He must find the children! He scampered along and finally fell in a heap on the ground from complete exhaustion. He rolled over, cursing his aching body for one more burst of strength. His searching eyes caught the silhoutte of a bark hut by the river's edge. Instinctively, he sensed Lydia. He clamored to his feet, dragging his long rifle behind him.

He fell headlong into the hut, searching madly in the shadows for any sign of his wife and children. To his amazement a faint, but familiar, odor caught his attention. He smelled their faint odor! He swore it! He crawled out of the cabin and tumbled down the bank, half expecting to see his wife and children huddled along the bottom of it. Only a few canoes greeted him. He kicked them angrily with his feet, sending one spiraling into the current. Exhaustion finally overcoming him, he fell to the rocky beach.

"Wait!" a voice shouted from the bank above. "We may need them!"

Covenhoven plunged down the bank and caught the canoe just before it gained the main current. He pulled the canoe back and tugged it up to the beach. Gasping and groaning he too collapsed in a heap of exhaustion.

"They've taken them," Boss mumbled to him. "They

were just here, I can feel ‘em! Smell ‘em!” He tried to struggle to his feet only to collaspe again. “Damn *Copperheads* took ‘em right out from under my nose!”

“No, damn it!” Covenhoven said. “You’ve done all you can! No one could’ve done better!”

“I shouldn’t have left ‘em, damn it,” Boss sobbed. “But Denison promised to get them back! I had to go for him and his soldiers.”

“It’s neither his nor your own fault!” Covenhoven said, rolling his head along the beach. His exhausted body fought with each of his movements. None could do more than he and his rangers. Thirty miles in one day through such a dismal wilderness. This expedition rivaled all he heard of Roger’s Rangers in the last war. No one could do better! He looked over to his crestfallen fellow. “Get a hold of yourself. We shall find them on the morrow.”

“No,” Boss said. “That half-breed Ester’s taking them to Fort Niagara or worse! I’m going back to the Hudson and gather my own people. We’ll get them!” He let his head fall to the beach. His eyes closed immediately and he drifted into a deep sleep, despite his anguished soul.

Covenhoven sat and listened. A slight rustle sounded from the village, but no more shots rang in the night air. He drew a long breath and fought against closing his tired eyes, for he knew if he closed them he too would fall into a deep sleep. Not yet, he mumbled to his aching body. Not yet!

He sat up and looked to the swirling waters at their feet. A fish jumped, making a splash just to their front, and giving him a start. He took advantage of the slight burst of energy caused by the start and grabbed ahold of one of Boss’ feet in the water. He tugged it out of the water to the beach and slowly rose. He took a swig from his near-empty canteen and stumbled back to the village.

Exhausted men with bloodshot eyes greeted him. He fumbled toward one of the fire pits now blazing to life from an ample supply of wood thrown onto it. He bent down and picked up a flaming pine knot and stumbled toward the large cabin in the center of the village. An ornamental porch sat over the door of the fine hewed-log structure. Someone of importance dwelt here, he reasoned. A Queen! He kicked open the door and prepared to toss the firebrand into it. A hand on his arm immediately stopped his movement.

"Don't you think we should wait 'til we've had a look around?" Franklin asked him.

"It's the fiend Ester's place for sure," Covenhoven answered.

The name made Franklin's bloodshot eyes widen. "All the more why we shouldn't put it to the torch 'til we've had a chance to look about it."

"Be my guest, fine sir," Covenhoven said, taking a step backward. His stomach felt queasy. His legs cramped. Every hair on his head cried for sleep, but he fought against the demand, at least until this demon's palace went up in flames.

"None would like to see it burn," another Wyoming man said, walking up to the two men in the doorway, "as well as the one who inhabits it, as we." He ushered the two exhausted officers aside and stepped into the cabin, holding a flaming pine knot in one hand and a pistol in the other. He kicked through the blankets and skins on the floor, angrily rifling through the selves over the hearths at each end of the cabin. Fumbling in the dim light he stumbled over something in the center of the floor. A grotesque idol, made in the image of something from neither heaven or hell, spilled from its coveted place on a stump in the middle of the cabin. He looked down at the thing through his tired eyes and backed through the door, repulsed by it.

"Well, Roswell?" Franklin asked the man.

"There's nothing this side of heaven and hell in that place," Roswell Franklin said. "Burn it, let its stench foul the nostrils of Satan himself!"

Covenhoven tossed the firebrand into the door and tumbled back from it. Roswell Franklin stepped behind him and tossed his own pine knot into it. Smoke soon rolled through the door. Sheets of fire followed, shinning through thick columns of billowing deep black smoke. Cheers rose from the gathering scouts and rangers.

"That's all for this night," Franklin said. "We'll wait 'til morning and light. There's cattle out there and our own plunder about this place. We'll burn it after we've reclaimed all we can."

No protests sounded from the exhausted men. Some already collapsed and snored by firepits, the sides of cabins, and inside them.

"We'll need a watch," Covenhoven said, barely able to keep his eyes open. "Parole is 'victory', countersign is or 'death.'"

"Me and Roswell here will see to that," Franklin said, watching the flames illuminate the mountains and reflect off the face of the Susquehanna. "Waited a long time for this, would like to watch it burn."

"And I as well," Roswell said, lifting his rifle to his chest. "I would very much like to fell one of those who killed Captain Stewart, if any of them be fool enough to show their faces!"

"Prisoners," Covenhoven muttered before collapsing next to a fire pit. "Prisoners. We need to know the rats' strength. Prisoners." He nodded off for a second before suddenly springing back to life. "Wake me and I'll spell you in a bit. Keep a watch out for the horse, they'll be back. Remember, prisoners!" This time he nodded off into a deep sleep, his snores adding to the chorus already polluting the air.

"We'll see about prisoners," Roswell said, walking toward the north end of the village. "We'll see just as they saw about prisoners at Wyoming!"

Chapter Thirty Nine

Ester stared down at the gems bedecking her horse. Torn from her victims, each reminded her of the individual circumstances from which she had acquired them. Each of those memories now haunted her on her people's lone trek through the wilderness. All, at this moment, seemed for not.

Silence now prevailed over the souls following her to the glen. No children cried anymore, no widows wailed, and no warriors whooped.

She thought of leading them to Chemung, but reconsidered, fearing it to be the Yankee's true target. Too much foul blood flowed between the two peoples now for anything but a fight to the finish. Now the war seemed one of annihilation.

Her eyes looked to the raven feathers braided all along her horse's mane. They swayed and flowed naturally on its neck, for a woman had taken great pains to ornate her Queen's horse. In the pale light of the moon their bluish-black hue glittered. She lost herself in their strange beauty and rode in a trance. She needed beauty to sooth her thoughts now, for no thoughts came to mind but horrid ones.

Her horse stumbled on a stone and neighed, breaking the silence and the mood. A sea of eyes shot to their Queen. She shook her head and waved them to go on, reining her horse to the side of the trail.

Something brushed along her leg and she gazed down at the hair wisping in the wind. She put her hand down to the great string of scalps, fourteen in all, taken in retribution for her son's death by the Yankees, and watched while one fell loose to the ground. She did not dismount to retrieve it. Too much blood had flowed from her hand in revenge. Somehow it did little to ease her grief. It seemed to only intensify the pain. Oh, my Gencho, she thought. He was the last vestage of her beloved husband Chief Eghobund, now lost well before his time. She felt her eyes water and let the tears flow freely, turning her head away from the line of Indians walking before her. They had enough pain. She did not want to add to their apprehension.

A sound echoed through the trees. Some bowed heads raised and let out an anguished gasp, while others trod steadfastly forward, ignoring the mysterious noise. A few warriors rushed back toward the disturbance, peering into the darkness of the trail behind them. They looked anxiously around and to their Queen sitting deathly still on her great black mare. Someone in Wyoming lost some fine horse flesh when Ester claimed the beast, they thought. One of them noticed the hair and bent down to it. He gingerly picked it up and handed it to Ester, though her head still turned away from him.

Ester hastily wiped her eyes and accepted the scalp, carefully tying it to the string of others. She swallowed hard against her grief and cracked a half smile down to the brave.

The brave did not speak, but only stared deeply into her eyes. His gaze broke to the white flag of a deer tail bobbing behind them and crossing the trail, no doubt the culprit causing the mysterious noise. He let out a sigh of relief which gave way to anguish again. He stared back up to the Queen with hollow eyes.

"Jogo, Roland," she said to the pot-marked face staring soulfully up at her. His eyes pleaded for an answer to this all, but she had none. She rolled her heartbroken eyes from him and slowly trotted up the trail.

Roland Montour stopped, turned with the other braves and stared down the trail. A dim light flickering just over the crest of the trail behind them caught all their eyes. They knew what it meant. All they owned now went up into flames by the hands of the revenging Yankees.

Roland fell to his knees, angrily pounding the ground. Throwing his head back, he let out a long mournful wail. His brother John walked slowly toward him and knelt down beside him, bowing his head in grief. Tears of rage and anguish flitted down their cheeks.

Ester reined her horse to a stop and turned back to them. "John, Roland, my blood!" she called down to the brothers in their native tongue. "Rise! Be strong! Our day will come again, for this one is lost. When Seneca come we see! They shall help us drive the *Yank-ee* forever from this land! *Par le fer et par le feu! Avoir de l'estomac!*"

The other braves turned and solemnly walked toward the retreating line of souls. John helped Roland rise and both slowly walked past the Queen. Noticing the Queen did not follow, Roland barked out an order to a pair of braves who immediately trotted back to her.

Ester ignored them and spurred her horse up the steep side of the trail. She plodded through the dark forest and came to the top of the mountain. The braves dutifully kept pace with her.

She reined her horse to a slight clearing in the trees and gazed down at the valley below. The braves stood on either side of her and gazed down into the valley, sharing the same grief filling their queen's eyes. All watched the lone fire flicker in the heart of their village far below them. Only one building burned, to their relief, but they knew which one-Queen Ester's castle.

Ester watched the flames silently, suddenly recalling all she had forgotten in her haste. The prayer idol which her husband crafted with his own hands to represent all he knew of the Great Spirit most definitely burned in the flames. She had kept it in a coveted place in the center of her castle in the center of her village. She thought it only fitting, for he remained the center of her universe even in death. Now her universe passed into nothingness.

So much lost of those whom had trod this ground for hundreds of years now went up in flames, she realized. All she had carefully preserved of that past now turned to ashes. All put to flame by the hands of a new invader, one the likes any Indian nation had never seen-the *white-eyes*. She thought of the bark tablets the great prophet Neolin had made with his own characters etched in them after watching the Moravian missionaries read from their *book*. Around the great fire at Tioga he had preached his word to many a great chief, nonetheless greater than the great Ottawa Chief Pontiac. Neolin, who for years stood at the southern door of the Iroquois Confederacy despising all the treacherous *white-eyes*. He whom had blown dust into the Penn's negotiator New Castle's eyes. New Castle, believing in the great medicine man's power rushed back to Philadelphia; there to expire a month latter, all the while muttering about Neolin's power. All of the wampum that told of this now rose to the heavens in flames. She only hoped the smoke on which they rose into the great sky carried the magic back to Neoilin and the countless other great men whom had made their homes at Tioga. Perhaps then they could help from the world beyond. For on this world, all they had been now fell to the wayside with the unrelenting tide of the *white-eyes*. She shuddered to think of it.

The braves looked up to the grave Queen, noticing

glittering tears reflecting the moonlight from her cheeks. They turned, both gazing at the flickering fires and the silhouettes of the avenging demons in their light. They both swore an oath of revenge in their native tongue.

The Queen looked down to them, suddenly feeling nauseated by the sickening call for revenge they represented. She fingered the scalps and suddenly jerked back her fingers as if they burned hot from the flames of hatred. Taking them did nothing but fuel the Wyoming Yankee's revenge which in turn fueled her revenge. She realized the futility of it all and thought it a vicious circle, never to end until the universe itself ended.

She shook her head and muttered Eghobund's name.

The braves' eyes glowed in recognition of the great chief, fueling the rage burning in their hearts.

"Jogo," she said to the angry braves while reining her horse back toward the trail. She did not turn again to gain one last look at the grief behind her. She stared straight ahead, focusing on the anguish of her people. It demanded her full attention now. She let the darkness of the night engulf the troubled memories and sights behind her and hoped it remained forever in the darkness beyond.

Chapter Forty

Roswell Franklin meadandered through the cabins on the northern edge of the village. The intense fire from the Queen's castle crept into the shadows of the trees well to his front. He sat, watching the trees for any telltale movement, clutching his rifle tightly in his hands. Every now and then he looked for Captain Franklin, supposedly sharing the guard duty with him, but gave up after the first hour.

Snores, groans, and occasional lip smacks filled the air behind him. He silently scorned the others for making such a racket while he tried to concentrate on his duty. Still, the thought of their exhausted sleep played at his own tired soul; but someone had to watch, he kept telling himself.

He fought to keep his head from bobbing and took a great gulp from his canteen. The harsh rye whiskey burned his senses awake with its force. Prisoners, he suddenly remembered, they called for prisoners. He scanned the whole perimeter of the village, carefully pacing around it, staring into the treeline illuminated by the great fire. He imagined if he wanted to gain the village and snatch a Rebel's hair how he would go about it. His eyes fixed onto a low ridge just to the west of the village. Scrub oaks dotted it. A few cattle milled about the plain just beyond it. One could follow the ridge right to the edge of the village, spurt forth and club a sentry before he knew what had hit him. Quite a feat, no doubt a warrior could gain much stature in accomplishing it.

He slowly crept to the edge of the ridge. Finding a nice clump of brush, he melted down into it, all the while watching the opposite side of the ridge while scanning the perimeter every now and then. No, he reasoned, if they are coming, this is the way. This is the trap, sit tight and still and you shall have some sport before long.

He removed his wide-brimmed slouch hat and sat it down next to him. He felt at the mud on his face. It felt a bit dry, but still clung to his cheeks. Easing down, he crouched with his hands on his rifle before him. He squinted his eyes, wishing to make the whites of them as small as possible. The Indians, the wily hunters at home in the forest, had awesome eyes. But he did too, he told himself, for his life depended upon it.

Fighting against his heavy eyelids he moved his knee over a sharp stone protruding from the ground in front of him. He placed his knee just atop it, applying just enough pressure for the pain to keep his eyes open. Sometimes pain worked as a partner in hunting, especially this foe.

He sat, listening to the crackle of the fire and a occasional beam falling from the cabin. The hoot of an owl sounded from a tree on the mountain not far away. He listened intently, relaxing once the owl took to the wing and swooped down onto something. He watched it rise into the moonlit sky again. Its huge wings pounded in the wind. A long snake slithered and rolled its body against the its talons. After watching it disappear in the trees he lowered his eyes and looked all around him, drawing his tomahawk ever so slowly from his belt. He carefully placed it within easy reach while still clenching his rifle in his other hand.

Out of the corner of his eye he noticed a faint movement up the ridge. He sat perfectly still, waiting out the spector. A twig moved, just slightly, but from the ground, not the wind. He stared in the direction of the twig, trying in vain to make out anything in the darkness. Another twig beside it moved. He drew a deep breath very silently. His white knuckles clutched his rifle. He watched the faint glimmer of light from the fire to his rear dance among the scrub brush. After what seemed a lifetime another twig moved; this time but a few yards away from him. He dared not move a muscle or blink an eye, for he knew someone watched him just as intently.

His old friend the owl swooped down from the tree, flapping it huge wings just above the brush along the ridge. He ignored it. His foe did not. A pair of white eyes turned toward the sky for a heartbeat, exposing the head, and after careful examination, the rest of the wiry body crouched in the brush below.

Now he cursed his own breath, not wishing for anything to betray his presence to his closing enemy. He pressed his knee ever so slightly against the rock. He must sharpen his senses! He must be alert! He mustn't flinch a muscle!

The white eyes stared in his direction for the longest moment before turning away, much to his relief. He remained rigid, wishing for the brave to move but a few feet more before he struck. He must know if any others followed. He must only strike when certain of victory.

The brave moved one hand along the ground and then the other. His black paint made him appear a mere shadow, except for the white paint around his eyes. He crawled painfully slow. He needed to gain the end of the ridge, then he could strike. Then at least one white eye would know his anger. The more he passed the spot which made the nape of his neck tingle, the better he felt. Somehow he sensed something there, even though his eyes alerted him of nothing. He moved one hand forward when suddenly stars flashed across his vision. He stumbled, feeling his hands lose all of their strength. His knife and tomahawk slipped from his grasp.

Enraged, he rose, flailing with his hands at the unseen demon clubbing his head. His fingernails caught some flesh. He dug them into it with all his might. A scream followed another thud. Yet another blow struck his head, making his neck bend backwards unnaturally. A metallic taste flooded his throat. All went dark.

"Damn it!" Roswell exclaimed, throwing down his clubbed rifle. He instinctively grabbed his bleeding arm and stared at the brave lying motionless in front of him. Looking down, he kicked all about the Indian's arms, seaching for the weapon which had torn his flesh away. Crouching down, he picked up the brave's knife and tomahawk, instantly noticing no blood shinning on them. Frustrated and fit to be tied, he picked up the brave's hands. Something curled and dangled under the brave's fingernails. Skin! "Damn it all," he said, wraping his bleeding arm with a rag. "Hate to see what he would have done with that tomahawk, the accursed rascal."

A movement to his rear flung his head around to face a new threat. Boss Strope stood holding his rifle up to his shoulder, aiming at the brave. His bloodshot eyes glared down at him. He took a few steps forward.

"Damn it," Roswell said, picking up his rifle. "You'd be best to announce yourself before coming up on a man like that, especially in these parts."

Boss glanced over at him, noticing the blood dripping down his arm. "Did the rascal get you?" he asked.

"Ain't nothing," Roswell said. "Well, we got us a prisoner, if'n he lives, that is."

"The next air he'll breathe is in the firey pits of hell!" Boss said. He leveled his rifle on the Indian's head and pulled the trigger. An empty click sounded in the still air. "Damn river's fouled all my powder!" Boss exclaimed, raising the weapon again and pulling back the hammer. It clicked again to no effect.

"Now, just hold on," Roswell said. "That brave's my prisoner."

"If'n you've a hankering for his hair it's yours!" Boss said. He flung his useless rifle aside and drew his long knife. Putting a knee to the back of the brave, he grabbed his head by the narrow strip of hair running down the middle of it. The hair quickly slipped through his fingers. "Damn Indian's head's full of grease!" he said, wiping his hands on his trousers before grabbing the hair again. A loud moan stopped him.

"He's still breathing," Roswell said. "Colonel wants a prisoner. You best back off, Boss."

"You mind your place Lieutenant Franklin, and I'll mind mine! Lydia's blood's most likely all over this buck's hands! My children's too! All of them! Damn these *Copperheads*!" Boss said. He placed the blade to the groaning Indian's neck. "You fine-haired rascal! Prepare to meet your maker!"

"Strope!" a voice sounded from behind the men. "Roswell's right! We need a prisoner! You best drop that blade!" A click sounded in the air.

"You'd kill a white man over a damn savage?" Boss asked. He did not look to the voice. His bulging and blood-shot eyes remained fixed on the brave. A quick hand to his shoulder stopped his shaking hand from pulling the blade across the brave's neck. Another hand reached down and gently took the knife from his hand. He looked up and gazed at the man before him in amazement.

John Franklin smiled at him. "It'll be alright, Boss," he said. "Been a trying time for us all, but we still got to follow orders. We ain't out of this yet, you know. Could be this here Indian can tell us a heap about what we're facing. Might even bring us word of your people."

The last words echoed through Boss' mind. "You're right," he said, backing away from the brave. He lifted both his hands to his face and stared at them. "This war makes murders of us all."

"Ain't murder in the line of duty," Franklin said. He pulled a length of rawhide from his pouch and bent down to bind the brave's hands.

"Good job," Covenhoven said, appearing with a group of others woken by the commotion. He patted John Franklin on the shoulder while watching Strope with his eyes. "Do you think he'll be alright?"

"Hard to tell," Franklin said. "Hard to tell if any of us will get out of this the same as we entered it. War is the heart of the demon, it is."

Covenhoven looked over to Roswell. The man stood erect, but clearly so exhausted a gust of wind could easily knock him over. "Here, I'm spelling you, Roswell, get some sleep. You're going to need it. And good job, by the way. The colonel will be proud."

"Pride, hell, he can have it! Should have let Boss have his way!" Roswell said, stumbling back toward the village. He stumbled to a nearby cabin. Finding a bear skin within it, he collapsed in exhaustion upon it. "Damn skin smells like hell!" he exclaimed for all to hear. "Just like a *Copperhead!* Whole damn place smells like hell!"

"This is hell," Covenhoven said, looking to the faint glow beginning to shine over the mountains to the east. "And come light, we're going to gather all the plunder we can and the rest is to be put to the flame like all hell!"

Chapter Forty One

Captain Carberry watched the dull glow of the sun tease the treetops to the east. He paced back and forth in front of his exhausted horse, glancing to the rear of the small Indian village his horsemen occupied. Nothing moved save the branches of the trees swaying in the cool morning breeze. The scouts must have stayed at Ester's Town, he reasoned. He did not blame them and beamed with pride at his saddle sore but staunch Light Horse. His backside burned as readily as theirs, but still no hint of complaint rose from any of them. He could only imagine the footsore scouts struggling with each step. All performed admirably. No one could ask more of them.

He felt at the pouch on his side and walked over to his men. Some rose groggily from the ground in front of their horses. Others lie silent and still, but all had tied the reins of their horses to their wrists so as to be instantly ready to rise and mount at a moment's notice. A few of the horses moved and lifted the reins, waking their masters.

Carberry pulled a rough map from his pouch and laid it on the ground. He took off his hat and sat it next to the map. Running his fingers through his hair with one hand he fingered the map in the pale light with the other. The men gathered around. "We are here," he said, pointing at a the map, "Shawnee Village, the map reads." He looked to the far end of the village. "Chemung is but a few miles distant."

"I don't believe any of the foot followed, sir," one of the men said.

"Yes, it would seem, but saddle sore is certainly different from footsore," Carberry said. He lifted his canteen and took a drink. It sloshed almost empty. Taking a piece of ash cake from his haversack he eagerly bit down on the crumbling biscuit. Pieces fell all over the map. “That is how the Indians are,” he said. “They are sprinkled all around and can strike from any position at any time. Dogged pursuit, cold camps, and sure-shots are the only way to counter them.”

“Well so far so good,” a man commented.

“It shall be full light soon,” Carberry said, rising and folding the map. “I hope all of you have had some rest and the guard was spelled, for we ride again this day, probably harder than we have so far.”

“The men can take it, sir, but the horses are about played out,” his sergeant reported. “Fodder is so scarce in this land.” He motioned toward one of the wild grape vines clinging to a tree nearby. A horse nibbled at it. “If it weren’t for the wild grapes and the scrub growing under the trees, they would have nothing. That damn Indian grass at Shesequin’s too rough to make anything but a broom. The rest is wild rye, none good for a horse. We need to find a good pasture of English grass.”

“Yes, I am aware of the situation, Sergeant,” Carberry said. “I think the flats held some promise, from the livestock milling about when we swept through Ester’s Town.”

“We just need to stop and let them feed.”

“In that, Sergeant, lies the problem.”

Carberry plunged the map into his pouch and nodded toward the trail. “Right now we need to take a long look at Chemung before we turn back to Sheshequin,” he said. He grabbed his mount’s reins and pulled himself up and onto its saddle. “I shall take two with me, keep a strong guard posted and let the horse feed as much as possible until I return, which should be shortly.”

"Yes sir," the sergeant said, doffing his hat. "What if the scouts show up?"

"I doubt they will. They are all exhausted, each one. I durst say the good colonel and all are still at Shesequin as we speak. Our mounts' four feet have far outdistanced them. Coupled with our exuberance for the fight, it has carried us far to their front. By the grace of God we should not retreat without gaining a glimpse of our enemy about Chemung."

"No sir, we should not."

"Nor shall we."

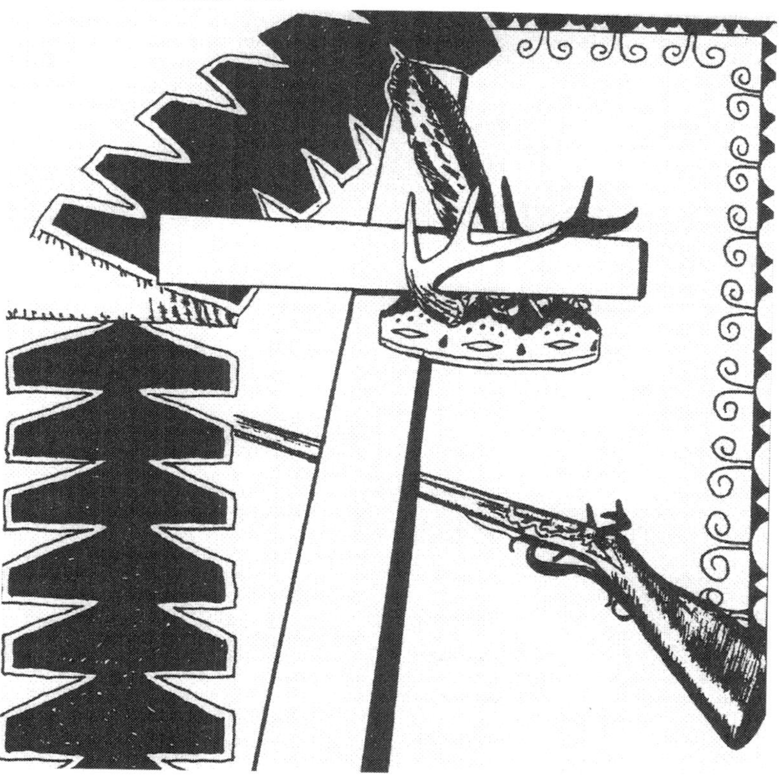

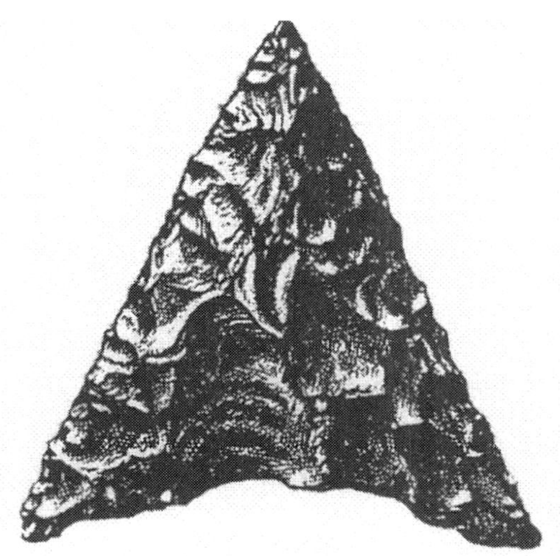

Chapter Forty Two

Captain Carberry stood aghast by the sight before him. He looked back to the two horsemen accompaning him and waved them to slow down, putting his finger to his lips. He dismounted, passing his horse's reins to the nearest horseman behind him. Gingerly crawling forward, he crouched down behind a small bush on the crest of the steep mountain before him and scanned the plain below him.

One of the horsemen carefully dismounted and past the reins of his horse to his fellow, ignoring his indignant look of protest. Leaving his disgruntled comrade to tend the horses, he crept silently to the side of his leader. His eyes grew wider than the captain's. Dozens of cabins spread across the plain below in the early morning light. Smoke curled into the sky from many fires. A huge corral to the north of the village overflowed with horses. Early morning sunlight glimmered and danced across the face of the Chemung River to the left of the village. Great overshadowing and ancient trees graced its banks. Numerous round, lush, and green fields of corn, beans, and squash dotted the bank behind the trees. Pastures of fine English grass crept from the river to the edge of the village. All seemed vibrant and alive, especially the many men darting to and fro among the cabins, corrals, and fires. Green coats and hunting shirts intermixed with dull brown buckskin, painted bodies, and the bright colors of the clothing of Indian women.

"They seem excited," the soldier said.

"Yes and I am afraid it is because of our little force," Carberry said. He took a long moment and carefully counted green coats and hunting shirts. The soldier followed his lead.

"Must be at least two hundred and seventy Tories alone down there," the soldier said.

"Closer to three hundred," Carberry said. He nervously looked behind him and all around the densily wooded mountain. "We should take care, no telling what shall pop out of the forest, this close to their nests and all. Be sure to keep the horses quiet."

"What's that," the soldier asked, dropping the spy-glass and squinting his eyes. He pointed to a squad of trotting horses thundering into the village from the north trail. Indian children and dogs scattered for safety from them. Many angry women's fists and scorns followed the haughty group. They reined their horses in front of a tall man in a fine green coat and plopped down from the saddle before their horses completely stopped.

"In a hurry, whoever they are," the horse soldier said.

"Here," Carberry said, "give me that glass." He bent down under a nearby bush on a large flat stone beneath it and steadied the spyglass, carefully focusing on the squad of rangers. He watched the arms of the newly arrived horsemen, especially those of a small wiry man, wave contemptuously at the man who greeted them. His manner and exaggerated movements betrayed a man full of himself and his own importance. Carberry watched him a few seconds more and slowly lowered the glass. "Walter Butler it is," he said, "Indian Butler's son and true traitor to our cause if ever there was one."

"Are you sure, sir?" the soldier asked, cupping his hands over his eyes to shield them from the sun.

"Look at the way he swaggers and banters about like a fine Banny rooster. How such a small frame can hold such a big head is beyond me. He is full of himself, cocksure and a braggart. I am only happy it is he down there and not his father, for then they would probably already be on the march for us."

"Do you think he has a clue to our true number?"

"No, or he would certainly march. Even the most vile coward would march if they knew the true state of things."

"Lucky for us he does not, sir."

"Luck is something one makes for himself."

Captain Carberry stood and took a few steps to other side of the bush. He stared at each section of the plain for a few seconds, commiting all he could of the lay of the land to his memory. "With a few hundred more men," he said, "as we were supposed to have, and couple of small cannon, we could lay waste to this whole village and beyond for twenty miles! Oh, for once to be properly provisioned and armed!"

A commotion in the center of the village caught their attention again. A huge chief, barrel-chested and so tall he towered over the whites and Indians alike sauntered about, thudding his chest and screaming to the heavens above him. A growing number of warriors milled about him, joining in his war whoops.

"That is trouble," the soldier said. "He looks as one who means business, and may not fear what numbers he faces. Must be Seneca. He'll incite them, no doubt. We're on his land, not the whites."

A sense of dread flowed through Carberry. He slowly looked to the sky, noticing the sun already rising high above the trees. "We've worn out our welcome," he said. "We best make haste to report to the colonel."

The soldier nodded and both men backed away from the bush, watching the ground below for any telltale sign that they had been spotted. In no time they backed to the man with the horses and flung themselves into the saddle. The soldier minding the horses quickly mounted his own steed. He did not ask for an explanation, for the fear in each of the men's eyes gave all the answer he wished to know. He adjusted his saber, pistols and carbine to have them ready for action at a moment's notice before turning his mount and following the others.

At first they painstakingly walked their horses down the mountain, careful not to disturb the slightest bush or twig lest its snap betray their position. Their wide-eyes took in every movement. Their ears perked at every noise. The welcome sight of the open trail just ahead broke all their apprehension. They thundered down to it and tore it up under mad hooves in their haste to gain distance.

If caught here and now an unimaginable death awaited them. That certainty dug the spur into the horses' flanks and brought the whip all the more mercilessly down on the their backs. Nothing but a full gallop would do until the haunting dread at their heels faded with distance.

They had seen the enemy, his numbers great and his fading resolve glowing back to life in front of their eyes. A empty feeling crept through them with this knowledge, only to be lessened by distance; the further the better.

Chapter Forty Three

Colonel Hartley put down the biscuit he held in his hand and looked toward the sound of thudding hooves approaching from the north. He put his hat on his head and rose from the fire he shared with Captain Bush. Checking his brace of pistols, he walked toward the guards posted at the end of the village. Bush followed.

Soldiers groggily walked around them, some coming to life at the sight of plunder brought forth by others from the cabins. It invigorated many more from their exhausted sleep all around the village.

All eyes, busy gathering plunder or not, searched the horizon, none more anxious than the group of huddled prisoners. They clung to one another and looked to the preacher for assurance. He only offered a quick prayer from his ner-vous lips.

"Be still," Hartley said to them all. "All is well. It is propably just our Light Horse. Eh, Captain Bush?"

"Most likely, sir," Bush answered, nonetheless quickening his march to the sound of the hooves, just as the good colonel. He strode a few paces and whispered to the colonel, "should we not assemble the troops?"

"No, no, my man," Hartley said. "They are already half out of their skulls with worry, especially those poor souls we liberated last night. Do not worry, if there is any mischief I am sure we shall all meet it with..." He paused and stopped, noticing the plume of feathers atop Carberry's leather cap. "See, it is Carberry, with two men."

"My God," Bush said, "where are the others?"

"We shall find out directly by the way they are riding hard for us." The colonel took a few steps and stood a rod behind the sentries, who stood smartly with their weapons held at the ready. He folded his arms and awaited the horsemen.

The sentries took a few steps forward and called out "Victory!" to the horsemen.

Carberry rode steadfastly toward the colonel, ignoring the sentries. He took off his hat and slapped his horse's flanks with it. Their trot increased rather than slowing to the challenge of the sentries.

The sentries stood fast and raised their rifles across their bodies, blocking the advance of the horsemen.

"Victory!" one of them called.

Carberry ignored them, slapping his horse again with his hat.

The sentries quickly maneuvered to block the horses. They stood rigid and gripped their rifles lengthwise to block them.

Carberry reined his horse to a stop at the absolute last moment, barely missing plunging into the guards. Dirt flew from their hooves into the faces of the stubborn sentries.

They didn't flinch a muscle.

"What?" Carberry screamed, "are you mad or drunk!?!"

"Victory!"

Carberry shook his head and muttered, "or death," before spurring his horse forward.

The sentries pushed against the horses, forcing them back.

"Look here you square-headed Yankee!" Carberry said. "Make way!"

The sentry with a red cloth pinned to his shoulder

stared defiantly at the captain. "Victory!" he said.

Carberry gritted his teeth and muttered "or death," again.

"What was that, Private Terry?" one of the sentries asked.

"Sounded like a foul wind blowing from some Pennamite's butt!" the prvate answered. "We best get down wind."

"You obinstinate Yankee rascals!" Carberry said. "Make way at once!"

The sentries did not move.

"Colonel!" Carberry finally yelled past the sentries, "I have pertinent information! Must we play this foolish game?"

Hartley did not say a word, silently considering the angst among these men. For all intensive purposes only a truce ordered by Congress after their last battle at Rampart Rocks in December Seventeen Seventy Five kept them from each other's throats. In that battle-of men in these very ranks whom had faced each other on opposite sides-two hundred and fifty Yankees beat back an invasion force of seven hundred and fifty Pennamites; some of the Yankees only armed with pitch forks and scythe blades fastened to poles. The bitter Yankee-Pennamite War still pulsed through each of their viens, caused by depredations on both sides. Only their mutual enemy united them, and a cause, a cause that rose above their differences and somehow threaded them all together. He decided to play on their faith in their common cause, one which united even the bitterest foes at the moment.

"They are only about their duty, Captain," he said. "Give Sergeant Baldwin the countersign and all shall be fine, and be pretty damn quick about it! The enemy is out there, not here, both of you mind that! Remember America, my good men, she's greater than any of our petty differences!"

"Or death!" Carberry said, bending his whole torso forward and spattering the sentries with his spittle.

"Very good, sir," Baldwin said, smartly stepping aside.

"Damn square-headed Yankee vagabonds," Carberry muttered under his breath. Disgusted, he whipped his horse through them.

"Did you hear something, Terry?" Baldwin asked.

"Just that foul Pennamite wind again," Jonathan Terry said. "Perhaps he should blow some smoke, relieves what's cooped up even the tightest buttocks."

Hartley fought a smile from forming on his face and shook his head toward the sentries.

They took the hint and turned back to their duty.

"Damn those fools," Carberry said, plopping down from the saddle in front of the colonel and captain. "There is a time and a place for formalities and damn it it's not here in this accursed wilderness! Who the hell did they think I was? Indian Butler?"

"Now, now, Captain, they're doing their best to maintain proper military bearing, we are still an army, no matter in what forsaken place," Hartley said.

Captain Spalding and Colonel Denison suddenly appeared from the corner of a cabin, forcing Carberry to curb his anger in the face of the two powerful Yankees. He too realized they needed to fight one enemy at a time.

"Chemung is swarming with Tories as we speak!" Carberry said. "Seen them with my own eyes! We gained Shawanee Village last night, three miles up the Chemung River from Ester's Town. I left my men there and advanced with two men to a mountain overlooking Chemung. They are forming, at least two hundred Indians gather with the Tories under Young Butler," Carberry reported.

"What of the Wyoming Rangers?" Denison asked.

"They are about Ester's Town, too exhausted to march any further last night," Carberry said. He shook his head, anticipating their next question. "The town's abandoned. Ester's on the hoof. Who knows where? The scouts are gathering what plunder they can in canoes, nearly two dozen, I believe. I left the balance of my men to drive the cattle and horses we've captured and to form a rear guard." He looked all the men in the eye. "They have a prisoner, also, an Indian, looked a little rough but he was still breathing last time I saw him." He caught his breath and looked deathly into Colonel Hartley's eyes. "Sir, Chemung, sir, better than three hundred Tory Rangers alone there with at least two hundred savage braves!"

"My God," Hartley said, rubbing his chin. "Three hundred? They must think our numbers great or they would have swooped down on us by now, for sure. This we shall use to our advantage!" He picked up his canteen and shook it. A little whiskey sloshed in it. "What say you, gentlemen, our rations are almost depleted and a great fatigue plagues our ranks. We are no match for five hundred fresh men at arms. We must get as much rest as possible this day and then gather as much provisions and plunder we can carry."

All of the officers nodded.

Hartley nodded back at them. His eyes widened and stared at something behind the officers, causing them to turn about immediately.

Dozens of columns of smoke curled into the air from the north. Smaller ones joined the billowing columns just over the trees, rolling and black.

"The scouts and horse will return shortly," Hartley said. "They've put the torch to Ester's Town. I hope the smoke will only convince our enemies we intend to advance and put Chemung to the torch also, for all depends upon it, gentlemen. All depends upon it. Come, let's get at it! Send parties out to all the cabins about the river, for all are nests of Tories and savages. Collect all we can carry and burn the rest!"

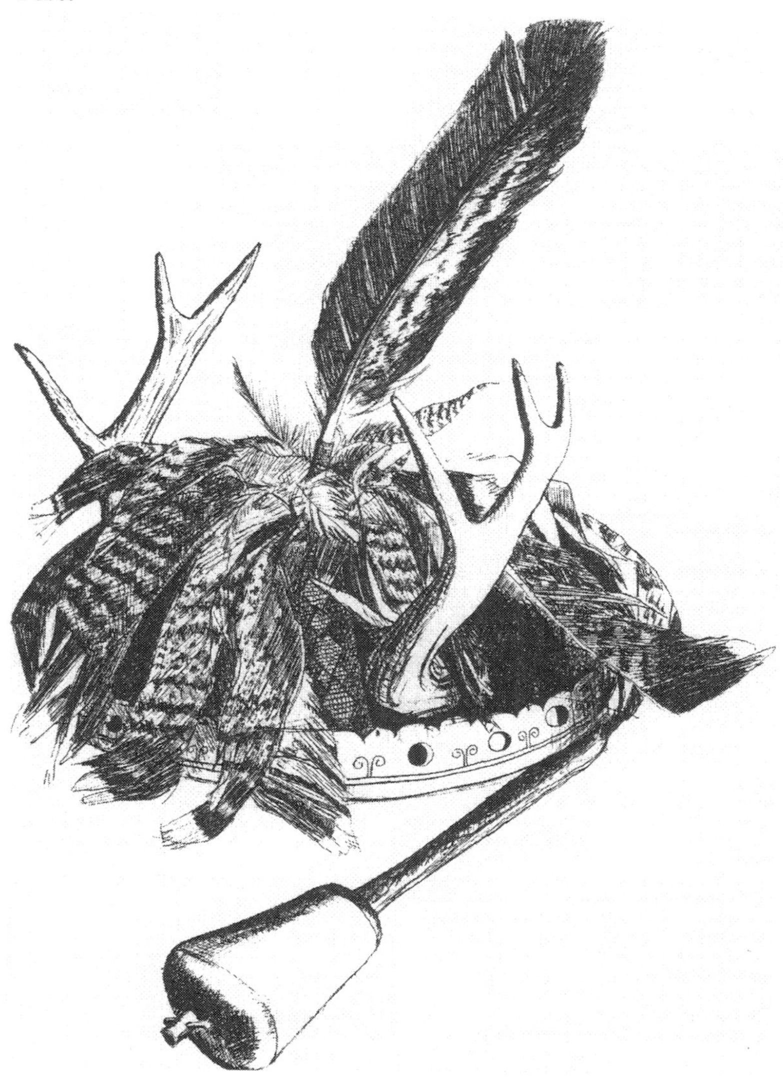

Chapter Forty Four

Colonel Hartley eyed the crestfallen brave forced to his knees before him. He clasped his hands tightly behind his back and paced back and forth, never breaking his gaze on the brave. All around remained silent and watched in anticipation of the colonel's, or the brave's, words.

The one eye of the brave not swollen shut followed the haughty eye of the white chief. His body ached from the blows and rough treatment from the hands of the scouts, but he did not utter a word or groan, refusing to give them the satisfation. Back in his mind; somewhere beyond the pain, he thought of the terrified look in his wife's and children's eyes. It is why he risked venturing so close to the approaching *white-eyes* while the others fled with the Queen to the glen. He needed to strike at the devils and return with a scalp, thus enticing the others to turn and fight. But the devils caught him. His heart sank pondering his fate. He only wished for the *white-eyes*' chief to draw his pistol and relieve him of his disgrace. But the *white-eyes* only watched him. What sort of torture is this?

Hartley finally stopped pacing and walked to the man. Noticing the brave's red and swollen eye and the great gash crusted over with dried blood on his head he stepped back and raised his lower lip. He looked over to the liberated prisoners and waved his hand at the man examining them. "Captain Smith," he called, "see to this man."

"Man?" Doctor Smith said under his breath. "The good colonel uses the word rather loosely."

The recently liberated man he examined nodded his head, giving the doctor leave to follow the colonel's order.

"Well, orders are orders," Smith agreed, slowly rising from his kneeling position and walking over to the brave. His eyes looked down his nose at the black-painted miscreant. Letting out a grunt of disgust he gruffly pushed the man's head to one side to get a better look at the gash and his eye. He grunted again and put both his hands to the brave's jaw, forcing his mouth open. "Still has his tongue, Colonel," he reported. "He can talk." With that he rose, tipped his hat, and marched back to the civlivians.

"Yes, indeed," Hartley said. He shook his head and stood full in front of the brave. "Do you think he understands English?" he asked both Captain Franklin and Covenhoven.

"He's a Delaware, probably of Ester's band, a Muncy, Wolf clan," Covenhoven answered. "Most of them know enough English, what with having to trade with civilized people and all." He looked to all the eyes of circling them and nodded.

A few nods answered his, but most stared grimly at the face of the foe who caused so much havoc and devastation in their lives.

"How many are about Chemung?" Hartley bluntly asked.

Defiance glared back at him through the brave's lone eye.

"It is best you answer, my fine fellow," Hartley said.

Silence again answered him.

"I'll get the painted pig to squeal!" Boss Strope said, advancing with his long knife drawn.

Captain Franklin and Colonel Denison immediately stepped in his path, blocking his way and shaking their heads.

"What?" Boss said. "With all due respect, Colonel Denison, my fine sir, you have spoken nary a word on this whole expedition! Are you, sir, to relinquish your rank so willingly? You know what they did! You know what they have cost me and my own!" He looked to the many eyes watching him. "You know what they've done to all our familes through their treachery!"

"Back off, private," Denison said. "Colonel Hartley is in charge of this expedition. You will follow his orders and treat him with the respect due an officer of the line or, damn it, you shall face the lash when we return to Wyoming!"

Boss angrily looked down at his knife and threw it to the ground in front of the brave. It stuck straight in the earth a hair's breadth from the brave's knee.

The brave did not flinch.

"Pick up that knife!" Denison said, unmoved by the blatant act of defiance.

Boss stared him straight in the eye and turned away in a huff. Had the whole world gone insane? Had they forgotten the field at Wyoming!?! Let all Iroquois be damned!

Franklin bent down and picked up the knife.

"My apologies, Colonel," Denison said, giving a slight bow before stepping back into the circle of men around the brave.

Hartley gave a slight nod and stepped toward the brave again. "Tell us what you know," he said. "It is all I ask."

"Go hell!" the brave gasped, spitting onto the ground at Hartley's feet.

Many a soldier took a step forward, only to be waved back by the colonel.

"We," he said, "are not the barbarians and will not act as such!" He bent down to one knee and stared into the brave's eye. "Come now, speak, and you may see your wife and children again this very day. I offer nothing but peace, and extend the white feather to your chiefs. A great many soldiers follow, if you speak now, you may curtail much bloodshed."

"Kill the heathen rat!" sounded from the ring of

soldiers.

"Silence!" Denison ordered.

A series of muffled taunts filled the air.

"You Bostonians ones to die this day!" the brave screamed. "Five hundreds Young Butler's men await you at Chemung! As many braves as leaves in trees! You go to Chemung! Not come back with hair!"

"Well," Hartley said, "this is what I meant."

"You *white-eyes* fools!" the brave continued. "One you come, Van Alstyne, and warn of your approach! Many brave come to lift your hair and knock you on the head! You die soon!" The brave spat once again and stared with all the hatred he could muster in his lone eye back at the Rebel colonel. "You Bostonian, *Yank-ee* chief, die."

"I," Hartley said, "am not of Boston, but of York." He put a hand to his knee and rose, waving for Captain Bush to meet him. "A quill and parchment, please," he asked. "I am sure Captain Butler, or indeed Brant himself, can read and relay our message to the Six Nations." He cast a wary eye back at the brave.

Strong hands on each of the brave's shoulders pushed the infuriated man back down, but he still struggled vainly against his bonds.

"Just sit still, my fine fellow, and we shall be with you presently," Hartley said. Lifting up his coattails, he sat on an upturned stump of a log one of the soldiers placed before a plank supported by two corn mortors. Bush placed the parchment upon the plank and handed the colonel a quill while holding an ink well in his other hand.

Hartley wet the end of the quill with his lips and dipped the quill in the ink well. He hurriedly scribbled on the parchment for the longest moment. All watched anxiously from the circle. With a self-satisfied grunt he finally rose, giving the parchment one more look before passing it to Bush. "Make a copy of this for the Council of war," he said to Bush. "And be quick about it, if you will, fine sir."

Bush took the stump vacated by the colonel and hastily went to work.

"The Six Nations," Hartley said, walking back to the circle pondering all he had written, "have killed many women and children, and ruthlessly tortured many prisoners! We know of this treachery! All know of it! It cannot be denied! The chiefs at Chemung must listen and come to parley about these matters which must be resolved before peace can once again be shared among our peoples! If they delay in sueing for peace I tell you all their country shall be put to the torch and feel the cutting sword of justice!" He stopped and looked directly down at the brave. "They must agree to parley before the sun sets over yonder hills or I swear by oath all shall be put to the fire and sword. Many come after me. They shall be here soon. Chemung shall be put to the torch as Ester's Palace was! No peace shall be made with the Tories unless they renounce their misguided alligence to the Crown! King George is the truest tyrant of all the world! If the Tories persist in their misguided allegiance, their farms shall also be put to the torch! The fate of the Six Nations and the Tories rests on these words." He took the sealed parchment Bush eagerly handed him with a self-assured nod. He looked to both of the men holding the brave and waved them away from him. They slowly released their hold on the brave. A dozen rifles leveled on the brave. Grim eyes stared down the barrels.

The brave looked down to the ground in shame and slowly rose.

"Are you to behave, my friend?" Hartley asked him.

He nodded without looking up from the ground.

Hartley motioned for one of the men to cut the thongs binding the Indian's wrists. Both men stood perfectly still as if not understanding the gesture.

Looking sour, Franklin stepped up, cutting the thongs.

The brave rolled his fingers and shook his wrists. He lifted his hand and wiped the blood from his swollen eye before stumbling toward Hartley.

A dozen rifle locks clicked in response.

The brave stopped and held out his hand.

Hartley handed him the parchment. "Go," he said, "take this to the Chief of Chemung Village. Tell him of all you see. I tell you more come with the thunder trees and are as many as the tall grass about this place." He turned and spread his hand toward the great sea of Indian grass growing on the plain north of the village and along the riverbank. "We are as strong as the rough grass too, as it stand straight against any wind that blows against it, so shall we! Go! Now!"

The brave still did not look at the man. Instead, he lowered his head even further and slowly stumbled toward the trail leading through the waving Indian grass. His steps gradually increased through the village, growing into a trot. All eyes watched his back disappear over the crest of the trail through the grass.

"Well," Denison said, walking over to Hartley. Both stood silently watching the crowd disperse. "Do you think your ruse worked?" Denison finally asked.

"I don't know," Hartley said, barely loud enough for Denison to hear. "I have only seen the Six Nations through one brave's eye, for the other was swollen closed with blows of anger. You have delt with these people before, what do you think?"

"I think, sir," Denison said, "you have done a fine job

of it so far." He looked to the lingering columns of smoke still rising in the air to the north. "Ester will not be happy, and I must admit seeing her castle in flames does a heart good, especially one which has suffered so from her betrayal. I think they may cower this day, but the eyes of their scouts shall ascertain our true numbers by the morrow."

"Aye," Hartley said, "I think the same." He looked around at the tired soldiers assembling plunder around him. "We shall fill all we can in the twenty eight canoes we have captured and fill all the pack-horses' backs. The rest shall be put to the torch. We shall gain as much rest as possible this day, and maintain a strong guard, before returning to Wyoming by way of the Susquehanna. It is the best way to return with the cattle, horses, plunder, and civilians. It shall be at the long trot, every step, after this day." He paused and looked to the north. "No word of Colonel Morgan's riflemen or Colonel Butler with the Fourth Pennsylvania. I had hoped to join with them here and then hasten the march as to meet the enemy about Chemung, but alas, they have not deemed it fit to rendezvous with us. But, nonetheless, we shall stick to our new plan of march."

"It is a reasonable plan, sir," Denison said. "I concur."

"I am glad," Hartley said, gazing to the tall mountains surrounding them. "But you are right, many eyes shall soon gaze upon us from the mountains. Our only hope is our little ruse, but if it comes to it I would put up any of my men to thrice their number."

Denison noticeably jerked at the words. He heard them before-at the Battle of Wyoming-he prayed for a different outcome this time. "I pray it shall not come to that," he said, "but if it shall, these men shall give them all the hell due to them from their rape of Wyoming. That is for sure."

"Amen to that," Hartley said. "Amen to that."

Chapter Forty Five

Flames from dozens of blazing cabins cast a dull yellow glaze upon the smooth face of the Susquehanna. A small fleet of canoes paddled silently along the river, breaking its glassy face with ripples and slight splashes. Grim faced men in tri-cornered hats, round hats, and wide-brimmed slouch hats paddled the canoes, all looking downstream and beyond the twisting mountains.

Mounted men whistled and herded livestock down the trail along the shoreline of the river. Heavily armed men on horses galloped all along a meandering column of men and civilians. Beams crackled and fell in their wake. None turned, save the horsemen bringing up the rear, to revel in the devastation in their wake. Each of their eyes and hearts now focused on departing this Indian country for safer havens downriver; namely the fort at Wyoming.

Captain Bush's musicians played no lively airs, for their backs lay burdened with packs of plunder. The preacher at the head of the civilians exclaimed hallelujah with almost every step down the trail, most likely because his back bore no bundle. His burden lay in delivering his flock safely down the river, he explained. He needed all his strength of limb and spirit to accomplish the arduous task. The bundles on the backs of his flock seemed not to discourage the veracity of his praises for the Lord. The Lord's ways are indeed mysterious, he explained to the questioning eyes of the soldiers.

Colonel Hartley spurred his horse to the head of the column to escape the rants of the preacher. He silently wondered if the man did not play an act for the eyes of the Indians he knew watched from the mountains above them.

The Indians feared a touched man and allowed him to do as he pleased, as long as he stayed away from them. The Lord does work in mysterious ways, he thought, trying to block the thought of the man out of his mind and focus on the trek ahead. Wyoming lay a full eighty miles downstream. If this accursed stretch of wilderness proved any bit as difficult as the Sheshequin Path he wondered how in God's name any of them could manage it. But try they must, for they had no other choice. Their fate lie in God's hands.

He reined his horse to the side of the trail before it rose over the steep Narrow Way and waited for the pack-horse train. He glared down at the still mumbling preacher passing him, wishing he practiced the virture of silence being golden, especially now. He watched young Lord Butler pass and nodded his head at him.

Lord nodded back and gestured to the lone sack of flour on the pack-horse behind him. To Hartley's horror he noticed only a few small kegs of whiskey on the pack-horse immediately following it. Plunder of all sorts sat bundled on the horsebacks of the rest of the train. He only wished the Indians' dogs had not been so thorough at devouring the Indians' stashes of food before skedaddling from their villages. The dogs had served their masters well. Plunder slowed their enemy's retreat. Food hastened it.

"Is that all that's left, son?" he asked Lord, riding up to him from behind.

"I'm afraid so, Colonel," Lord answered. He lifted his hand and waved toward the herd of cattle. "But we've got plenty on the hoof, if need be."

"Yes, son, I guess we have," Hartley said. "But what of drink?"

"Well, we'll just have to put our trust in the Lord as the good preacher says and hope he protects the water from putrid fever."

"Quite," Hartley said, spurring his mount forward. He rode to the foot of the trail and pondered the steep climb up the Narrow Way. Already a few men stumbled and fell down the edge of the trail. He looked to the advancing column of civilians and cattle with dread.

"Captain Spalding!" he called to the nearest officer in line.

Spalding stepped from his place by the side of his men and marched up to the colonel. "There's a spot just a ways back I think we can ford with no problem," he said, anticipating his commander's words.

"Very well," Hartley said with a smile. "See to it! Turn them around, I fear an ambuscade awaits us up this steep path, or worse."

"Yes sir," Spalding said, turning away to bark orders. He suddenly stopped. "But there's Breakneck Hill on the east side a few miles down, just as steep, it is."

"But the way is much more better after that, Franklin has told me," Hartley said. He lifted his eyes to the sun rising over the river. "And besides, our tawny friends shall not expect us that way. It'll throw them off a little, perhaps enough for us to get the hell out of here with our hair."

"Sound reasoning, sir," Spalding said, turning to covey the new orders of march.

"Yes," Hartley said under his breath, "I hope it is only sound enough to work, for I fear we may need all of God's graces to get out of this scrape. I do most certainly indeed!"

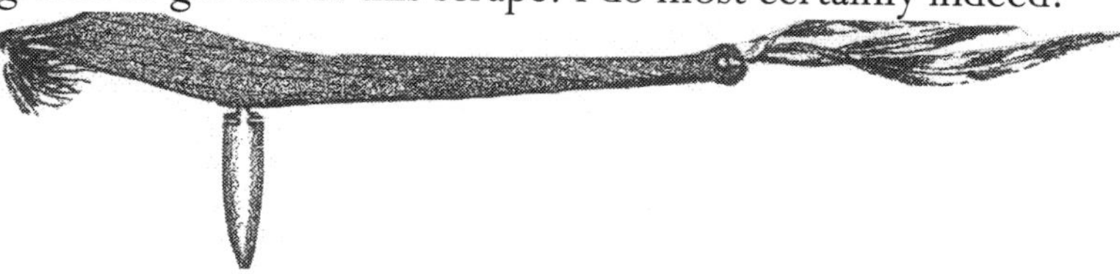

Chapter Forty Six

Painted men darted from the forest, rifles and spears held ready for action. They dodged in between the burning cabins, searching madly all around the ruined village for any lingering *white-eyes*. But to their disappointment none showed themselves. With sharp hoots they called back to the treeline along the edge of the mountain to the west of the village.

Indians emerged all along the treeline, at first a mere trickle, but soon a flood of miserable and mourning souls. Women wailed upon sight of their burning cabins. Wide-eyed children stumbled about in a daze. All they had known in their entire lives now rose with the thick colunms of black smoke billowing in the air. Many cried. Many stood in shock.

One, a middle aged woman, bedecked in bright flashy garments and silver trinkets, stumbled crestfallen to the center of the village. After a while she stopped, staring blankly down at the pile of ashes lying before her. She collapsed to her knees and let out a long, slow, mournful wail. Great tears flooded her eyes and flowed down her pale cheeks. She pulled at her long black hair in her grief, flicking her fingers to let strands of it drift in the wind. In no time more women joined her, making a semicircle around the ashes of the Queen's castle. The same soul wrenching wail crept from all their aching souls.

Warriors stood for a time and watched, embarrassed and ashamed no *white-eyes* paid for this treachery with their blood. Several of them flung their heads back and let out their own mournful cry. A growing rhythmic thud, slow at first, but increasing with the wails, echoed through the air. At first few eyes turned to see what caused the thud, but with its increasing volume more eyes turned to it, especially the warriors' eyes.

Chief Wamp stood tall beside a slightly charred post. His empty eyes stared dead ahead, seemingly at nothing. His hand rhythmically thudded the post with a war club. More and more warriors crowded around the aged chief. Finally satisfied he drew enough of them, he ceased pounding the post. Slowly, he let the war club fall to his side. His other hand slowly emerged from under the blanket wrapped around his torso. He stretched his arms wide in the air, pushing the blanket from his back. Bright war paint of white, vermillion, and black, showed in swirls all over his body.

He lifted his other hand into the air with the war club and spoke in his native tongue. "Brothers! My warriors! Be brave! Be strong! All is not lost!" He turned slowly about for all to see his painted body. "I wear the colors of all the wars I have seen! Many battles! Many scalps! The day is not lost!" He pointed the ball of the war club to the sun still low on the horizon. "I say let the woman stay here and mourn! Let the men follow me to meet the white demons before they retreat to Wyoming! Many defiles await them along the trail! We have seen their numbers from the trees! They are no more than ours! The *white-eyes* of the King say wait! Wait for what? Their escape? I say if Young Butler is too afraid to walk when his numbers are so much greater than the devils' then let him stay behind with the women! For that is where he belongs! But all true warriors shall follow me now down the river. The *white-eyes*' way is long! We know many ways to get ahead of him! He is hindered as always, by his greed! Let us all take up the hatchet and knock him on the head! He is tired! We are strong! He shall pay for his deeds! Come! Follow me!"

Another chief, Panther, rose in front of Wamp and let out a horrific yell. He bared his teeth and hissed. His head turned wildly to and fro. His bulging eyes glared into each warrior's soul he encountered. His feet began to stomp the ground in a mad rhythm reminiscent of Wamp's thumping of the post. He danced back to the post and gave it one loud and sharp whack with his own war club, splintering it into pieces. "This is how we shall strike the *white-eyes*!" he screamed, collapsing to his knees. He bowed his head to his chest and let out a slow wail. His head rose slowly back. His wail increased in tone. He jumped at the end of the wail, shaking his body in a spasmodic frenzy of grief. "They have struck our hearts! They have struck our women's hearts! They have struck our children's hearts! Let us strike their dark hearts!"

A medicine man appeared from nowhere and danced around the two chiefs, pulling a reluctant pure-white dog behind him. He jumped, yelled, and lifted a flaming firebrand from one of the burning cabins into the air. Two younger warriors hastily threw some wood into a clump before him. He flung the firebrand onto the wood and hissed while the flames grew. With a slow turning hand he waved at the two young warriors. They brought forth three long poles and placed them over the fire, interlocking them at the top.

The medicine man bent down to the dog and cradled the wimpering beast in his arms. He pulled a thick leather thong from his pouch with one hand and looped it around the dog's rear feet. He let it down, tugging and pulling at the thong around the dog's feet while it tried to crawl away with its fore paws. In one great sweeping arc he lifted the dog by its feet and tied it to the tripod over the fire. The dog whined, jerking madly against the thong to no avail.

Wamp slowly drew a long knife from his belt and walked up to the struggling dog. His aged but strong fingers reached to the dog's muzzle and clamped it shut while his other hand guided the knife across its neck. Blood flowed copiously down from the flailing dog's neck, sizzling on the fire below it in great spurts with each new spasm of the dog.

The medicine man stood before Wamp and the dying dog and lifted one hand high in the air, with the other he flung gun powder and tobacco onto the sizzling flames. With a high pitched wail he declared the war sacrifice a success. The great spirit would be pleased and after each warrior partook of a piece of the flesh he would come and make a tobacco pouch of the dog's skin. This the medicine man declared most earnestly.

Panther screamed at the top of his lungs in pure delight. Many warriors joined him.

Wamp stood holding the bloody knife. He gazed at all the enraged eyes beaming back at him and stopped to crack a slight smile when his eyes met another's in particular.

Wamp's wife smiled back at him. Her face still glowed in his memory of the first time he saw her. He closed his eyes and breathed in the memory, wishing to forever etch it in his mind's eye and silently hoping to recall it if he should find himself breathing his last on the battlefield. For he fought for her, their children, and their grandchildren. He fought against the conquerer. He fought against the land-crazed and greedy *white-eyes*. For all they touched turned to ashes.

The sight of the ashes clouded his vision. He forced his eyes open to his wife's beaming smile. Taking his knife from his belt he cut the first piece of flesh from the dog. He chewed it slowly and swallowed hard against it. This I do for you, he tried to convey with his eyes to his wife. For you I fight the demons. For you I would die.

Wamp's wife recognized the deep stare and often wondered what burned in her husband's soul when his eyes glared so. It remained a mystery to her, but she felt fine with it, for some feelings escaped words. She did as she always did at the look, she smiled.

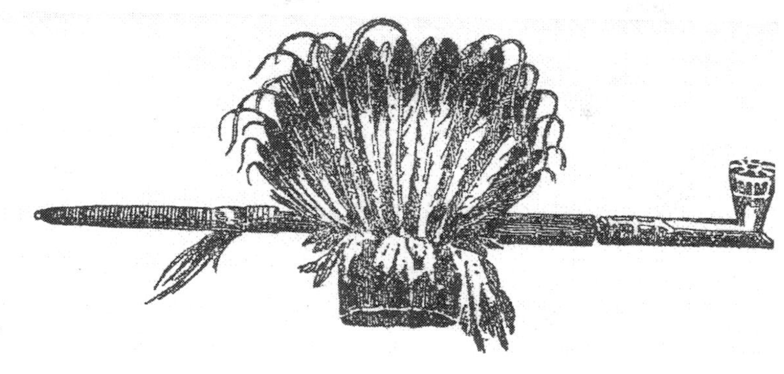

Chapter Forty Seven

Dark flowed the Susquehanna, dim the haggard souls trudging along its banks. Haunting the light of the pale moon; its glow the only luster in this foreign land. Sullen the eyes staring down to the hard ground from bent heads. Hours ago the sun left them and retreated to its safe haven in the sky. Here they trod, seeking the haven of the fort at Wyoming, but alas, a vast distance lie before them.

No more did the exhausted children walk. Long ago they hitched rides onto soldiers' shoulders. Great bundles of plunder torn from the backs of the pack-horses made a place for their mothers, also, too worn to tread another step.

But onward they must tread; for death followed close behind. No one knew this more than Colonel Hartley. Who but a soldier knows the willing emotions forcing one tired foot after another forward? He raised his nodding head and stared in contempt at the shadows under the great trees surrounding them. He knew they wait there; if not at this very moment, soon. They wanted to kill him. They wanted to kill all whom followed his lead. He fought to open his squinting eyes and rubbed them again. He felt the large bags under them and thought he must be an awful sight. Gazing at the haggard souls trudging trance-like around him he knew appearance meant nothing to anyone now. Only life meant something. Only its promise kept them marching.

A bleary-eyed scout stumbled along the line, stopping at the colonel's side. Hartley looked down to him and let out a grunt.

The scout nodded and wiped his face with his hand, waving his other forward. His long rifle stood a full foot and a half from the sling on his shoulder; for a second Hartley had the peculiar thought of placing a banner onto it. He shook his head and wiped his burning eyes again. "What is it man?" he growled. "Out with it!"

"The Moravian Indian Village at Wyalusing's just ahead," he said, pointing at the creek crossing the trail ahead. "That's the Wyalusing Creek just there, once we past it, it's not far at all. Covenhoven says the village's clear, been abandoned some time now, but a few of the cabins survive."

The scout put his arm on the colonel's horse and leaned his tired head against it while he walked. "We all got to rest. Come thirty miles since Sheshequin. Can go no more, some of the men dove in the river at the sight of the canoes and swam to them. Pulled plunder out and let it sink or float down the river while they crawled into the canoes. All them's beached down at the village. Even the paddlers are exhausted."

"Yes, but they've had it much easier than us," Hartley said. "They'll be the guard when we reach the village." He lifted his canteen to his lips and drank it dry. "Empty," he said. "As is my haversack. We'll have to slaughter a beef at the village and cook up what flour is left into ash cake. From then on we'll live on the beef."

"Fine, sir," the scout said, pushing his head away from the horse's flanks. "I'll push ahead and relay your orders."

"You do that," Hartley said. He never felt so tired. This trek rivaled all he endured with Arnold in Canada and at Crown Point. Such men, he thought, to endure this without complaint. The preacher complained more than any of his rank and file. Oh, these men. Six Nations beware, for there are legions from where these men came! Attack you bold devils and even in their exhausted state these men shall rip your hearts out of your chests! Yes! These men! He looked to the pale moon, knowing its light also shone on the fort at Wyoming. Somehow he found comfort in the thought. What lack of sleep does to a man's mind. They must rest! They have gained all the ground anyone could through this tangled wilderness. It must have gained them some advantage from their pursuing foe. It must have!

He let his horse ramble down the trail and into the village like the tried souls all around him. Men collapsed onto the grass. Some kicked in the doors of the cabins still standing and plopped down inside them. Soon an exhausted mass of humanity lay all about the village.

Hartley slid down from the saddle and staggered over to one of the great fires already blazing around the village. He plopped down on the grass beside it and curled into a tight ball, not caring who saw him. The sound of creaking logs being torn from the walls of some of the cabins made him open his eyes for a slight moment. "It's alright," he mumbled. "Tear it all down, burn it all. Raze the whole place so it will be but ashes when we resume the march on the morrow."

No one heard his mumbles over the crackling flames or the bellowing cattle. No one would care anyhow. For survival took over the reins guiding everyone's souls now. Instinct ruled them now.

Chapter Forty Eight

Painted demons, drifting from the forest everywhere, jarred Colonel Hartley awake. His eyes shot open. A dream he quickly realized, just a dream, thank God. His heavy eyelids fell closed again, leaving him somewhere between conscious thought and dreams. But soon the sounds surrounding him; crackling fires, groaning men, baying animals, and sizzling meat over fires, shook him back to reality. He wanted to lie and wait just a few more seconds, perhaps drift back into his uneasy sleep; but alas the nightmare followed him. He lay with his eyes closed for a few more winks. Thoughts started drifting through the veil of exhaustion clouding his mind.

Here, in the midst of Indian country, sixty miles from the nearest American settlements, with many bands of hostile Indians skulking about their flanks and rear, they sat. The boldness of their movements and the rapidity of their march led their enemy to greatly overestimate their strength. The enemy found no time to rally for defense. But that had changed. Their weakness had been discovered. Hundreds of Butler's Rangers and Johnson's Royal Yorkers gathered at Chemung alone. Adding Indian forces to their number meant certain annilihation for this small band of courageous men. Men whom trusted their lives to his leadership, he realized. The weight of the burden kept his eyes closed, but soon he swallowed hard against it and opened his eyes.

The haggard and ragged souls tramping around the village brought the full weight of their situation down hard on his shoulders. He sat, stiffened his back, rubbed his eyes, and rose. He adjusted his hat and pulled his coat tight at his waist and looked regally about him.

Few of the exhausted eyes recognized him. The nearest sat around a fire picking at great hunks of beef burdening a spit over the flames. The smell inticed his senses. He strutted to the spit and drew his knife, cutting a large piece from the chunk of meat. He took one great bite and then another before the burning sensation in his stomach ceased. Wishing to find anything to wash it down, he reached for a gourd of water sitting by the fire. He took a long drink, noticing the faint bite of whiskey in it.

"We put what whiskey that's left in the water," a soldier by the fire reported to him. "It might take care of the putrid fever within it, leastways, we'll all know soon enough if'n it didn't."

"Quite," Hartley said, lowering the gourd back down to the ground. "The beef is fine anyhow," he added.

"The scouts slaughtered the best," the soldier said, taking advantage of the rare opportunity to speak freely with one of such high rank. "Fear'n that it might be their last and all, last meal that is."

"Now see here, my fine fellow," Hartley said, placing one hand on his knee and turning toward the soldier.

The soldier blanched, knowing he crossed the line with a high ranking officer.

Hartley noticed his fear and shook his head. "Just mind your tongue," he said, "we don't need such talk right now, especially around those poor captives. The thought of returning to captivity among the savages must be most distressing to them to say the least." He nodded his head to one of them he recognized by the fireside. "We will make it to Wyoming," he added, standing tall, "if we have to fight every forsaken inch of the way, we will make it." With that he wandered to the other fires, silently taking assestment of the men's manners and attitudes. All seemed to greet him with confidence and a self assured manner; much to his relief. There is always one bad apple, thinking of the brazen soldier who first spoke to him, even in this fine lot. He did not hold it against the man though, for he knew a certain amount of doubt plagued all their minds, no matter what they said.

He drew his watch from his pocket and ignored the admiring look from all the eyes around him; especially from those of the frontier. For those whom rely on noon marks above a cabin door, the fancy time piece remained a coveted oddity indeed. Taking out his watch key he wound it and read its face. "Nearly nine o'clock in the morning. My God, we must get ready to march." he said.

Tired heads bobbed in agreement.

"Captain Spalding," he said across the flames. "How are things?"

"Well sir, most of the men got some shuteye and the ones who were spelled from the watch last night are the ones still resting about. I've ordered all to check their firelocks, for we may have sport today." Spalding answered.

"Very good, Captain, and I am afraid you may be right about sport on this day." He looked to a few mud-caked faces sitting around the fire. Nests of yellow jackets stumbled upon the trail yesterday had done their work. "Has the mud drawn the sting out?" he asked one of them.

"It's helped, but if it ain't that it's someone stumbling over a rut and landing crossways on his tomahawk or the other falling this ways or that, twisting their ankles, wrists and such," the man answered.

"Yes, it has been rough going to say the least."

"There are many claiming lameness and some are just done tuckered out," Spalding added to the man's coments. "Many have twisted an ankle and wrist, but no broke bones, as of yet."

"And how are the men of the regiment?" Hartley asked, turning to Captains Bush and Walker .

"We're holding out fine sir," Walker said. "We got a few stings and twists but we are fit to fight."

"That is fine, for you all," Hartley said. "We shall have to fit what lame we can in the canoes and on pack-horses. We have at least two day's march ahead, make sure enough of this beef is boiled for that. Let's get things in order and prepare for the march, I wish to get going as soon as possible. The further we get from Chemung and the closer we get to Wyoming the better I will feel. What say you gentlemen?"

"Huzza to that," the captains said. "Huzza to that, sir."

Chapter Forty Nine

Colonel Hartley rode up and down the assembled column of men. Barely one hundred and twenty fell in the line of march, he noticed with a long sigh. Glancing across the green plain and to the riverbank he scratched his head watching the dozens of men filing into the canoes. Some he knew only pretended lameness, but he let them board the canoes just the same. A loud neigh turned his head to the others astride the backs of pack-horses just behind the advance guard of an officer and fifteen men. Several children sat atop oxen, their mothers sitting on pack-horses just behind and to the sides of them. Horned cattle milled about them all, herded by a few of Captain Carberry's Light Horse. The remainder of the Light Horse sat evenly divided between the advance and rear guards.

Hartley stopped and turned his horse about. He stared down at the officer in command of the rear guard.

"We'll make it just fine sir," Captain-Lieutenant Sweeney reported to him.

He smiled at the valuable officer and the eager faced lieutenant standing beside him.

"I've five runners," Lieutenant Van Campen said, nodding his head to the men behind him. "Each is as fleet of foot as the next. If we run into mischief you'll know about in a quick hurry, sir."

"Yes, no doubt, Lieutenant," Hartley said. He looked to the once fine Indian village and tried to imagine what it looked like in its heyday, reflecting on the emptiness of war.

Many of the cabins, especially the larger ones, sat halfway dismantled. Wide spaces shown between some of the walls. Some fine cedar singles and beams lay scattered about near some of the cabins. They had been torn apart to make timber for rafts, Colonel Denison explained to him, on Lieutenant Colonel Dorrance's expedition to to save the few families up river the previous winter. Now the work would be finished, he thought, waving a hand to the scouts who stood about the buildings with flaming pine knots.

With sharp yells they flung the pine knots into the cabins near them. Grabbing more pine knots from the fire-pits they moved fast and furiously from one end of the village to the other. After they completed their task all of them converged just in front of Hartley. With a satisfied nod from him they scattered to form flanking parties on each side of the column. It had been a beautiful town carved out of the heart of the wilderness by people with no more intention than living in the peace they preached from their bibles. Now all the visions of peace went up in flames. They rose with the memory of Wyalusing into the heavens; it's haunting and shadowy memory the only place of peace on this war-torn ground now.

He spurred his horse forward, first riding by Captain Murray's men who formed the Third Division. After saluting them he rode past Captain Spalding's men who formed the Second Division. He also saluted them, before finally taking his place in front of his regiment, which formed the First Division. He looked down to Captain Bush's muscians and nodded his head. Drums promptly beat a strong rhythm of march along with the shrill of three fifes. The spirited music brought new life to the men of the ranks. All stood a little taller.

He glanced down at his watch. Twelve o'clock;

noon, as good an hour as any, he thought, casting a defiant gaze up the mountain to their front. The enemy undoubtedly lie in wait for them. How many, he could only imagine, but if they wanted a fight they would get it. With a grim eye and a stiff upper lip he drew his sword and pointed it to the trail leading up the mountain.

Following the colonel's lead the officer in the advance guard pointed his own sword ahead of him and took the first step of the march. Every foot behind him stepped in perfect cadence to the beat of the drums, wishing to display their determination to any Indian eyes skulking in the trees somewhere around them.

This little army proved equal to any fight, filled with a resolve that pounded in each man's chest. None of their feet would stop marching until they met the gates of Camp Westmoreland, come hell or high water. Damn any Tory, British Regular, or Indian who stood in their way. They had come too far and suffered too much for it all to go for not.

A new-born spirit, the *American spirit*, emboldened this new people, born of the old but molded anew from this new land. It forged their hands, their lives, and their spirits.

The world never witnessed their spirit before and it frustrated description even in those hearts in which it beat so strongly, but nonetheless it lived, and would live as long as they did, changing their hearts and their descendants' hearts forever.

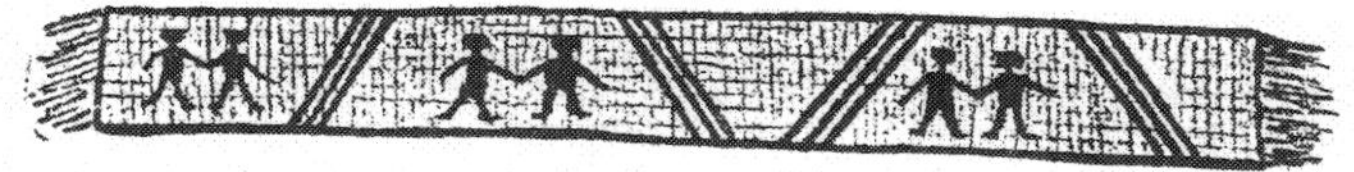

Chapter Fifty

Columns of smoke billowed into the air on the plain behind them. Dark and mercky shadows within the great forest lie ahead of them on the rocky face of the trail. None turned to look back, save the rear guard, but faced forward with grim faces full of resolve. Onward to the music they marched, stepping lively with some even singing in the face of the unknown.

Then, as the hornet strikes sudden and quick, flashes of fire erupted in the faces of the advance guard. The flankers yelled and opened a scattering fire. Indian war whoops answered their call. Captain Stoddert calmly ordered the advance guard to 'present' and a breath latter ordered 'fire!' A wall of fire burst from the line of the advance troops. Leaves fluttered. Branches cracked in the thick brush ahead of them.

Colonel Hartley sat resolutely on his mount in front of his regiment, totally confident in Captain Stoddert's ability to handle the threat. If he called for assistance it would be sent posthaste; if not, he could continue on his own.

The anxious eyes of the rank and file did not share their commander's appraisal of the situation. Heads bent around the column, straining to see the fight atop the mountain ahead of them.

"Just keep your places," Hartley called to them. "Watch the flanks and if need be we shall advance!"

Everyone watched the puffs of white smoke drifting through the leaves. Perked ears listened to hoots and hollers from the dark folds of the forest. The preacher, overcome with grief, dropped down from an oxen and knelt with a bowed head, beseeching all of heaven to come to their aid.

"Just mind yourself, preacher," Hartley said to him. "Save your request for heavenly assistance for latter, for we may need it more then. I suspect this is just a ruse to draw us into an ambuscade. Some of us have learned from Oriskany." He stopped and gazed back to the Second Division. "And Wyoming, I might add."

"We've learned enough to give 'em hell in their own land!" a voice boomed from the ranks.

"Save your spirit, man," Hartley called back to him. "You may find greater need of it before this day is done, I durst say!"

A wild ball whizzed through the trees to the left of the column, leaving a trail of fluttering leaves in its wake. Women screamed from atop pack-horses and oxen. Wide-eyed children stared at the stauch colonel, sitting resolutely on his horse without fliching.

"All is fine, dear souls," Hartley assured them with a nod. "Just be still and this shall pass." He barely stopped uttering the words before all fell silent to their front. A faint Indian war whoop sounded in the distance. After it silence prevailed.

A man ran pell-mell from the front of the column and stopped dead in front of Hartley. “Captain Stoddert’s compliments, sir,” he reported. “We put the runs to them, sir, Captain Stoddert wishes to know if he should pursue them?”

“No, certainly not,” Hartley said. “If they wish to run about and play their games let them, for we are wise to their tricks. We are not following the rascals into an ambuscade. Continue the march downriver with all due haste, if none are wounded, that is.”

“Not even a hair on any of their heads, sir,” the runner reported. “The scouts are looking to see if we put a ball in any of them as we speak.”

“Tell them to proceed no further and to resume their flanking duties,” Hartley said.

“Yes sir!” the runner said, lifting his musket in a hurried salute before scampering up the trail.

“They’ll strike again,” Colonel Denison said, riding up to Hartley. “They’ll strike from ambush and when it’s least expected like the snakes they are.”

“Yes, Colonel,” Hartley said, “but we have a remedy for snake bite! It’s swan shot, buck and ball.”

“Quite a remedy,” Denison said.

“Oh, I think it quite effective, I bet more than a few of the rats in that fight are dealing with stinging lead in their backsides as we speak.”

“I hope so, Colonel, I hope so.”

“I know so, my friend, I know so.”

Both let a slight smile creep across their faces at the thought and quickly erased it at the sight of the curious eyes of the ranks passing them.

“But it’s not over yet, Colonel,” Hartely added.

Chapter Fifty One

The sun climbed high into the sky and turned hot, seeming to awaken every insect and other pest for one last forte. Gnats rose in droves and hovered in clusters around the heads of man and beast. Ticks dropped from trailside brush, growing fat from the blood of many an unwilling host. And always the greatest threat, Indians lurking in the deep shadows of the everpresent forest, plagued everyone's thoughts. They already flitted about their front and stung once, now all hoped their swat good enough to keep them at bay.

Colonel Hartley fanned his hand through the sea of gnats plaguing his face. Annoyingly, they flit about his eyes, seeking its moisture. He ran a finger into the corner of his eye to clear it of their foul presence. He rolled them along his cheek and flicked his fingers, just in time to open his eyes to a new swarm. "My God," he muttered under his breath, "is every pest of the world here today?" He almost wished for the torrential rains to burst forth from the heavens again but his wrinkled and cracked feet beseeched him to reconsider his wish. He wondered if his feet would ever heal. Part of the rigors of campaigning, he consoled himself, knowing this march may be the axis on which his life turned one way or the other. Fortune or famine lay in it for him and all his troops, he feared.

His eyes fell to one of the scouts kneeling by the trailside. He dumped water onto a bare patch of dirt and swirled it about, making mud. He promptly smeared it all over the backs of his exposed hands and neck. "Damn Poison Ivy," he said, noticing the colonel. He angrily waved toward the shiny leaves growing all along the right side of the trail. They stretched and crawled all over the limbs of many of the trees. Falling pine needles and leaves caught in the tangle of ivy vines and formed weird and heavy shapes. The matting of vines stretched as far as the eye could see into the forest, giving the trees a strange apprearance of some new form of threatening beasts rising from hell itself.

"You flankers do your best," Hartley said, noting the difficulty of the ground and their fatigue. "It is all I ask of any of you." Another cry from the line made him and everyone else look to men in the ranks slapping at their bodies.

Another nest of yellow jackets must have been disturbed. All of this, Hartley cursed under his breath, with an enemy posed to strike at any moment. It seemed the children of the forest had entreated their Gods for help and they had responded by causing every manner of pest to descend and plague their foes.

Slapping at a bite on the nape of his neck he turned his open hand and stared at the great glob of black flesh smushed into it. Horseflies now joined the assault. He felt his horse's tail flail against its rear flanks. Its loud neighs of frustration echoed along the trail. But the sound echoed alone, save those recently stung, for not a grumble sounded from the troops plodding along beside him. "Such men," he said on a sigh. "Such men." He swallowed hard against his parched throat. Another problem of which he heard no complaint, thirst. Even though they marched on full bellies of beef few drank the only thing left to them-water. Some had mixed what little whiskey remained in their canteens with the water, hoping to stave off putrid fever, but most declined to drink it. Thirsty, tired men, but not a murmur of complaint rose from their dry throats. "Such men," he whispered again, wiping sweat from his eyes. Sixty miles to go, his scouts told him repeatedly. Sixty miles of hell. He thought of the men in the canoes and envied them. "We must push on," he muttered under his breath. A few eyes in the ranks looked to him. "We must push on," he said louder, hoping to ease their apparent concerns. "Push on! We need all good men to their duty just now! The enemy is all around! We must keep on!"

A man stumbling just to his rear rolled down the edge of the steep trail. He quickly rose to his feet, searching madly for his fallen musket and hat. In his exhausted state he barely noticed the odd angle of the tomahawk stuck in his belt. The red spot growing from it made his eyes widen. Amazed, he dropped both hat and musket and grasped the tomahawk, carefully pulling it from his thigh. "Just a scratch," he reassured himself.

"Here now," a sergeant called down to him. "Be still, I'll be down directly to help." The sharp crack of dozens of rifles stopped the sergeant dead in his tracks. He lifted his own weapon and listened. Another volley, followed by war whoops and sporadic rifle shots, echoed through the air. The sergeant hurriedly met the wounded man and helped him back to the ranks, all the while being assured by him of his need for no aid. "Just a scratch," the man countered the sergeant's concerned look at his wound. In no time both took their place in the ranks paying little heed to the 'scratch'.

"Form up!" Hartley called to the troops, drawing his sword and pointing it to the front of the column. "We shall make short work of them!" He spurred his mount up to the crest of the trail and quickly surveyed the ground. A slight ridge rose above the swale from which puffs of white smoke ascended in the air.

He cast an eye to Captain Stoddert busily ordering his troops forward in good order along with some scouts. "Good job, Stoddert," he said under his breath. "Keep them busy and we shall flank them." Trusting in the competent officer to keep the enemy engaged, he rode back to his awaiting troops, reassuring the nervous preacher, women, and children while he rode through their number.

"Second and Third Division!" he called to the awaiting troops, "Move to the left and flank the enemy! First Division form on me!"

Captains Spalding and Murray instantly barked out commands to their troops. Both led their troops up the left side of the trail and into the woods fearlessly, ordering those with bayonets to fix them on the march. Their backs quickly disappeared in the woods.

Hartley and the others stared into the depths of the forest swallowing them up, anxiously awaiting any sign of their progress. "You men form up right here," he ordered his regiment. "Fix bayonets! Refuse the flank, while the rest face forward. We don't know from which direction the devils may strike, we must be prepared!"

A sharp volley, followed by another, broke the haphazard sound of musketry. Soon great yells of triumph sounded from the woods-in English.

"They've broken them," Hartley said, perking up in his saddle and listening. No war whoops or spurts of rifle fire echoed through the air. A slight rustle to their left caused an awful moment of concern before triumphant brown-coated men appeared from the woods, followed by others in a wide array of civlian and military dress. Spalding marched proudly in their lead with Murray by his side. A self-satisfied grin stretched across both of the officers' faces.

"We put the runs to 'em for sure, sir," Spalding reported. "They'll be thinking about our little surprise all the way back to Chemung."

"Oh, I only wish," Hartley said. "But me thinks they

are about some other mischief. We, my good man, may have a sharper encounter before this is all done."

"Perhaps we should seek them out," Murray said.

"Where?" Hartley asked, rolling his eyes to the thick forest surrounding them. "They could be anywhere, and we have civilians, cattle and such to mind. No, it is best we be on our way with what we have, trusting in providence to deliver us from this hell."

"Amen! Colonel, Amen!" the preacher exclaimed, overhearing his words.

"Quite," Hartley said with a nod to the nervous man of the cloth. "This was only an amusement on their part, though your movement did put a cork in their bottle of mischief, for sure. Good job, very good job, for you all!"

He turned his attention to Spalding and lowered his voice. "Do you think you infilicted any losses on the enemy?" he asked.

"Hard to tell, sir," Spalding said, "the way they scatter and carry away their dead and wounded."

"Yes," Hartley said, nodding his head to Stoddert's runner approaching them. "Are there any casualties of Stoddert's men?" he asked the man before he reported.

"No sir," the runner answered. "It was getting a little hot when the Captain Stoddert said to hold fast and you would send a surprise into their flanks, then, pop! there was these men spilling out the woods! The enemy scattered like the wind! Sir!"

"Very well," Hartley said. "Give Captain Stoddert my compliments and tell him to resume the march at once. We had one man slightly wounded in an accident, but we are all well, and shall follow with all due haste. We must lose as little time as possible with the enemy. Perhaps in this we shall foil any of his attempts of ambuscade. So let's get to it!"

Chapter Fifty Two

Hawkins Boone stopped his paddle in mid-stroke and perked his head toward the shore. The man in the rear of the canoe, John Brady, compensated for the drifting canoe and stared at Boone in wonder. These Boones, all of them he heard tell of anyway, possessed a sixth-sense about things. None had a more keen sense than Hawkins, though, besides maybe his cousin Daniel in the Kentuck country. Brady lifted the edge of his paddle out of the water and listened for what alerted his friend's senses. Those in the canoes behind them also noticed Hawkins and also lifted their paddles from the water.

Silence drifted over the swirling face of the Susquehanna. No one moved in the drifting canoes except one or two bending down to their rifles. Hawkins slowly lifted his hat from his head and waved to the others behind him. He kept his head bent toward the riverbank, intently listening to something none of the others heard.

John Brady scanned the shore and let his hand fall to the pistol in his belt. He still didn't hear or see anything out of the ordinary, but he trusted his friend's senses. He drew a deep breath. Several sharp cracks from the mountain on the east side of the river caught his attention. He perked his head toward the noises. The further they drifted the louder and sharper the cracks sounded, joined by the faint cry of yelling men and the unmistakable cries of the rage of war. Everyone sat rigid in the canoes, anxiously waiting for the sounds to increase or die as the previous noises but a half hour before these shots.

They increased.

Hawkins Boone immediately sank his paddle deep into the river and paddled madly for the riverbank. Brady followed his lead, along with everyone else. Soon all the canoes sat beached silently on the muddy riverbank. No one spoke, but reached for their rifles and accoutrements.

Listening to the sounds of battle rising on the moutain before them, they formed into a long line, suddenly relieved or forgetting their so-called ailments.

All eyes ran up the line to Boone, who stood listening and staring up the mountain. He looked to Brady before turning to William King. Both men nodded at him. He nodded back and pointed forward with his rifle. The whole line instantly started up the mountainside, moving silently and gracefully as to put to shame any pack of wolves. All focused on the sounds of battle ahead and negotiated the terrain in perfect unision, leaving no one but two guards for the canoes behind, or anyone exposed to their front.

The abating sounds of battle did little to break their tight formation. Each a seasoned woodsman, they knew the importance of keeping together against the fury of their foe. Experience taught them to stand fast at the first shock; after which the Indians seemed to lose face and melt away into the forest. They seemed to have little stomach for a stand up fight one on one, at least from their experiences with them, of course with the exceptions of Oriskany and Wyoming. The exceptions played hell with their reasoning, but onward they marched.

A growing silence blanketed the mountain. Moving carefully so not to disturb the silence, they broke the crest of the trail and fanned out in every direction. Some carefully examined the trailside, while others combed over the apparent scene of battle.

Hawkins Boone himself seemed to be everywhere at once, from the trailside, front and rear, and to the battlefield itself. He finally stopped and surveyed the slight clearing to their front. Bits of paper from torn cartridges lay strewn all over the area, along with the other litter of every battlefield, bits of torn leather straps, neglected haversacks, a couple of hats, a stray buckle or two, and even a powder horn.

"They beat feet in a hurry," Brady said, scanning the clearing beside Boone. "But there ain't no sign of anybody hurt, thank God. From the looks of things they can't be far up the trail."

"Yep," Boone said. "They did beat feet in a hurry, rightly so, for the *Copperheads* are merely playing with them, slowing them to strike them at some spot they choose better up the way." He squinted his eyes and looked up the trail. "Colonel Hartley's right smart about it. He knows the foxes are circling the hen house. Thinks it's best to just keep moving fast as he can, leastways he might spoil a bit of their sport and get away from them before they're ready."

Brady nodded in conformation and to the others forming around them. "Ambush, as always," he said.

Hawkins nodded.

"There ain't no one about these parts, white or Indian," a gruff looking man in buckskin reported to him. "They's all gone down the trail."

"Over here!" a man called from back down the trailside. They all scampered down the trail and stood looking down at the man.

The man waved at some disturbed dirt and bushes. His hand flowed down to ground at his feet. He knelt down and raised a few leaves up in his free hand. He lifted the leaves to his face, smelled them, and tasted something on the leaves. "Blood," he said, lowering the leaves and letting them dance down to the ground. He lifted his rifle and looked all about the mountain. “It’s people blood, too, ain’t no horse or varmit, excepting maybe a Injun, but by it’s place it looks like someone was shot, fell, or was pushed down the bank and ended up here. Ain’t no blood trail after this spot, so I reckon he got the bleeding stopped.”

“Well they’ve drawn blood,” William King said. “Once they gets the taste of it there’s no stopping them, the snakes.”

“Could have been someone just fell,” Brady said.

“Was you a hearin’ the same ruckus we was a coming up here?” King asked. He shook his head and pointed at a small sapling cut in two by a ball just a few feet from them. “With all that lead flying it’s a miracle if no one caught a ball, white or red, Tory or Patriot!”

“That may be,” Boone said, looking down the mountainside to the river. “But we best get back to them canoes and get to paddling downriver to keep astride with them. I have a awful hankering that the Colonel just may need a miracle afore this day is done for many a tomahawk may be about his head! And he might just get a miracle from canoes on the river. So let’s get to it!”

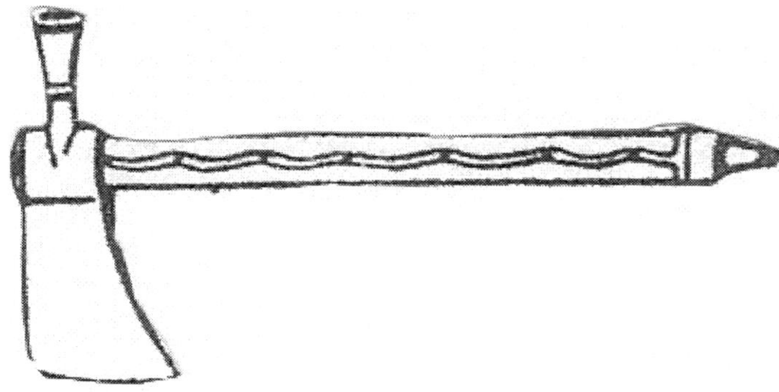

Chapter Fifty Three

The tight trail led into a thick marsh, made all the worse by the recent rains, but onward they trod. Stunted trees stood about the gnarled swamp. Lichen-covered rocks lay above the mucky water. Slimy blue-green algae covered the tree trunks in the morass. The mucky water smelled of rotting plants and soggy earth. Men's and horses' feet made a strange sucking sound with each step. All eyes stared to the other end of the trail and the promise of solid footing. The trees ahead seemed less dense and the ground rose slightly, showing hints of a rocky face. All wondered why on earth the trail cut through the swamp, but after looking to the sheer bank to the right cascading down to the river and the slight rill of water running through a tangle of vines and stumps along with trees covered with poison ivy to the left, the wonder escaped them. They bowed their heads and plunged through the soggy trail.

Hartley plopped down from the back of his struggling horse and sank knee deep in the muck. He let out a disgusted grunt and braced himself against the flank of his horse. He pulled one foot, then the other, from the thick mud. Besides a few eyes glancing his way, no one offered him any help.

They had their own troubles.

He lay his arms across the horse and took a few deep breaths. Watching Carberry lead his exhausted mount along the trail in front of him, he wondered of their effectiveness if trouble awaited them further up the trail. But they all ached and longed for sleep. The Light Horse behaved magnificently so far, and he scolded himself for his doubts about them.

The caw of several crows over the trees ahead of them made him roll his tired eyes toward them. They flew toward them and suddenly turned toward the river after catching sight of the haggard line of people, cattle, and horses struggling through the swamp. Even Hartley drew something of the fact they did not fly from the direction from which they originally took to the wing.

"Something has spooked them," Captain Murray said, trudging through the muddy water just to his side. "It'll be our friends calling upon us again, probably in those trees just ahead or there abouts. Trees aren't so thick there, but just enough to give some cover while firing on us on the trail below them." He lifted his rifle barrel toward the trees. "Bet my life on it, I would, yes sir."

Hartley watched the crows and digested the passing captain's words. No doubt they had merit, for Murray had a great knowledge of Indians and the same strange sixth-sense Hawkins Boone possessed. He nodded to Murray's men marching behind him. All of them perked their heads toward the crows, each pondering their warning.

Hartley's mind flashed with scenarios of battle. Mr. Stoddert, stern, competent, and professional, along with his mixture of riflemen, scouts, and militia, would be fine. Mr. Sweeney, just as capable, would be fine in the rear. If need be he would dispatch Captain Spalding and his hardy men to their aid. Each a fine shot, they could hold against thrice their number. He could divide Mr. Murray's men wherever needed along with the Light Horse. That left only the center with the cattle, civilians, pack-horses, and his regiment. Fine in proper line of battle against a red-coated and proper foe facing them, his men proved awkward at woods fighting. But with swan shot in each musket they would prove just as valuable. He liked Captain Spalding's idea of sequential fire, a necessity in fighting Indians who waited for their enemy to fire and then rushed them before they could load again.

Watching the men march past another thought burdened his mind. His responsibility for their well being played hard at his conscience. He tried to ration it away but it plagued him just the same. Here, if one fell, fifty miles from any help, he lay at the mercy of the land and savage; both of them as unforgiving and ruthless as the other. He must do his best, he told himself: For these men, and for himself. He rubbed his eyes and reassured himself of his plan before stepping through the muck again.

He let out a deep sigh of relief upon touching solid earth again. With his first step he stumbled over one of the many rocks and found himself cursing it. He pulled angrily at the reins of his horse but then let up on them, curbing his anger with his resolve. One must not lose his bearing, he told himself, especially when tested in such an inhospital place. He looked through the trees surrounding them. The ground stretched and rolled gently underneath the great branches of the ancient trees. It took on the appearance of a fine park, no doubt from the custom of the Indians burning the scub brush away by controlled fires, he reasoned. He had heard of the practice, but now witnessing its effect he admired it. No wonder the Indians fought so hard in their own country.

The rolling ground crested on a ridge just ahead, beyond it a spectacular view of green rolling mountains stretched under the deep blue sky. Such beauty, he thought, could only be inspired by the hand of the divine. All of the sudden the gnats and black flies seemed frivolous compared to the majesty of this place. Now he knew why the Wyoming people cherished this land so much. It must be fought for. It must be won.

The sharp crack of rifled guns broke him out of his trance. He looked to his front, seeing nothing, he realized the sounds came from the rear. He turned his horse aside and quickly mounted it, turning its reins toward the sound of the new battle. Hundreds, not dozens as before, of shots echoed through the air. He spurred his horse to Captain Spalding and immediately ordered, "Second Division to the rear!"

Spalding and his men sprang to the task, marching at the long trot to the rear. One of Van Campen's runners hurried past them with a look of horror in his eyes. They ignored him and with stern and grim looks ran steadfastly to the sound of battle.

"They are in force, sir!" the runner reported to Hartley.

"Yes, I can hear," Hartley said. "I am sending the entire Second Division to your support, tell Mister Sweeney to hold fast!"

"Yes, sir," the runner said, turning to catch up with Spalding's men. Screeches he never heard before, produced by fiends he thought only imaginable in his grimest nightmares, turned his head to the left of the line. A burst of mur-derous fire flashed from the trees all along the left, felling several surprised men in Hartley's front.

"Stand fast!" Hartley bellowed, yanking his sword from its sheath. He raised it and defiantly pointed it toward the trees. "Form on me!"

The men of his regiment dutifully obeyed, ignoring the men writhing in pain to their front. They formed a smart line and stood rigidly at attention.

"Make ready!" Hartley screamed. The whole line of firelocks flew from the shoulder to their front. "Present!" The firelocks leveled. Hammers clicked back. "Fire!" A wall of lead splattered against the trees, splintering saplings and thudding hard into branches and trunks. Teardrop shaped swan shot flittered through the leaves. Several groans sounded in the wake of the horrific volley, despite of the Indians ducking when they heard the colonel's orders.

"Captain Bush!" Hartley said, "Independent fire, but keep it sequential, one fire while the other loads!"

A new chorus of gunfire caught his ear from the front of the column. He glanced down at Bush and spurred his horse toward the new sounds. "Third Division follow me!" he said to the anxious men left standing behind the line of his regiment.

Stoddert stood full in front of his men, pointing his sword with one hand at painted men skulking in the bushes to their front while firing his pistol with his other hand. A half dozen men slowly advanced against the enemy with their officer, laying down a constant and steady fire.

Only Stoddert turned to look out of the corner of his eye at Harley galloping hard to them from the rear. "We have them well in hand here, sir," he reported over his shoulder. "We'll put the run to them shortly!"

Hartley glanced madly about, taking in all of the characteristics of the land. "They are pushing from the rear," he said to Murray. "Look to that ridge! If we gain it we can pour a broadside into them!"

"Yes, sir," Murray said.

Just before he finished speaking a runner from the rear-Van Campen himself-rushed up to him. "Colonel! They are driving us from the rear!" he reported. "We're holding, but it's getting hot!"

"Damn it but for those men in the canoes!" Hartley said, staring down toward the river. "Look at the lay of the land! But for a few more men we could completely surround them!"

"Surround them hell, sir, with all due respect," Van Campen said. "They're doing just that in our rear!"

A horrible shrill echoed through the air. Great blue-white clouds of stagnant smoke hung lazily about the ridge. The acrid smell of sulfur began to fill the air. Indians yelled from all quarters. White warriors screamed loudly back at them. Curses, taunts, and threats screamed forth in a dozen different tongues. Women screamed with fright from atop jittery pack-horses and oxen. Hearty prayers sounded between their yells from the terrified preacher. The Light Horse dashed in and about the trees on their exhausted and played-out horses, screaming and firing their weapons while brandishing their long sabers at the scattering foe darting in and among them. Men fell from horses and onto the ground, some painted, some in blue regimentals, some in buckskin, and some in breech-cloths.

The chaos of battle spread out everywhere before Hartley's eyes. He thought of his promise to himself and to his men. If anyone fell, he knew no quarter would be given, on both sides.

Watching two of Stoddert's men wrestle a huge brave to the ground and dash his brains out of his skull bore witness to that fact. The gleam of a knife shone in the choas and smoke. He watched it slice the scalp lock from the fallen brave's crown with one quick flick of a wrist. Before the two men rose from their gruesome task, spears and arrows rained down onto them. One screamed 'powder and ball doth settle all!' and knelt, firing his rifle. The other stopped dead in his tracks for a heartbeat. He turned toward Hartley, his eyes pinched together staring at a long rod protruding from his forehead. Before he could raise his hand a gush of blood poured down from the arrow and flooded his eyes. His body went limp and fell instantly to the ground.

No more would he breathe, Hartley thought just as a glancing blow from a feathered lance struck across his horse's shins. It jumped, nearly throwing him from its back. He gripped at its mane and steadied it by leaning forward and whispering in its ear. A shadow of a breeze passed his cheek followed by a whizzing sound. He brushed at his cheek and drew his pistol, firing at the painted men darting beween the trees to his side. "Pour it into them!" he screamed, joining his men in cursing the awful savages. "Send them all to hell this day!"

He watched his regiment fight the painted men darting about their front. They formed and fired briskly, matching the rate of fire from their foe fighting from behind trees. Several enemy balls peppered their ranks. Men screamed, twisted and fell in agony, spilling blood in great spurts onto the ground and one another. A few broke from the ranks and charged independently at shadows in the smoke and trees, some emerging victorious, others falling from a hail of angry lead.

"Stand fast!" Hartley screamed. "Don't let them drive you in! Stand fast and fire!"

Obeying, none ventured forth after hearing their colonel's order. Soon the bursts of flames from the trees lessened. Soon the yells sounded from behind, instead of their front.

"We've got to gain the ridge!" Hartley said. "They're concentrating on our rear!"

"Permission to flank, sir!" Stoddert asked, waving his sword to the opposite side of the ridge.

"Do as you see fit, man, but keep your hair, mind you!" Hartley said, turning his horse toward the mass of men scambling to gain the ridge. Arrows, bullets, and spears peppered them but they plod headlong to the ridge, knowing their very survival meant following orders.

"I intend to keep it but may lift a few of the Indians' locks!" Stoddert answered, leading a dozen men into the trees he so recently freed of their foe.

"Godspeed," Hartley called behind them. "Godspeed!" He quickly loaded his pistols and stared at the ridge ahead, hoping and praying he reached it before the enemy realized his designs.

Chapter Fifty Four

Captain Spalding stood tall at the apex of his line of men, directing their fire and reassuring them. Balls whizzed all about the line, striking the ground and thudding into the trees around them. "Keep it hot!" Spalding called to his men, "lay it into them! Hold them, damn it! Hold them!" He rolled his eyes to his left. Sweeney and his men stood firm, but a new rain of fire struck them, knocking several to the ground.

With loud yells and bulging eyes a group of Indians burst headlong into Sweeney's staggering line. Soon more poured one after another into the line. Rifles swang in the air at them, along with tomahawks, swords, and fists. Men of both sides fell and rolled to the ground in masses of flailing arms and legs. Screams and oaths in many tongues sounded from the smoky ground.

In the midst of the mayhem a slight tug at his arm twisted Spalding about. Glanced down at his shoulder he noticed a fresh tear in his brown regimental. He grabbed at it and pulled it up, to his relief finding no blood spewing from the tear. He looked to his right, seeing white men in green hunting shirts madly reloading their weapons and firing into his line. "To the right oblique!" he ordered his line. "Take aim! Fire!" A dozen rifles fired in unison into the brush to his right, delivering a hail of fire. One of the green-shirted men twirled about, clutching his arm. Others grabbed him and pulled him along in retreat.

Spalding glared at them. Madly reloading his pistol he called "Elliot! Terry!" to the two men nearest him in the line. "Scout the to the right. Make sure no more Tory rats are lurking there. Clear it if you can!"

Joseph Elliot and Jonathan Terry instantly backed from the line and ran to the right. Spalding watched them disappear and called to his lieutenant, "Jenkins hold them here! I've got to see Sweeney!"

Jenkins nodded. With grim eyes, he calmly loaded his rifle. He raised it and took careful aim at two of the painted men dashing from the trees toward Sweeney's men on his left. He fired. One of the braves tumbled and rolled on the ground, only to be quickly dragged back into the trees by his comrade.

Spalding nodded, praising the great shot with a wide grin. A spear flying from nowhere wiped his grin away. He flinched just at the right moment, watching the spear thud into the ground between his feet. He swiped it with his sword in anger, cutting it in twain. Lifting his pistol in his other hand he fired at the miscreants hiding behind the trees. "It's getting hot," he said to Covenhoven, noticing the awe in his eyes from witnessing the whole spear episode. "You want to come with me to Sweeney? We've got to coordinate our actions. They're concentrating on us, and I've seen some Tory rats sulking about!"

Covenhoven fired once more ahead of him and scampered over to the captain, reloading while he ran. Both men strode through the arrows, bullets, and spears flying and striking all around them. Smoke began to engulf the entire line, trees and all, and both looked apprehensively at the screaming braves darting about the trees.

Sweeney barely lifted his eyes from his front to acknowledge the officer's and scout's approach. A new wave of warriors burst forth and struck his line with all their fury. The crack of several men's skulls attested to their rage.

A large warrior strode through the smoke directly at Sweeney, sweeping the men's clubbed rifles aside with ease.

He gripped a tomahawk in his white knuckles, raising it high over his head to strike.

Sweeney's pistol clicked. No fire spurt from it to check the advancing demon of death. Instantly he raised his sword and spun about, deflecting the blow of the tomahawk enough so it just skimmed his cheek. He sank down and twirled about on his right foot.

In the same moment the brave raised the tomahawk again and bared his teeth at the Rebel officer. He drew his knife from his belt and raised it in his other hand.

Sweeney's sword, riding on the momentum of his twirl, struck up and into the brave's ribbcage.

The brave's eyes widened in shock. He cocked his head to one side, dropping both tomahawk and knife. His hands fell to the sword and he grabbed it to no avail. Blood flowed from his grip on the blade.

Sweeney raised one foot to the brave's thigh and slowly drew the blade out of his ribcage. A great spurt of blood sprayed forth on the brave's last gasp. His eyes rolling back in his head he fell hard on top of his slayer.

Both Spalding and Covenhoven rushed to Sweeney, gruffly pulling the dead brave off their exasperated comrade.

He quickly rose, covered with smudges of vermillion paint and peppered with blood. He wiped the blood from his eyes with his sleeve and greeted the officer and scout. "My God! They're pouring all they have into us! They're mad!"

"Yes," Spalding said, his eyes widening in awe of a new wave of red men charging from the trees through the smoke. He raised his pistol and Covenhoven his rifle. They both fired at the same instant, felling the same brave.

Sweeney turned around and quickly picked up his pistol. He aimed at the aged warrior in the forefront of the Indians and pulled the trigger. This time it sparked to life, but in his haste Sweeney jerked the weapon to his left. The ball creased the warrior's skull to the aged chief's right. The warrior fell backwards, screaming and clutching both of his hands to his head. Suddenly rising, he ran pell-mell back to the safety of the trees.

The aged warrior glanced back at him and turned about, his eyes full of purpose and anger. He screamed something in his native tongue so loudly it rose above the chaotic whir of battle. Darting forward, he carried a dozen or more warriors in his wake. Smoke swirled about his grisly painted body by the sheer force of his mad steps. He swung his war club savagely to his right and left, clearing a huge swath of Rebels before an equally angry volley felled several of the warriors following him. With great reluctance, he turned and retreated back to his own lines, all the while cursing the white demons.

Covenhoven fired into them and lowered his rifle to reload it. His eyes wide, he turned to the two officers standing next to him. "That chief said '*My brave warriors we drive them; be bold and strong, the day is ours*!'" he reported.

"Damn it, the bloody savage, I'll give him a day he'll regret!" Spalding said. He reloaded his pistol and backed with the line being pushed by a renewed burst of brisk fire. He fired along with the rest in the line and looked to his own line holding strong on the right. Before long they stumbled back until they fell out of his view, forming a gap in the line.

A new, furious wave, of painted men darted forward, plowing into Sweeny's caving line. Men met hand to hand in mortal combat. Several swarmed around Spalding. A long spear thudded into one of Sweeney's men at his side. The man fell to his knees, cursing all of heaven and hell.

His foe darted toward him, ready to finish his work with his upraised tomahawk. Spalding leveled his pistol him before a spine-tingling wail to his front instinctively turned his pistol to a crazed man bearing down on him. He fired, killing the man within an angry step of his front. Looking in the same blinking of his eye he watched Sweeney's man grasp and yank the spear from his bowels, twisting it in the same instant to meet the advancing demon to his own front.

The brave's momentum sank the spear clean through his bowels, popping it out his back. Instinctively, he reached forward and clutched the wide-eyed white man before him by his shoulders him in his death grip.

The white man's hands gripped the spear impaling his foe with his own death grip. Blood spilled out of the corners of his mouth.

Both men glared into each other's eyes while their life blood drained from each of them. The same look, eyes full and bulging, mirrored in each of their eyes. The furious glare melted into a gasp, spilling great globs of blood down from both men's mouths before both fell, their eyes still bearing the look of pure rage in death.

Spalding recognized the rage. He saw it many times

in battle. The rage born of the demon of war. Men wore it, living and dead in battle. All warriors shared it. It locked men's eyes in a tunnel vision to their immediate front in battle. Men's brains seemed to pour from their ears in the height of battle. They only looked to their immediate front, for in that moment all of life and death faced them and demanded their full attention if they wanted to draw breath after the fury of battle. Their blood flowed hot in their veins in such moments. They thought of nothing else. They left the larger sense of the battle to their captains. In their captains they trusted to deliver them from the madness and hell that is the fury of battle.

It all shone clear to Spalding in this instant. In this instant of madness and mayhem, of men screaming for the last time in the explosion of war. Of men dying by one another's hand. All they are, were, and hoped to be yanked away in this moment of rage; of battle. The terrible responsibility of leading men in battle choked his breath away for a moment, but in an instant gave way to clear thought. A plan immediately flowed through his mind. He suddenly felt alive and fully awake, staring down in wonder of his hands reloading his pistol without any conscious thought of his own. God's will, he thought, turning to Sweeney.

Sweeney stumbled backwards along with the rest of the line, swearing many an oath and waving his sword in the air. "Call your men to my support!" he yelled to Spalding.

"Wait!" Spalding said, "look about! Look to their rear! They are advancing with little regard for it! They are pushing us into this swale, but my men are still in place! If they keep moving to our left we can surround them and cut them to pieces!"

Sweeney let his sword fall to his side and peered about the madness engulfing him. Divide in the face of a superior foe? What nonsense ran through this Wyoming officer's mind? He gazed at Spalding firing his pistol and waving the spent weapon to the ridge on their right. Through the wisps of smoke men poured to the top of it, starting to lay down their own fire at the enemy. Hartley's and Murray's men! Now Spalding's plan made all the sense in the world. "Yes! By God! Yes! We can turn their own momentum against them! I'll send a runner to Colonel Hartley!" Sweeney gasped.

"No time for that, my man," Spalding said, gazing at the mounted man darting about the men forming on the ridge. "If we're to act we need to act now!" he added. "I reckon the good colonel's already figured out what we're about anyhow!"

Sweeney stole a glance up to the ridge and back to the enraged line of Indians darting about to his front and firing at his line. One of his men twirled about and fell to his side, almost bringing him down with him. A ball whizzed by his ear. "You're right Captain!" he screamed at Spalding. "Get to it! We'll hold here, be damn quick about your movement!"

Spalding nodded. Firing once more he ran back to his men, confident of his plan. This time the Indians advanced up the center. This time their confidence and impetuosity turned against them. Wyoming in reverse, Spalding thought, pouring down upon his veteran fighters and barking commands. "Odds with me!" he shouted over the roar of rifles and muskets, referring to his earlier division of his men into ones with odd and even numbers. "Evens with Jenkins!" All obeyed immediately, recognizing the potential of the movement just as clearly as their captain. The taste of revenge wetted all their palates. They thirst for it ravenously, feeling this time it would be quenched.

One of the mighty warriors of the "Six Nations."

Chapter Fifty Five

Elliot and Terry gained the tree line to the rear and right of their Division and carefully advanced into it. Both held their long rifles at the ready and darted from tree to tree, one covering the advance of the other. After advancing a rod or two Elliot stopped behind a tremendous tree and waved Terry to his side. "They've cleared out," he whispered to his partner. He peeked his head around the tree which they gathered behind and assessed the lay of the land.

"They've got a wounded man slowing them, if we run like deer I think we can cut them off before they gain their friends' company again." He turned and looked sternly into Terry's eyes.

Terry looked back to the smoke drifting through the tree's behind them and listened to the sound of the brisk fight to their rear, considering Spalding's orders.

"He said to clear it!" Elliot said. "They're Tory rats, turned against family and home! If we go back for help they'll escape. We've got a chance here man! I know you Terrys despise the Tories more than most, if'n that's possible," Elliot said. He watched Terry consider his words.

Terry's cold eyes stared back at him. His reference to his brother Parshall stung him deeply. What of it? Was he responsible for his brother betraying their ranks and joining the enemy? He thought not, and damn anyone who did. Didn't Elliot hear the story of Parshall seeking him out on the day of the Battle of Wyoming? No doubt remained to his purpose on finding him. The story of John Pensil slaying his brother Henry after finding him hidden on an island in the river rang true and deep to him. This war tore families and friends asunder. Its great purpose and meaning even rose above the sacred call of family. Its higher meaning changed the hearts of many, leaving life long friendships devastated in its wake. That purpose, either for or against, burned with equal intensity in the souls of the men on either side of it. A chance lie here to strike at the foe. He swore an oath to himself right then and there to fire no matter who's face shone down his rifle's sights. His sense of duty demanded it. "Lead on, damn it!" He said to Elliot. "Lead on!"

Both men dashed around the tree, running madly through the forest to gain the ground to the rear. In a few rods Elliot stopped, pointing down to a slight clearing between the trees running almost down to the river. The telltale sounds of the battle quickly mapped out the position of their foe in his mind. "They'll have to cut across this clearing to get back to their lines!" he said. "let's hope we've not missed the rats."

Terry nodded and leaned back against the tree Elliot hid behind. Both checked their rifles and leveled their rifles on the clearing. They waited, not moving a muscle, lest it betray their presence.

Now and then a spent ball spilled through the leaves around them, rolling and tumbling to the earth. Some smacked into trees and rolled down the bark to the ground. Both ignored the sounds, intently listening and searching the edge of the clearing for a rustle or movement in the brush to the left of the clearing. Just as the muscles in their arms began to burn from holding their long rifles up so long a twig snapped.

An Indian, painted half red and half black from head to foot, carefully stepped into the clearing.

Both men stared down the sights of their rifles at the Indian brave looking about, but held their trigger fingers still, knowing more followed him. They watched the whites of the Indian's eyes dart to and fro, ready to dispatch him if his eyes locked with theirs. Bigger bucks follow in the herd, wait them out. The bigger the buck, the bigger the trophy. To their relief, the warrior turned and slightly waved the barrel of his rifle to his rear. Several white men in green coats and hunting shirts slowly stepped into the clearing. None looked about, trusting the keen eye of the Indian to their own. One, two, three, and finally four stepped out, all casting a nervous look behind them before scampering down the clearing to regain their lines of battle.

Elliot cocked his eye from the barrel of his rifle over to Terry. "Wait until the last," he whispered ever so slightly, "we'll get the last, they're too great in number to chance getting them all. Let them clear out. The biggest buck is always the last of the herd!"

Terry stood firm, letting the silence of his firelock speak to his comrade's request. He searched every face of the white men, half hoping one of them shined familiar to him, while at the same time not wishing to know what face would catch his ball. All bore the taint of treason, regardless.

Two more enemy rangers stumbled into the clearing, each with a wounded man's arm over their shoulders. A civilian stepped behind them, fanning his rifle around, not seeming to share the rangers' confidence in the Indian's eye. Another pair of rangers stepped out to their rear. All stopped to catch their panting breaths for a moment.

The civilian remained tense and on guard.

"Secord himself," Elliot whispered on a harsh breath. Both he and Terry watched the elder Secord's eye skirt the trees. To their dismay the Tory's eyes locked with their's.

Both watched Secord's jaw drop in disbelief. Before the stunned Tory could mutter a word or raise his rifle to his shoulder flames burst from the tree. A ball whizzed past his ear, slightly creasing it before thudding into the shoulder of the ranger behind him. The man's feet flew straight in the air. With an anguished groan the Tory ranger rolled head over foot behind Secord. Another twirled about just to his side, clutching his arm.

An uncontrollable sense of panic raced through Secord's veins. He raised his rifle and fired blindly at the tree before turning and scattering into the trees opposite the clearing.

Elliot and Terry ignored the ball thudding into the center of the tree and calmly reloaded their weapons. A few more balls whizzed past them from the rifles of the few remaining Tories, but most of their number, including the Indian, scattered down the clearing or into the woods. The few remaining quickly tried reloading their weapons.

Terry stared resolutely at the paniced men, searching their faces, despite his oath. He recognized one, Moses Mount, another traitor from Wyoming, but the others remained clouded by distance and their rash movements.

"I'm ready," Elliot reported from the opposite side of the tree.

Terry looked down at his fingers instinctively going through the motions of loading his firelock while his mind and soul pondered his haunting thoughts. "Ready!" he answered Elliot's call, raising his rifle to his shoulder.

All of the Tories' eyes widened at the sound of the voices. One pulled his weapon up to his shoulder and pulled back the hammer, only to be cut down by Elliot's shot. He collapsed onto the ground to the horror of his friends. One grabbed him by the cape of his hunting shirt and his belt, roughly dragging him clear of the angry balls of the Rebel marksmen. The other wounded men hobbed along behind him, terrified and with a love of life fueling their hasty steps. Two Tories stood firm, raising their weapons to fire back at the Rebels to cover their wounded comrades' retreat.

Terry leveled his rifle on one of them and fired, sending him reeling about and tumbling to the ground.

Elliot let out a loud huzza at the shot. "It's a turkey shoot for sure!" he screamed, quickly reloading his own piece. A ball splattered into the tree just by his head, sending splinters into his cheek. "No," he muttered, raising his rifle to his shoulder to fire at the last Tory dragging his wounded comrade down the clearing, vainly trying to gain distance before the Rebels reloaded. "It's a damn Tory turkey shoot!" His eye tainted with a slight trickle of blood, he aimed and fired nonetheless. The ball cut a scrub oak in twain just to the side of the retreating Tory.

The Tory looked back, his wide-eyes betraying his absolute fear. Still, he tightened his grip on the cape of his wounded comrade's hunting shirt and dragged him along, cursing, but not abandoning the man.

"You ready or what?" Elliot asked Terry, wiping his eye free of the blood. He fumbled with a cartridge, cursing the trickle of blood flowing into his eye. "Fell the rat before he escapes!"

Terry took carefull aim at the wide-eyed Tory, seeing in his eyes many a peaceful day hunting and fishing along the banks of the Susquehanna in his youth. Many a trap had been layed between the two. Many a wrestling match. Many a meal enjoyed by both of them prepared by the hands of their dear mother. They had grown and lived together, sharing all the cold winters by the hearth, and many a summer's day swimming in the creeks and rivers. They had courted the same women and stood beside each other at weddings. They had grown through life together.

Now it came to this. Brother against brother. Oh, what would their mother say if this hand pulled the trigger and released the ball that cut down her son, even if he did betray her? Wars do not last forever. How is one to mend the broken hearts left behind in its wake by such acts of pure vengeance? How is one to live with himself?

"Fire, damn it, before he escapes!" Elliot screamed from the other side of the tree. He raised his own weapon and fumbled to prime the pan through the blood trickling into his eye.

Terry clenched his finger against the trigger. All of the innocence of his youth flashed before his eyes in a great puff of white smoke exploding from the end of his rifle. Another blast sounded from the opposite side of the tree, adding to the smoke. He blinked, waiting for it to clear and lowered his rifle, peering into the clearing. The back of the wounded ranger disappeared into the brush by the side of the clearing. A hat still spun in the wild rye grass of the clearing behind him.

"You just missed the rat!" Elliot said. "But you took the hat right off his head! I could swear I saw him wet his britches!" He leaned against the tree, put another cartridge to his lips and bit off the top of it. "Best load," he said to Terry, who stood deathly still by the treeside.

Terry nodded and slowly loaded his piece, all the while watching the clearing in awe.

"We wounded a few," Elliot said with pride. "They felt Wyoming lead for sure and I reckon they durst not come back for more!"

"Yes, they felt it at that," Terry said, proud of knowing he could perform his duty no matter what the circum-stances. Finally, the answer to a question which plagued him every since his brother's defection to the enemy rang true. He mused over the bridge in the soul from sense of duty to conscience, from soldier to civilian, and wished this war to end before another such test tortured his soul. He knew many shared his wish, but the war loomed far in front of them, overshadowing any thoughts of the future and that long ago time of peace. Too many scars and open wounds remained for it to ever truly heal, he thought.

"Best get back to the fighin' proper," Elliot said, ripping a length of cloth from his ragged hunting shirt. He handed it to Terry. "Bind my head?" he asked. "One of them just missed me, struck the tree and splinters got me."

Terry took the cloth, neatly tying it around his partner's head. The fury of the battle intensified to their rear, hastening his efforts to bind the wound. "Can you see to shoot?" he asked.

Elliot wiped the blood from his eye with his sleeve and smiled. "Damn right I can!" he answered. "And I intend to, this ain'y over yet! Don't you hear that storm? It's the worst of all, the storm of war!"

"Yes," Terry said. "And I feel it a might bit in my soul."

A rustle to their rear brought both of the men's rifles up and ready for action. They lowered them in relief at the sight of a great elk cresting the hillside behind them. It strode a few steps forward and stopped, sensing the men. It let out a snort and huffed away into the forest.

"There goes meat for a whole winter," Elliot said, shaking his head. Both of the men let out a sigh of relief and prepared to trot back to their company when another beast appeared in the same place the elk vacated a moment ago. This beast bore a stern-faced soldier on its back. It trod painstakingly up the hillside, purely exhausted and played-out, but forced on by its determined master. The man on its back lowered his pistol, recognizing the two men. He turned on his mount and waved down the slope.

A dozen or so men ran up the hillside, barely pausing to give a nod to the Wyoming men. A half dozen Light Horse rode along side of them. Both Elliot and Terry stared oddly at arrows sticking in some of the horses' flank muscles. They bobbed with each movement of the muscles, appearing as some grotesque ornaments of battle.

"You think they would have the decency to pluck those arrows out," Terry said under his breath at the fast moving group weaving through the trees.

"They would if'n it wouldn't cause them to bleed so," Elliot said. "If they yanked them now, while they're still at work, the blood would pour from them and bleed them out in no time. Have to do it when they're calm and out of this. It's the only way."

"Do you reckon we should join them?" Terry asked. "Look's like they're trying to gain the rear."

Another rush of movement to their left caught their eye before Elliot responded. They recognized the men moving among the trees immediately. "There's our lot," Elliot said, "we best get back to them, for it appears the tide of battle is turning and we're all going to strike to their left and rear!"

Both men trotted to rejoin their ranks, eager to strike again at their brazen enemy, confident this time victory lie with them. This fight they had to win, or certain death awaited them all, and each man seemed to sense it. Thus, both Elliot and Terry muttered a quick prayer under their breaths, beseeching God in all his mercy to deliver them from this macabre place and back to their homes fifty miles below on the Susquehanna, and away from this nightmare.

Chapter Fifty Six

Captain-Lieutenant Sweeney counted the moments under his breath, hoping he allowed enough time for Spalding to place his men on the flanks of the enemy and to his rear. The fire to their front increased, driving them back a few rods in spite of Hartley's and Murray's covering fire from the ridge. Even Spalding's men lost a little ground, despite their bold efforts and staunch example of the brave lieutenant in their charge. Upon each rush of the enemy he led his men in a bold countercharge, driving them back, only to have them lunge at them again in a few moments.

After a particulary hard rush Sweeney knew he had no more time. A quick, sharp, and simultaneous click turned his worried eyes about. He heard it before on the battlefield. It always brought chills down his spine. He stared at the sea of bayonets now glistening beneath the tapestry of nature's beauty on the ridge. The gold, red, and orange leaves somehow added to the desperation of the action. His wary eye followed the line of men on the ridge until they locked with eyes of equal determination. Knowing it to be too late to send a runner scampering up the hill by the increasing wails and whoops to his front; he found his answer in Colonel Hartley's cold eyes. Charge!

He raised his sword high, ready to order an all out charge when new and somehow more distinct war whoops sounded to his left. Along with them a new burst of fire poured into the enmy's flank, sending them falling back in confusion. Sweeney peered through the clearing smoke at the line of men emerging from nowhere on his left.

He immediately recognized the three men hooting

and yelling in front of the line. A smile grew across his face at Captains Boone and Brady, along with Lieutenant King. He looked up the ridge to Hartley, who apparently saw them also, for he waved his sword madly over his head yelling "Drive them! Drive them! Drive them into the river!"

Sweeney let out a great war whoop of his own and swung his sword forward. Drawing a deep breath he stepped in front of the line and yelled "Charge! Charge! Charge the *Copperheads*!"

His war whoop echoed along the line like a contagion, joining the already screaming men of Hawkins, Brady, and King. Hartley's and Murray's men joined the whooping advance, spilling down the ridge and rushing steadily into the enemy's faultering line. Jenkins' men added their own cries down the line to Spalding and on to Stoddert with the Light Horse.

Wide and anxious Indian eyes peered all about, suddenly realizing their exposed position. "*OONAH*! *OONAH!*" rang down their ranks-their unmistakable call for retreat. They spilled from the swale like a liquid through a funnel into the gap in the rear between Captains Spalding's and Stoddert's men.

Hartley spurred his horse ahead, galloping through his victorious troops, swinging his sword wildly over his head, beseeching them to press forward with all due hatse lest the enemy pour through the rear of the trap. The troops answered his call, running pell-mell into the retreating red men, slashing, clubbing, and shooting those unfortunate enough to be caught by the impetuosity of their charge.

To the rear Spalding yelled for his men to close up and join to the men to their right, but to no avail. The exhaustion and fatigue of their forced marches finally caught up with them, slowing them just enough to get but a few passing shots into the trees at the painted devils. The Light Horse-their mounts totally exhausted as well their riders-dashed in between the scattering red men in the trees, firing their pistols and swinging their sabers at the confused braves.

Stoddert, his men barely settled before the rush of retreating red men, fired and fought a few luckless souls, but most slipped through their scattered ranks. Alas, they faired no better than the Wyoming Rangers, but gained a certain satisfaction upon witnessing the brazen and previously undefeated warriors of the Six Nations scury away in defeat. Their victory could not be denied. They gained the field of battle. They drove the enemy.

The report of rifles and muskets soon faded along the mountainside above the mighty Susquehanna. On its high meadows men lay squirming in agony. Among its ancient trees brave warriors, both white and red, breathed their last.

Nonetheless, a wave of relief rushed over the exhausted victors of the battle.

A wave of disbelief ran through their vanquished foe.

After the last report of a firelock most of the victorious Rebels collapsed in exhaustion, both man and beast. They sat among the debris of battle, staring at the lifeless souls littering the field. Bloody and torn skull caps lay aside tri-cornered hats and wide brimmed slouch hats. Haversacks and pouches decorated with glittering pieces of silver and colorful porcupine quills speckled the ground. Broken firelocks sat side by side broken spears. Bent and broken swords lay in the grass along with tomahawks. The red color of blood peppered the leaves and matted grass. All had been a hubbub just a moment before; now all sat still and quiet as death hovered over the field of battle searching for one more victim among the groaning wounded.

Hartley slowly rode among the troops, too exhausted

to issue any orders at the moment. They had done enough, he told himself, let them catch their breaths, they at least deserved that courtesy.

He, of course felt disappointment that a lack of coordination allowed the enemy to escape, but they had barely done so, he reassured himself. Still, his mind played with the thought of driving them into the river. There they could have shot them like sitting ducks as the Tories and Indians had done to the men of Wyoming in the late battle. But no more could be asked of such men. They had trudged over impossible ground at the rate of twenty to thirty miles a day. Few could match that achievement and he knew it.

He sagged down in the saddle and watched Hooker Smith already tending to the wounded, directing men to carry this one or that one away, and to comfort others. He looked to the curious eyes of the preacher and his throng of women and children watching from the ridge. Their eyes bore a sense of wonder and disgust. Still no one, save Smith, spoke.

Captain Carberry rode his tired mount to his side and plopped down from the saddle, careful to avoid the arrows still sticking in the horse's flanks. "We did it," he reported. "They are on their way to Hell or Tioga, and they aren't looking back!" He collapsed to his knees and breathed deeply.

"Very well, Mr. Carberry," Hartley said. "You and your horsemen have behaved very admirably, as have you all. Every man performed well this day and I will be sure to mention you all most favorably in my report to Congress."

Boone, Brady, and King approached him and dipped their hats to him in salute.

"It is good to see you gentlemen have recovered from your lameness," he said, letting a slight smile stretch across his face. "Gentlemen you and your men showed up at the precise moment you were needed and in the exact spot you were needed. Your vigor added to this victory, and I myself, am most grateful."

All three men nodded their heads to him.

"Now," Hartley continued, "if you would be so kind as to find a place in your canoes for the wounded, I would be most grateful."

"Certainly, sir," Captain Brady said.

"Very well, see Doctor Smith, he shall direct you." He bowed his head slightly to the men doffing their hats to him and rode back to the men staggering into the field from the rear. He rode to Stoddert and doffed his own hat to the man before he could salute. "Mr. Stoddert, you sir, deserve the esteem of your country!" He bowed his head to the man and also to Captain Spalding. "Capatin Spalding your exertions shall be duly noted in my report to headquaters. You all acquitted yourselves with reputation. You all behaved well to a man!"

Spalding bowed his head to the colonel and rubbed his unshaven chin. "We best get moving, Colonel," he said. "We may have run off this lot but the whole Six Nations may be about Chemung now."

"Yes, quite," Hartley said. He looked around at the played-out men and horses and muttered, "Do you think they're up to it?" under his breath.

"They have to be," Spalding said. Stoddert bobbed his head in agreement.

"Very well, assemble the men and we shall be off, there are still some fifty miles between us and relative safety. There certainly is no safety here. We shall have to let the dead bury the dead, I'm afraid."

"Yes sir," both men said, doffing their hats in salute.

"By the way Captain Spalding," Colonel Hartley said,

pulling back on the reins of his mount to momentarily face the frontier officer, "does this place have a name?"

"Yes sir," Spalding quickly answered, gazing about the field of death. "We call it Indian Hill* 'round these parts, sir."

"Yes, quite appropriately named to say the least," the colonel answered with a nod, reining his mount around one of the dead painted men. "Quite!"

The battle had been won but the gauntlet still lay wide open between them and safety, and every man, woman, and child knew it from the preacher to young Lord Butler and George Palmer Ransom, drummer and teenage son of the late Captain Ransom killed in the Battle of Wyoming.

This day the young soldier struck a blow of revenge for his father. One brave lay dead on the field, felled by his ball. But this day, this victory, would not be complete until they reached Wyoming, nor would his thirst for revenge be quenched until more fell by his hand. He felt it. He knew it.

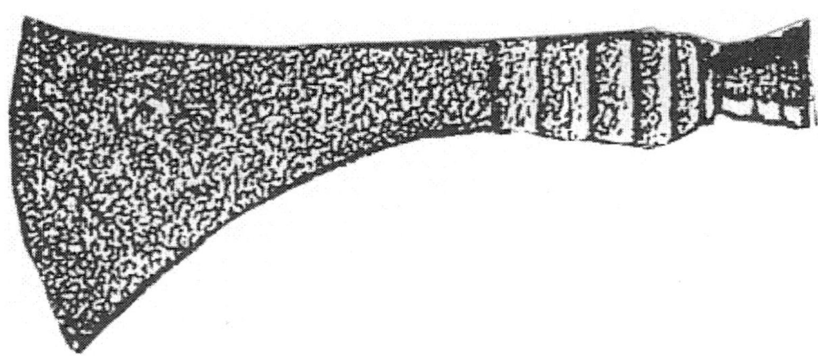

**Note: Indian Hill is located near present Laceyville, Pennsylvania.*

Chapter Fifty Seven

"Van der Lippe's farm," a Wyoming scout reported to Colonel Hartley. The colonel leaned against the pommel of his saddle and stared at the abandoned farmstead spreading out in front of them. Though the cabin sat burned to ashes part of the barn roof remained held up by a few charred, but solid beams. A few of the outbuildings appeared serviceable also.

Hartley leaned back in his saddle and gazed at the weary souls trodding along the trail and to the moon shinning brightly in the early evening sky above them. "We shall make camp here this night," he announced. "By my recollection we have come some thirteen or fourteen miles on this day's march. With two shirmishes and a pitched battle, I say we have come far enough." He threw one leg slowly over his saddle and gently slid to the ground. His aching feet burned. "Yes," he said, "we shall definitely camp here this night. One of you scouts signal the canoes to pitch here for the night. It shall give Smith time to treat the wounded, also. Tell him of our plans."

"Yes sir," the scout said, rambling off to the river-bank.

"Captain Bush," Hartley said, turning his head to the officer sagging in the saddle behind him. The officer lifted his head up and pushed his hat from over his eyes. "See that a strong guard is posted."

The tired officer nodded his head and barked some orders to the ranks stumbling behind him. Two sergeants loudly repeated his order. Under the unforgiving eye of a staunch corporal several reluctant men marched from the ranks to the perimeter of the farm. The corporal promptly posted them, giving each a stern look warning them to remain vigilant.

The remaining column of men, women, children, pack-horses, livestock, and oxen, slowly spread out on the fields around Van der Lippe's farm. Women lifted sleeping children down from perches on top of pack-horses. Other women carrying children in their arms slid down from the backs of moaning oxen.

The Light Horse gathered near the barn, immediately constructing a makeshift corral to tend to their wounded mounts. Arrows still protruded from several of their flanks. They neighed and whinnied while saddles and blankets slid from their sore backs.

Fires promptly lit the entire plain. Soon their flames danced in the night sky, sending great bursts of sparks high into it. Their crackle brought a sense of comfort and security to all.

Hartley walked up to one of the fires staring blankly into its flames, his mind full of thoughts of the day and the day to come ahead. He barely noticed Colonel Denison walking up to him.

Denison eased his rifle down in his hands and took off his hat, wiping his sweaty brow with his arm. Exhausted, he plopped down next to the fire and joined Hartley. His eyes followed Hartley's to the flames.

"Wondrous, isn't it?" Hartley asked, rolling an eye to Denison. Such reflection on the mysteries of life eased his mind of the troubles of the day.

Denison said nothing. He too let his mind drift into the heavens with the flames. The face of a lad standing on the other side of the fire tore his eyes from the flames. He raised an eyebrow and asked "What is it Lord?"

"Sirs," Lord Butler said, easing his way around the fire. He held something loosely wrapped in a cloth. "I have your ration of beef." he added, passing the cloth to Denison who slowly unwrapped it.

Looking to the fire he scratched his head, finally deciding he hungered too much to attempt to reheat the boiled meat. Besides, taste mattered not on expeditions such as these; only nourishment. He ripped off a piece of the meat and immediately gnawed on it. Tearing off another piece, he handed it to Hartley.

"I am sorry but the whiskey is spent," Lord said. "But no one has gotten sick from the water, yet, that is." He handed the men his canteen. "Filled it from the well," he explained. "It should be good. And by the way, all the flour is gone, too."

Neither of the men said a word. Their eyes blank and empty, they continued pondering the flames and gnawing on the tough meat.

Lord noticed their fascination and cleared his throat. "Mr. Priestly has a new theory on '*dephlogisticated air*'. He refutes the theory that combustion is accompanied by the realease of phlogiston. His work on the mystery of airs is quite interesting. It is a wonder what such great minds as he, and his friend Doctor Franklin, are dwelling on these days."

Hartley looked up from his tough meat and slowly to Denison. "Colonel Butler makes sure his children are well read, does he not?" he said.

"Quite," Denison said, shaking his head at the lad. "To us it is just flames, lad," he said. "Some are content to leave the mysteries of God to God. But others fear not to seek his light in them. I say let them search, my day is too filled with life to dwell on such matters."

Lord smiled and bowed his head, graciously departing the fire to attend his duties.

"He does a fine job as Quartermatser," Hartley said. "I'll give him that. As to Mr. Priestly and the great Doctor Franklin I shall take him at his word." They both chuckled. The sounds and groans of wounded men and frightened horses neighing soon quelled their sense of humor. Both men tore and gnawed at the incredibly tough meat and stared into the flames again. "I must say I am quite anxious to finally meet Colonel Butler face to face," he said, swallowing a huge chunk of meat. "The page relays a man's thoughts, but alas, man is more than his thoughts alone. I look forward to meeting one whom sired such a fine lad. I shall also be glad in many other ways to finally reach Camp Westmoreland."

"I shall also be most glad, and I must say relieved to finally end this trek through the wilderness," Denison said. "Most assuredly," he added, lifting Lord's canteen up to his nose and sniffing its contents. Shrugging his shoulders he took a long drink from it.

"Tastes fine," he said, passing the canteen to Hartley.

"We drank worse than this in Canada," Hartley said, taking a long drink. An ear splitting yell and a series of curses gave him such a start he jiggled the canteen and jerked it from his mouth, dropping it to the ground. He bent down, looking over his shoulder to the makeshift shelter Hooker Smith had constructed to perform his duty as surgeon.

Denison stopped eating and peered back at the convulsing man held down by three other stout men while Hooker Smith stood over him. Another man forced a thick piece of tough leather between the patient's teeth, pleading with him to bite down tight on it. The man's terrified eyes glowed in the eerie light, alive and full of intense fear. His cries crept through his clenched teeth.

A glint of yellow sparkled from the bloody blade of a saw shaking in Hooker Smith's hands. The doctor cursed and yelled for someone to wipe the sweat from his brow. Cursing and grabbing firmly on the man's leg with one hand he steadied the blade and performed the necessary task amid muffled cries. The pale yellow light reflected in his grim eyes. He narrowed them in the light, full of intent to perform his duty.

The leather suddenly slipped from the man's mouth, letting all of his anguish ride on his loud cries. All became silent from the spine-tingling wails.

Hooker Smith's curses paled in the man's cries.

Finally, they forced the leather back into the man's mouth, relieving all in the camp.

"There is always the surgeon's butchery after battle," Hartley said, letting his hand fall limp with the meat. He sat down and lifted his knees up to his chest. Bowing his head in between them he let the meat fall from his hand. On a harsh breath he whispered a prayer.

Denison, suddenly losing his appetite as well, rolled over and faced away from the surgeon's table. He stared at the dancing flames before him, thinking of the slain souls they left behind on the battlefield today. Listening to the man's tortured cries and pleas, he could not help but wonder who were the luckier; the dead or the wounded?

Chapter Fifty Eight

Crowds of people gathered on the green at Wilkes-Barre, anxiously listening to the music of the approaching column. Colonel Butler ordered all of his men to form into two ranks on opposite sides of the road and waited patiently in between them, pacing back and forth and fidgeting with the hilt of his sword. His eyes remained locked on the road. His scouts reported the approach of the column two days ago and his imagination flashed with visions of their hardships. But they won a major victory, burned four villages, and came back with tons of plunder and livestock. Quite an achievment to say the least, especially since every foot of the march lay in enemy territory for the most part. In fact, he had doubled the scouts and patrols in anticipation of the column's return. He would not fully breathe easy until they stood on the green before him. He looked to the cannon on the north end of the green, making certain the officer commanding it remained alert and ready for action.

The officer noticed his commander's stern gaze and barked a few expletives at his men. All stood taller after being dressing down by the officer. After he had completed his tongue-lashing he looked to Butler, who nodded his head in confirmation of his actions. The sharp banging of drums and shrill of fifes turned his head back to the road. The haggard, but proud column, finally marched into view.

Hartley sat tall in saddle just ahead of the muscians. His eyes stared straight ahead and his stiff neck held his head high. Men in ragged and torn blue regimentals closely followed the muscians, led by the always regal and immaculate Captain Bush. His regimental, cocked hat, and trousers stood out among the men-including Hartley-for showing little of the tears and soil so prevalent on the others' clothing.

Bright eyed civilians, liberated and glad of it, gazed upon their counterparts of the wilderness post with a strange fascination. The Wyoming civilians stared back for a moment, but most turned their eyes to the cattle, oxen, horses, and pack-horses loaded with plunder. Many clamored along side of the plunder and cattle, trying in vain to recognize any of it as their own. The gruff actions of the Light Horse detailed to guard the plunder and herd the animals kept their fingers at a distance. A few harsh words announced their ire, but the sight of the proud Wyoming men marching with their chests jutted out and rifles held tightly at their shoulders turned their critical words into a chorus of cheers. Captain Spalding graciously doffed his hat to the praise and thanks poured onto his men.

A voice from the river announced the arrival of a fleet of canoes, turning many eyes to it. A few anxious merchants, chief among them Mathias Hollenback, darted down to meet the canoes at the landing. He greeted and shook each of the men's hands departing the canoes and offered deep sympathy to the wounded souls lying prone in the canoe bottoms. Between his words of praise he managed to drop in a few hints as to the value of the plunder. The answers he received brought a great smile to his face which quickly faded when one of the men told him with a fine smirk all could be obtained at auction, by the highest bidder. Hollenback burst into a rage, only quelled by the request of some of the men asking him to help lift some of the wounded from the canoes. After helping with a few of the moaning and suffering men, his tongue fell silent of complaints.

Mixed emotions followed the men of the expedition into camp. Many of the Wyoming people broke out kegs of whiskey, rum, and ale, of which each man gladly partook in consuming his fair share, but their haggard and careworn faces quelled any sense of celibration. They seemed just glad to be alive and free of the torturous marches and threat of Indians and Tories pouncing on them from any direction and at any moment. Most sank down onto their blankets around fires soon after setting up their camp. They gladly accepted the many gifts of food offered to them from the grateful citizenry and the garrison.

Captain Bush even declined an invitation to dance, sighting his saddle sore backside as the main reason for his polite refusal. Disappointed women, newly arrived and hearing of the light-footed officer, graciously accepted his reason, with the stern promise of a dance the next night.

Hartley watched the crowd of disappointed women and chuckled, along with Nathan Denison. He noticed Colonel Butler turn his nose to it all. He eagerly shook the man's hand upon finally meeting him, but seemed a bit put-off with his no-nonsense manner. The man immediately asked for a full briefing of the whole expedition and seemed indifferent to the praise of his son, young Lord Butler.

In spite of it all Hartley accepted his invitation to use his quarters for the night and found the man most gracious when not under the eyes of his men. They dined, drank, and talked of small things, easing Hartley's mind of its troubles.

As Butler threw the last log on the fire and graciously

offered a last toast, his eyes drew tight with the same dour look of earlier in the day. "For all your accomplishments, which are in themselves great and deserve much praise, I fear you have only given the Six Nations a strong slap when a full beating is called for. A slap may sting for a bit, but does little to hurt the foe, it only fuels their resolve, if anything." He sat his mug down on the table and bowed his head to the exhausted colonel before walking over to the door. Lifting the latch, he stopped. Looking back over his shoulder he said, "I fear if Congress does not act by sending more reinforcements quickly they may have their frontier much lower than they expect." With that, he locked eyes with Hartley before slowly lifting the latch and excusing himself for the night.

A man of deep insight, Hartley thought, plopping down on a featherbed, and of true words. Despite the comfort of the bed after sleeping on the rough ground with barely a blanket to cover him from the rain and cold, Butler's words echoed through his mind. Yes, he thought to himself, if the enemy should take Wyoming, New York, Pennsylvania, and New Jersey will realize its importance too late. He reconsidered his own his plans he decided upon after the battle. Butler was right. It was not enough. He hoped Washington true to his word, and be quick to dispatch a larger expedition to this region. No, he would not depart for Philadelphia as he had planned. Much danger still lay in these mountains, hills, and vales.

He would stay until it passed. Conscience demanded it of any man of honor. But at the same time his tired body made him realize mortal man only had so much to give.

Chapter Fifty Nine

The men settled into a state of calm for the last two days. Backs and feet welcomed the brief respite. Among the women hints of faint smiles gradually began to replace the dour looks of fear so prevalent on their faces as of late. Children, overjoyed by the new sense of calm, started playing again. Their chuckles and laughter once again resounded around Wilkes-Barre. Eyes looked away from war and to the domestic pleasures of life. The harvest occupied many conversations. Optimistic hints of planting for the next season ran among certain circles.

A faint ray of hope began to shine, and all welcomed it, though every heart still stopped beating upon hearing any suspicious sound and every eye darted to any sudden movement in the brush. All reassured themselves and each other against their apprehension, though. Colonel Butler's scouts would be sure to alert the settlement upon the first sign of trouble. Surely the enemy would not be so bold as to strike against these men in arms, now rested and well fed, who had given them such a thrashing in their own country. No, per-haps they had won at least a brief respite from the raids and constant harrassment.

New praise grew for Hartley's little army on this almost full second day of peace. He accepted it in the spirit of hope shared by all, but deep down inside his soul he still cast a wary eye to the surrounding mountains, as did all.

But on this bright morning all seemed well, enough so he gracefully accepted Colonel Bulter's invitation to stroll along the green. The two men slowly walked along the river, mindful of the pistols in their belts. Nonetheless, Hartley attempted to lighten the mood by sharing pleasantries and small talk.

But Butler seemed anxious, not of the lurking threat of the enemy, but rather of a something altogether different. As other minds thought of the harvest, planting and such, his mind fluttered with a grandiose dream as of late. Reaching a fine and clear spread of green grass he marched boldly about, taking wide steps as if surveying the land. Hartley grudgingly tried to keep pace with the man's spirited walk but finally stopped, letting Butler take a few more great strides before saying, "Yes, it would be a fine place for a new fort."

Butler's eye lit up at the words. He turned, stretching his arms in a wide arc. "I am so glad you, a man of vision, see what I see," he said. He took a few more steps to one side, spreading his arms wide again. "Here shall stand the walls, solid, two rows of fine logs laying horizontally with a space between, six to eight feet, filled with well tamped down earth!" His eyes rose up the imaginary walls as if they already stood. Knowing his determination by the glitter in the man's eyes, Hartley had no doubt this vision would become a reality. He walked up next to him and nodded his head.

"Yes," Butler said, "thus formed the walls shall be carried to a full height of seven or eight feet! And all around the inclosure formed by the wall, a platform, or bench, will stand, enabling our men to deliver their fire over top the walls. All around the outside shall be a ditch, beyond that, an abattis, formed by setting firm the tops of pitch-pine trees, trimmed and sharpened by the axe, pointing outwards." He took a few more steps and waved his arms in a circle. "Here, an embrasure, along with several all around the walls, from which cannon may be fired! All the corners of the fort shall be rounded, as to give a sweeping arc of fire, and flank all sides! Inside the enclosure, which should be about a half acre, barracks for the garrison."

He stopped once more and strode to the southeast, leaving Hartley standing and watching wide-eyed at his enthusiastic vision of the new fort. "Here shall run a timbered, and thus protected, access to a copious spring of water at the margin of the river, just as Forty Fort had." He took a deep breath and gazed up the river. "Two small blockhouses shall be constructed on the upper side of the fort, across the plain, to shelter those who cannot be accomindated in the fort proper." He took a step back toward Hartley and stared with sparkling eyes at the whole sweeping vision as if it already existed. "This shall be done before this month is finished. I know these men, my men, they've all strong backs and are up to any challenge. That they are. Besides, they know it may be paramount to our very survival, what with the lackluster response of Congress."

"Oh," Hartley said, "I assure you our greatest minds are considering the Wyoming question at this very moment. Such a great movement as they have planned shall take time. My little slap, as you call it, shall be nothing compared to the sledgehammer blow coming, I do most earnestly assure you, fine sir."

Butler looked at him with a raised eyebrow. He only hoped they survived to see the day of which the good colonel spoke. Both of the men stared at one another, gauging the sincerity of each other's words.

The report of several rifles abruptly broke their stare. Both men shuddered and gazed across the river. War whoops echoed over the water. Screams of terror followed the whoops from the far bank, soon joined by women's cries of concern from the camp.

"My God, my God, they're back!" Hartley gasped.

"Who did you send over there?"

"No one," Butler said. "Whoever they are, they are not of this garrison."

Hartley blanched. He had been too lenient for the past two days, letting his men roam and mingle with whoever and wherever. Now some poor unfortunates paid the price.

"I have standing orders none are to go to the west side of the river," Butler said, starting to turn back to the camp.

Hartley turned with him, meeting the officers and troops rushing to meet them. "What is going on across the river?" he asked before any of them could speak.

"Four of Captain Murray's men crossed the river!" Captain Stoddert reported.

"Crossed the river?" Butler asked. "What in heaven's name for?"

"Wild potatoes," Stoddert answered.

Hartley rolled his eyes, remembering the others killed outside Fort Muncy on the same quest. These damn Dutchmen and their lust for wild potatoes, he thought. Will they ever learn? "Follow me at the long trot!" he ordered, running up the riverbank. All of the troops and officers filed behind him. Upon reaching the crest of the bank they spread into a strong defensive line. All scanned the opposite bank for any sign of the men.

"You left a guard at the camp?" Butler asked Captain Spalding, who searched the opposite riverbank intensily with a spyglass.

"Of course, sir," Spalding said, keeping his eye to the glass. His hand immediately pointed to the opposite bank. "There!" he said, waving to the troops nearest him. "Stand ready!"

Both Hartley and Butler stared in the direction he pointed, along with all of the eyes of the troops.

A bush rustled on the opposite bank. Dozens of rifles and muskets leveled on the movement.

"Hold your fire!" Hartley ordered. "We know not if it's friend or foe! Just stand fast!"

A man burst from the bushes, spilling down the bank in a tustle of flailing arms and legs. Bareheaded and seemingly unarmed, he quickly stumbled to his feet. His eyes grew wide and he cast a horrified gaze over his shoulder before plunging into the swirling Susquehanna.

"Get to the canoes!" Butler ordered some men near him. "Get out to him before he's swept downstream!"

Several men darted down the bank to the canoe landing. Pouring into the canoes, they paddled madly into the river, rushing to the terrified and exhausted man smimming for his dear life.

The man plunged one arm after another into the water, his feet kicking up a storm of water in his wake. He kept swimming headlong toward the opposite shore, either too terrified to stop, or not hearing the pleas of his rescuers to stop so they could pull him into one of the canoes.

He swam past the first canoe to the amazement of the officer within it. The officer bent down, barely missing the man's shoulder. His fingers ran across a fresh red spot on the crown of the man's skull, trailing trickles of red in the water. Absolute terror shone in the man's bulging eyes.

The officer leaned back in the upsetting canoe, leveling it again to the relief of the men manning the paddles. He stared in horror at his fingers. What hell is at play here? he mumbled to himself. War cries raised his eyes to the approaching riverbank. "Drop those paddles and grab your muskets!" he ordered. He called to the next canoe to pluck the man from the water and turned his eyes toward the scrub brush on the far bank. The stark and absolute terror in the man's eye flooded his mind's eye. Whatever caused it lay in wait there, waiting to pounce and strike. Their number could be legion or a half dozen. Whatever their number, these cold hearted killers waited just ahead of he and his men in their rickety birch bark canoes. They would not get them without a fight, though, he promised himself, drawing a pistol from his belt.

A call from behind broke his gaze at the riverbank. He looked back to the other canoes. Men waved them back and pointed to the far shore, shouting they had the man. Louder yells from the men watching from the far bank distinctly ordered him back across the river.

The men immediately replied to the order from without word from their anxious officer, dropping their muskets and regaining their paddles.

Nonetheless, the officer nodded at the paddles sinking into the water and leveled his pistol at the bank until the canoe turned about in the swirling waters. His heartbeat stopped for the blinking of an eye from a glimpse of red paint and feathers through the brush. He lifted his pistol, intent on firing if he caught sight of the hellish demon again, even though he knew the devil to be well out of the range of his weapon.

"What?" the man grasping the rear paddle asked, increasing the rapidity of his movements upon noticing the glint in the officer's eye.

"Nothing," the officer muttered. "Just keep paddling!"

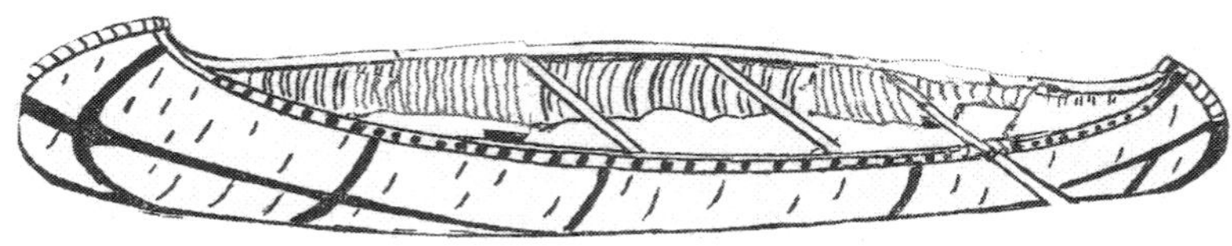

Chapter Sixty

"Poor man," Hartley said, watching the trembling man's lips trying to mouth an explanation of what he experienced across the river. Butler stood staunchly beside him, quietly listening to the man mutter in German. Captain Murray bent over the muttering man, trying to take in all his words while Hooker Smith tended to the wound atop his head.

"Well, I don't know Dutch," Smith said, rising from the bed, "but it'll be best to let his wound air. He's been creased by a ball along his arm, as well. He'll have plenty to tell his grandchildren after this is all done and over, though. He'll make it just fine, he will at that."

The man ceased muttering and turned a grateful eye to Smith. He swallowed hard and managed to mouth a thank you before collapsing into the bed from pure exhaustion.

"Just doing my job, is all," Smith said with a smug smile. He collected his things and passed the two high ranking officers. "He'll be bald, but he'll live, there's worse things that could have befallen him." With that he excused himself and marched to the other beds in his makeshift hospital.

Murray slowly rose from the bed also, reassuring the man in his native tongue. The man's eye opened wide. Tears streamed from his eyes and he muttered, "Mien Goot! Mien Goot!" after the officer. Another of Murray's men promptly took his place, reassuring the distraught man.

"Says they came out of nowhere, a full dozen of the rats, and struck them down before they could blink an eye," Murray reported to the officers. Both nodded. Hartley nervously rubbed his chin. Butler fanned his hand for the captain to continue. "He was keeping guard a few paces away from the others while they dug up the potatoes. The ball for him only creased his arm and he spun about. The savages in their bloodlust fell upon his luckless fellows, stabbing and firing point blank into their bodies, screaming like demons all the while. He rose, fired, and hit a large one in the shoulder. The big Indian barely moved in spite of the force of the shot. The other Indians swarmed down on him but the big one called them off, must've been some chief or somebody of importance, for they obeyed him. As they parted he marched through them with his war club raised and struck him down. He held up his rifle to shield the first blow, but the chief was so angry the blow splintered both the club and rifle. He stood with the two pieces in his shaking hands when the chief struck him down with another club quickly passed to him. All He saw was stars and then he felt the cold earth beneath him. He felt the Indian's knee on the small of his back and a shearing sensation to his head. He said he heard a terrible ripping sound all along with the sensation, and realized it was the sound of his own scalp being torn from his head. The chief took a few steps back and held his bloody hair up, yelling and hooting for all get out when he saw his chance and bolted. The next thing he remembers is being pulled from the water. A hell of an ordeal to say the least."

"Indeed," Hartley and Butler both said at the same time.

"Thank you Captain," Hartley said. "You may return to your men. Tell your men, and all the volunteers from Northumberland, along with Captain Bush's company, to cook three days' provisions for the march to Fort Augusta." He pulled his watch chain and looked at the time piece in his palm, ignoring Colonel Butler's stunned gaze. "Be ready to march at four o'clock this day."

"Yes sir," Murray said, doffing his hat. He promptly turned and trotted toward his men, barking orders for all to hear. Surprised eyes all shot to the hospital before the booming voice of a sergeant scolded them to get about their duties.

Hartley put the watch back into his pocket and raised his lower lip. He rolled an eye to Butler. "I shall leave half my regiment here with you, sir," he said. He slowly stepped from the hospital and gazed sullenly at the mountains. "I am responsible for all the posts from Nescopeck to Muncy, and from thence to the head of the Penn's Valley. All of this vast frontier, from Wyoming to the far Allegheny Mountains. I have my little regiment, your men, along with two classes of Lancaster and Bucks County militia, barely enough, to say the least. If the Indians are bold enough to attack here, where the most men are assembled, what of the other posts spread all along the Susquehanna? I must attend to my duties sir."

Butler bowed his head, suddenly ashamed of his selfish nature. "Of course, Colonel," he said. "I understand."

"I shall return as soon as possible, Zebulon, most likely from Fort Jenkins, with provisions, cannon, and ammunition, if all goes well." He rubbed his eyes and let out a long sigh. "It is the best I can do, we must make due with the tools available. If there is an attack at Muncy or below, do not be surprised to receive orders to come to our assistance. But if not we must secure our posts for the winter. It is too late for another expedition even if we had fresh troops. "

"Of course, the snow lays two feet thick when it comes and stays well into March," Butler said. "And we shall come immediately if called, if even by snowshoe, I assure you. All are grateful for your leadership on that incredible trek through the wilderness and tremendous victory at Indian

Hill. It has done far more good than you realize. Perhaps more in men's souls than any other thing, but alas, that may be the most important thing, for in the end, all comes from the soul."

"Thank you, Zebulon."

"Of course I would have liked to accompany you, but orders kept me at this post."

"We must all obey our orders, and I appreciate your understanding, for these troubles are not over, but may be just beginning anew."

"We shall raise the new fort before the month passes, I assure you. But it may be short of proper cannon. I shall await you to solve that problem."

"And I assure you all, I shall do my damnest."

"I know you shall."

"You men of Wyoming possess much grit and raw determination. As great as any I've ever encountered and the most determined belief in our country's cause. Even General Washington has commented upon it. I've heard him with my own ears. He is as proud of the Wyoming Rangers as I am. Be strong, as you always have against the foul winds blowing from every corner of the wilderness, for I promise you others do know of your struggles. Wyoming shall not fall as long as one of you breathes, I believe that. Stand strong ye men of Wyoming! Stand strong!"

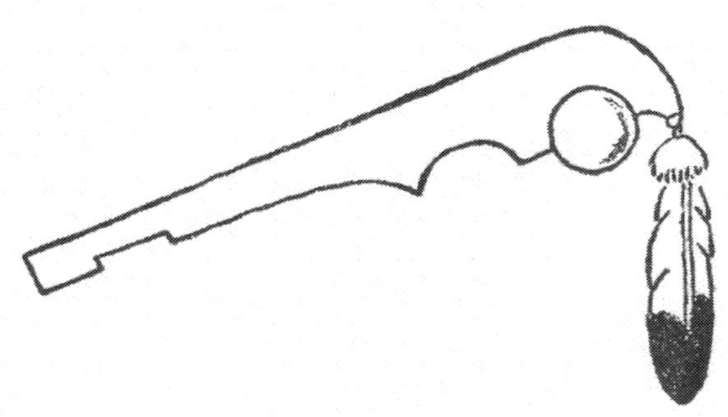

Chapter Sixty One

Chemung resounded with wails of triumph upon hearing the huge chief's boasts of slaying three Rebels and scalping a fourth. He paraded around the war post, thumping it with his war club with each new twist of his tale. Warriors whooped in delight when he raised several small hoops with hair stretched across them. He jutted out his chest proudly and pointed at the bruise and cut across his upper arm. A Bostonian's ball had grazed him but he did not even flinch when the ball struck, he bragged, adding how he fell upon the shaky white devil and fell him, lifting his scalp before his prayers to his demon God gave him the strength to run. He did not pursue him, though. He had his hair. He would claim the rest of the devil in due time. Now that he and the Seneca had arrived the shame of Indian Hill would be forgotten. The valor of his acts would not.

Gucingeratchton, brave war chief of the Seneca,

strutted through the gathering of wide-eyed braves after his declarations and to his cabin, full of himself and his brave deeds of this day. Before entering the door held open by his beautiful wife, he turned and promised another strike at the white devils soon. The honor of the Six Nations demanded it. This time none of the lying Yankees would survive. The Yankees broke their solemn word and struck at the belly of the Six Nations like the cowards they are! Word of the white chief Denison joining the march infuriated him, he proclaimed loudly, especially since the white chief had promised not to raise arms against the Six Nations ever again. He lied. And this letter written by the white chief Hartley accusing them of killing and torturing women and children at Wyoming must be addressed, as all lies must! With that he turned and disappeared into the cabin with more hoots and whoops following him.

All did not share his enthusiaism, though, among them the crestfallen Queen herself. She watched the whole spectacle with a wary eye. A fear rose in her heart. A fear that all changed forever. A fear of the might she herself had seen in the cities of the *white-eyes*. Their numbers seemed endless. Their resolve and fanatiscm made her wince. She braved a smile to the few curious eyes glancing at her before excusing herself. Turning, she strode slowly to the river. Its flowing waters always calmed her at such moments. She needed them now more than ever, she thought to herself.

Finding a grassy spot by the swirling Susquehanna she sat and watched it flow before her, wondering of the waters and of their great quest for the sea. She wished she could fling all her sorrows and concerns onto the waters and let them carry them far away. The world seemed to shrink around her and her people. No more could they freely canoe all the way down the river to the sea. No longer did the river seem a friend, but an enemy, carrying the settlements of the *white-eyes* along its banks. Oh, for the days of her youth when the vast expanse of land seemed too endless for any one people to claim for their own. The world had indeed shrank: her world at least.

A nagging feeling at the nape of her neck broke her melancholy train of thoughts. She glanced out of the corner of her eye to a woman standing patiently behind her. She did not have to turn to see her whole face to recognize her.

"*Auweni*? Oh, Lydia," she said, bowing her head to face the waters again. She fought to hold back the tears threatening to spill down her cheeks. Raising her hand she tried to slow the white woman's advance, ashamed of her tears. "*Alakqui*! You jogo," she said, "to Fort Niagara!"

Lydia stopped in her tracks and bowed her head.

"No safe for you and childs," Ester continued. "Much hatred, too much. *Quilawelelendam*!"

"Yes, I know," Lydia said, wanting to plead for her return down the river to Wyoming but knowing the fruitlessness of such a request. No one would be going down the river from Chemung but on a war footing. She looked to the river and to the great trees drooping their branches over it, sighing at the beauty of it all. She wondered just how that beauty compared to the cities marring the coastline and quickly quelled the thought. You have been too long among the savages, she scolded herself under her breath, get a hold of your thoughts!

"You been too long," Ester said, hearing her faint whisper. "I done all I can for you. Young Secord, Cyrus, going Niagara, get more provisions, you jogo with him. *Vivre vieux*!"

Lydia's eyes widened hearing the good English rolling off the Queen's tongue. In grief all things flowed more easily, she reasoned. "Yes," she said, wanting to reach out and take the Queen's hand to thank her but thinking better of it. This Indian Queen had destroyed their home and sent the men folk to who knows what hell in Canada. Now she sent her and her innocent children to the same fate. But at the same time she knew without the Queen's protection they would all have been killed or she at least separated from her children. That meant something. "Thank you!" she said on a gasp of emotion before turning away holding her hand to her cheeks to check her tears. She stopped a few steps away and turned, wishing to find better words to express her gratitude but none could pass the growing lump in her throat.

Ester heard Lydia stop and looked down to her own hands. They suddenly felt tainted with the grime and blood of vengeance. "They cry for vengeance! I have had vengeance with these very hands! Still it does little to ease the grief of my son! Much blood flowed, but none cleanses my heart of its pain! No! It will never! Jogo, dear Lydia, *par Dieu*! I hope you find Boss and be happy! Is all I can do! Jogo!"

Lydia took a few steps forward, reaching her hand down to the Queen. In the shadows on the Queen's face Lydia noticed tears streaming down her cheeks before she gruffly rubbed them away with her arm. The bells and trickets on her clothing jingled in a strange rhythm that seemed out of place.

"Jogo!" Ester demanded, waving her jingling arms behind her. "*Le mieux est l,ennemi du bien*."

"I can hear the pain of your broken heart," Lydia said on a whisper. "It flows to the waters and spreads across the very heart of the land. It weeps with your beleaguered soul. Once more I thank you, for I know you have done all in your power you could do. You are caught up in this as we all are, may God have mercy on all our souls!"

A cry of pure anguish poured from Ester's soul. She waved her arms behind her, fighting her tears to no avail. She collapsed face first into the grass, clutching it as a dear child just about to die. This land, as she knew it, as her people had known it for thousands of years, would change soon, and with that part of it would die, never to reborn but in the vague memory of its conquerors. She, nor no one, white or red, seemed able to stop it. Fear flooded her whole body. "*C'est dommage*," she cried. "*C'est fait ! Frapp'e de stupor! Hartley foius-moi le camp*!" She wept profusely for the earth and her people. One way of life had to die to make way for a new one; one she feared more than death itself. This brought a grief that pulsated through her very being as if cojoined with the trembling earth itself.

She feared nothing but death itself could ease this grief. Nothing.

This revolution, as they called it, changed all. This revolution touched all, even the very earth itself. Nothing would ever be the same in its passing. Nothing, the whole world wide.

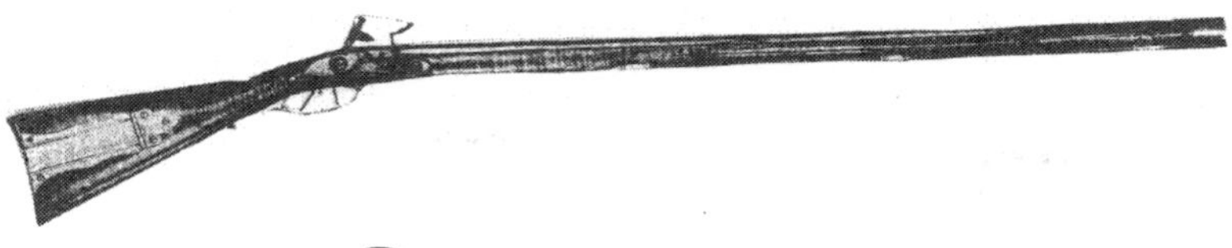

Chapter Sixty Two

William Jameson looked about the land, taking in the full beauty surrounding him. Birds chirped and sat among the bright colors of Autumn's leaves. A few clouds drifted lazily through the blue sky above him. Breezes teased the ripe grain in the fields below him. All seemed at peace. Perhaps finally, the Indians holed up for the winter, he hoped. Anyways, he put off checking the conditions of things at the ruined homes of his brother and father in Hanover too long. Snow would fly soon, he felt its warning in the bite of the breeze cutting his cheeks. This had to be done, and now.

He heard the echo of axes and timber falling to his rear. He marveled on how the fort Colonel Butler had ordered built came along so famously. Almost all of the walls had been raised. By the end of the month it looked to be finished; meeting the colonel's goal he barked to the ranks each night after another hard day's toil. Their lives and future depended upon it, he told everyone so much they tired of hearing it. The Six Nations would not sit idle, he preached, come spring they would strike. How strong we stood against them depended entirely on how strong of a fort we had! Something in his words struck home, for everyone, including he, worked their fingers to the bone constructing the new Fort Wyoming.

The colonel's warning grew in credence upon sight of the burned and charred remains of homes Jameson passed along the roadside. It sent chills down his back. Desolation amongst beauty, he thought, glancing down to the rifle laid across the saddle of his horse. His mount seemed to share his feelings, lifting its head and perking its ears to let out a loud neigh. He gently patted its neck and leaned forward to whisper reassurances in its ear. It calmed the beast, but only added to the tingle haunting the nape of his neck.

The truth of Colonel Butler's words rang loudly in his mind. Looking behind him he thought of his friend Asa whom accompanied him for a while but turned back to the fort on some trifling excuse. Perhaps he should have gone with him, he mused for a moment, thinking of the Indians and Tories. They would be back. They had been back. Suddenly he felt totally alone and isolated. He eased back and looked over his shoulder, letting the sounds of those raising the fort reassure him.

Only a mile or so, he thought to himself, and you will be there. He carefully and slowly looked all around him. Nothing moved in the trees or in the bushes. All seemed quiet-too quiet. No birds chirped. The caw of a spooked crow echoed among the dull thuds of distant axes. His eyes followed the black bird flying over his head. He wished for a moment to have its eyes and therefore its view, but quickly scolded himself for being so apprehensive. Colonel Butler ordered scouts to constantly patrol the whole valley and beyond; in fact, he reasoned, looking down at the fresh footprints in the muddy road, one of the scouts preceded him no more than a hour ago. Too much real fear haunted Wyoming; do not add to it with an imaginery one, he thought. He tightened the reins and gripped his rifle more firmly nonetheless. Flicking his knees together against his mount's flanks; he increased its gait.

An overwhelming feeling stopped him at the crest of a slight hill. Before him the road meandered through a clearing before bushes funneled it to a crossing through Buttonwood creek. The sugarbush seemed very thick along the funneling path to the crossing, he noticed for the first time. It apparently had never bothered he nor anyone else before; but now times had changed; everyone's eye seemed a bit more keen to such dangers. A savage could burst from the brush, do his terrible work, and disappear in the blinking of an eye. He must report these funneling bushes when he got back to the fort. This brush must be cut back because of the potential threat it harbored.

He scanned the brush ever so carefully, looking for the slightest movement. Reaching down, he cocked the hammer back on his rifle, ready to lift it and fire in an instant. His muscles tightened. He perked up in the saddle and looked all around, watching his horse's alert ears for any sign of distress.

An enormous crack from a great falling tree rang through the air. His horse danced around to face the sound, almost felling him from the saddle. Scolding the beast, he tightened the reins in his fingers, balancing his wobbly rifle on the saddle again.

He reined his mount back toward the creek and looked around; this time not for any savages, but for any friendly eye watching him. He would not want word of his overreaction and fumbling mount to get back to the fort. What would they think? With that he gritted his teeth and spurred his reluctant mount forward, despite its neighs of warning. "Be quiet," he said, spurring it to a trot through the bushes. "In a few more trots we'll be beyond it! We mustn't let fear of every bush cripple us!"

The words barely escaped his lips before a force knocked him from the saddle. He rolled head over heals into the mud, madly groping for his rifle through the stars flooding his vision. He stumbled to one knee, blinded by the mud in his eyes. Another whack struck his skull. He collapsed backwards, looking vainly through the mud at his retreating horse. Another strike knocked him full on his back. His head ached and burned. Mud oozed into his gaping wounds. Raising one of his wrists, he wiped the muck and blood from his eyes, only to see a painted demon bending down over him.

Bared teeth stretched across the hideously painted face. The glint of a knife blade flashed in his eyes before he felt a sharp blade about his head. Instinctively, he burst to his feet and ran. He clamored through the woods, ignoring the snapping branches in his face. His feet fumbled along rocks and fallen timber but never slowed in their quest for life. Screams and yelps sounded in his rear. A whizzing sound brushed by his ear, followed by the crisp report of a half dozen rifles. He ran for dear life, his mother, family, and all he held sacred.

Blinded by blood, ooze, and muck in his eyes, he focused on the thud of the axes and ran toward the noises. Life awaited among them; along with safety and freedom. He ignored the pain, plowing into the trunk of a tree. He wheeled around it and kept plodding forward; he had too. The yelps grew fainter in his rear. The axes sounded more crisp to his front. Soon the groan of oxen and the familiar rhythm of men's voices grew along with the thuds.

He stumbled forward, now alert to the many pains about his body. His shoulder burned and felt wet with blood. His fingers crept up his shirt to find a hole in his flesh, but it did not compare to the sheer and agonizing pain about his head. He felt air on parts of his body he knew should never feel such sensations while he lived. It felt strange among the pain; a sensation he knew few ever felt. It scared him down to his toes. Tears cleared his eyes. His mouth mumbled "Mother, Mother," through his fluttering lips. The sounds of safety grew closer.

He ran and ran, collapsing when the sounds of safety boomed in his ears.

Gasps and shouts of alarm flooded his ears. The sound of rushing feet closed around him. Shock and disbelief hung on every word of his familiar language but he did not care. Safety lie in their tones, along with the hope of dear life.

"What is that he is mumbling," one voice asked close to his ear. "Is it Mother?"

"What's about his skull? His brain?" another shocked voice asked.

"Back! Back!" another strong voice boomed. "Clear the way!"

Through his pain he recognized the voice of Hooker Smith and never thought he would be so glad to hear the boisterous doctor's voice again. "Save me," he begged through his delirium. "Save me."

"What's that?" a voice asked. "What's that he's saying?"

"He can speak?" another voice asked in astonishment.

"Yes!" Hooker Smith's voice boomed. "Now shut up so I can hear what he's asking!"

All fell silent. He felt a hand gently lift his head by the back of his neck and gasp.

"What is it son?" the voice belonging to the hand asked. He felt the hairs from the man's head bending down to hear his faint words on his lips.

"Save me, dear doctor, save me," he muttered on a tortured breath. He felt the hairs lift from his lips and opened his eyes to see the shocked doctor's eyes mirroring horror.

The doctor shook his head and gently nodded, noticing his gaze mirrored in the man's terrified eyes. "Of course, son," he muttered. "Of course."

The doctor carefully lifted him to an awaiting cart. "Be gentle as you can!" he called to the driver. "And you," he ordered the man cradling the shattered skull. "Be mindful of his head, that's his very brain oozing out from that tomahawk wound, keep it still, and bandaged, for God's sake!"

The man nodded and the cart slowly pulled away.

Hooker Smith stood and caught his breath for a moment. Many surrounding him did the same. He reflected on the sheer horror of Jameson's ordeal and wondered of the man's great strength. "My God," he finally said, "if he can be saved, I will save him, for if a man wishes to live so badly, well, he shall." He climbed onto the saddle of his awaiting horse, silently knowing the brave man's wounds to be mortal. But one must keep faith, he reasoned, looking at the sea of shocked faces around him. The isolation of their settlement in the middle of this harsh wilderness loomed in each man's soul.

"We must keep faith," he said, turning his mount to follow the cart. "For faith is all Wyoming has, now. Faith and one another."

Chapter Sixty Three

Colonel Hartley stood on the platform surrounding Fort Muncy's walls calmly surveying the land. The sun rose slowly over the trees from the east, its bright rays already threatening the frosty air and grass. Bright leaves danced on the breeze in the tall trees. The river shone brown with wisps of crisp fog about its face. Bald Eagle Mountain stood regally in the distance, its splendid grandeur overshadowing the landscape. Smoke rose from the chimney of the stone fort of Wallis, beckoning him with its promise of warmth and good food. But he stood firm, being a good example to the men bustling about in the early morning.

A loud crash turned his head below the platform. A huge hewn log tumbled to the ground with the curses of Captain Walker's men following it. Walker himself walked over and put his foot atop the log, reassuring his men and ordering them to lift the log into place again. "Winter's a coming," he said on a frosty breath. "The sooner we get these barracks done the quicker we'll be out of those damn ragged tents about Wallis' and around our own warm hearths. Now let's get to it!"

Hartley watched the men eagerly return to their work. The log quickly rose into place to the cadence of their work song. The call for more echoed through the gate to the oxen team pulling another log through the open gate.

These men had heart, if nothing else, Hartley observed, watching them work enthusiastically in their threadbare uniforms and small clothes. He shook his head and reminded himself of the pleas he had sent to Congress for provisions, pay, and clothing. Only ammunition came in abundance so far, but he had received promises. Promises do not fill bellies and clothe backs, though, he thought.

The sharp rap of a drum tore his eyes to the two squads of men parading at the far end of the stockade. He looked with pride at the two officers drilling the men; sergeants recently promoted to ensigns for their distinguished bravery in action on Indian Hill. He knew Allison and Thornbury to be deserving of the rank and expected great things of them in the future, as he did of Carberry drilling his Light Horse on the green about Wallis' house. Technically still only a lieutenant, everyone on the expedition and now referred to him as Captain Carberry, and Hartley expected formal commissions for all three to arrive in the next batch of dispatches. Everyone in these ranks recognized them with their new rank despite of what a lackadaisical headquarters called them. And that is all that seemed to matter to the three men anyway. So here on this frontier post their titles were Captain Carberry, Ensign Thornbury, and Ensign Allison. And rightfully so.

"Do you think they are about?" Captain Bush asked, walking up the ladder to Hartley. He stopped at the top of the ladder and gazed over the pointed logs to the woods beyond them.

"Oh, they are there," Hartley said, "skulking and lurking about, watching every move we make." He turned away from the captain and scratched the back of his neck. The fingers of his other hand's fingers played nervously about the butt of the pistol stuck in his belt. "I durst wager, fine sir, that there are more Indians within one hundred and fifty miles of this place and Wyoming, then within like distance from Fort Pitt where so many men are posted. I have written Congress requesting another regiment be sent to Wyoming, lest they all find their frontier far closer than what they imagine."

Bush rolled an eye toward him.

"I assure you what I have written can be relied upon," Hartley said watching two sergeants stroll through the gate. "What are they about?"

"Just on a stroll to check the brush over there," Bush said, blowing into his hands to warm them against the chill. "I ordered it," he added. "As soon as the barracks are completed I shall have it removed. Swampy ground over there. Walker says it was cleared before the expedition, but it grows fast."

"As does everything in this bush country," Hartley said. A yelp and a shout turned his head quickly back to the sergeants. Stunned, he stared at the painted man smoothly cutting around the crown of one of the men's heads. The other sergeant seemed to have vanished into thin air. "There!" he shouted, raising his pistol and firing a wild shot at the demon. Before the smoke from the pistol cleared the devil vanished.

Bush swirled about and flew down the ladder, landing with a thud. He shouted and waved at the men spilling through the gate, directing them to the fallen sergeant.

Dozens of men fanned out immediately into the brush, leaving the frustrated captain standing and running his hands nervously through his hair while he watched the brush. "What the devil!" he called back up to Hartley. "They were just here! Where in the hell could the have gone? And what of the other sergeant?"

"We've a wily foe, Captain," Hartley called back to him, carefully reloading his pistol. "Here in the blink of a eye and gone by the next heartbeat."

The rumble of hooves trampled the ground. Carberry galloped headlong at the head of his Light Horse, saber drawn and with grim determination in his eyes. The horsemen flew by the foot soldiers and burst into the brush and woods beyond it, screaming and hooting as loudly as any Indian. They soon returned along with the bedazzled foot soldiers, sharing the same baffled look on all their faces.

"They are still about, indeed," Hartley said under his breath. "I fear it shall take more than our feeble numbers to curb their acts against us. I fear for the innocents caught in the midst of this terrible upheaval. Nothing will lessen it but complete destruction of one or the other. This I know. This I fear. God help us all."

Chapter Sixty Four

"Well there you be, young Jenkins," Abel Yarington said, grinning at the lieutenant before waving over to the man on the opposite shore of the Susquehanna. "He's secured the tow line." He stepped onto his new ferry, looking down at its creaking bottom with concern before nodding at the anxious men standing around the carts aboard it. "Never ye mind the creaks, she's new," he said. "Be fine after she's broke in like a new coon-dog or woman is all!" He turned and motioned to a man minding an oxen attached to the other end of the rope after it wound around a huge tree trunk. "Pull!" he ordered the man.

With the sharp crack of a whip the oxen moaned and trudged ahead, dragging the rope taunt. It sprang from the brown water. Abel reached out and grabbed it, making sure it guided easily through eyes of the rail on the side of the ferry. After watching it guide freely through the rail to his satisfaction he glanced over to the lieutenant standing by a group of canoes filled with well-armed men. "We're ready," he said, "now just get ye lot over there ahead of me." He watched the man on the opposite shore eagerly climb back into his canoe and paddle back toward the safe side of the river. "If there be any savage in wait, I'll be pulling hard for this shore again," he added. "Ye best make sure it's good and clear. Wave back to me when it's so."

"Sir," Jenkins said, pointing the barrel of his rifle up to the early morning sun, "it is true the day is young, but many a brave soul waits over there to be properly buried, by his own people and not by the cruel hand of nature." He stepped into the canoe waiting for him and nodded to the ferryman. "Best we all set out at the same time, that ways we'll all be getting there at the same time and get about our work. I want no time wasted by the timid in case there be trouble. This may be the only day allowed us. I want to get as many buried proper as possible."

Yarington sneered at the insinuation and pulled hard on the tow rope, motioning for the others to lend a hand on it. "Then be about ye business, sir, and don't be looking over ye shoulder for us, for we'll be right behind ye, smug rascal. We'll see they're all buried proper."

"What's that you say?" Jenkins asked.

"Just do ye part and I'll be sure to do mine," Abel Yarington said. "If ye lose your hair, so shall I, but don't be imparting any reluctance on my part, fine sir!"

"Then pull that rope and mind your tongue, you're still in the employ of the army, you know," Jenkins said, waving his arm toward the far shore. With that canoe and ferry swept across the river in one long continuous line. It only slowed once, to meet the man in the canoe paddling from the opposite shore; and then only long enough to tie his canoe to the ferry and pull him aboard it.

In spite of the eagerness of the ferrymen, they slowed just before the shore, letting the canoes land before them. The men in the canoes ignored them. Their eyes remained locked on the trees and bushes lining the shoreline. The hoots, war whoops, and glowing fires from the west shore every night heightened their anxious feelings; plus the plight of the three Germans killed just a fortnight before their present expedition. The wails and pleas of the poor scalped survivor haunted their minds, sending a loathsome, but familiar chill down their spines. Nonetheless, they fanned out all along the shore and marched forward in perfect military fashion, led by their stern commander. Under the watchful eye of the ferrymen and civilians on the ferry they soon disappeared into the trees and brush.

All aboard the ferry stayed perfectly silent, listening intently for any telltale sounds of distress. After a while rifles rose in some of their hands while others turned around on the rope, ready to pull on it with all their strength in anticipation of a hasty retreat. “Ye just hold fast,” Yarington told them, slapping at their white knuckles clenching the rope. “I meant what I said. If that brash young rowdy loses his hair, so shall I, but I’ll not be pulling this ferry away from this shore without taking as many of them across safe as ye. If ye can’t wait then swim, damn ye!”

Jenkins suddenly appeared on the shore, waving the ferry to land.

“See,” Yarington said, “told ye all it’d be fine, and ye still got ye hair, ain’t ye!”

None of the men laughed at his remark but just pulled steadily on the rope. The forest and trees that had once been so familiar to them now seemed completely foreign, as if conquest had totally changed the very nature of the ground itself. Somehow the horror of what happened at the battle remained embedded in the soul of the earth itself, sending out a lingering warning to all who dared to step upon it again. Every man felt the feeling. Every man let it swell in his chest and swallowed hard against it, anxious to be about their duty. They remembered friend, father, and son, all lying on that field for so long, and the shame of it swept away and subdued the anxious feelings. Their long overdue debt to their brethren overrode fear itself.

Soon the carts creaked forward, surrounded by Jenkins’ vigilant soldiers.

Along the way they all stopped to face the ruins of the strong fort they had constructed in a time that seemed so long ago. Nothing but the hint of one of the cabins within its wall greeted them. Jumbles of logs lay piled in heaps, some half-burned. Others lay split and hacked so as to never rise in defense of Wyoming again. The demolished fort harkened of the complete devastation that lay ahead of them. None one spoke. A whisper would have seemed a yell. The creak of a cart finally broke the stares at the fort and they continued on in a veil of silence.

Alert eyes watched the trees all along the road leading from the fort. Flankers investigated every suspicious bush along the roadside. Fingers itched to pull the locks of the rifles back in the blinking of an eye. Onward the silent burial party marched, listening, watching, and bracing themselves for the shock of the sight of the carnage that lie ahead of them. Upon reaching the first bend in the road the soldiers in the lead stopped. They raised their hands and signaled for their officer to step forward.

John Jenkins lifted his head high and jutted his chin, silently hoping the remains to be too unrecognizable to identify. He thought it best, gazing up to the sun high in the sky. August had been dry. Perhaps before the September rains the bodies had dried. Perhaps this body would not be that of his friend John Murphy, whom he had cheered when they marched out of Forty Fort's gate on that hot July day to collide with a fate too horrible to imagine still, after all this time. He looked to the eyes watching him march to the front, knowing they harbored the same fears. Some of their fathers lay here. Some of their dear friends lay here. Some of their sons lay here.

Jenkins looked down at the three bodies spaced but a few feet apart, one with an upraised arm in the direction of the fort but a few rods up the road. Had it been this poor soul's last act to reach and pray for someone to deliver them to the fort? But alas, no one came, and here he died, hoping against all odds.

He lowered his rifle and bent down to the body. Dry, sickly gray, and splotchy yellow skin covered the face staring up to him with empty eye sockets. The clothing draping the dried skin of the skeletons lie mostly in tatters. The sleeve of the upraised arm blew in the breeze. Upon closer look a bit of metal glistened in the sun from one of the fingers of the bony upraised hand. He gently held the hand and slipped the ring from its finger. The rigid arm fell loosely to the ground, seeming to give up the ghost for the promise of burial for a body now long overdue to return the dust from whence it came.

He raised the ring to his eyes and twirled it about, carefully looking for any telltale marking on it. Many eyes now watched him.

A gasp came from one of those standing near him. "That's Perrin Ross's ring!" a man said. He took a step forward and knelt next to the lieutenant.

Jenkins handed the ring to the wide-eyed man.

"Sure enough is," the man said. He stumbled to his feet and looked at the other two bodies lying close by. He took a few steps next to the body lying face down on the ground. Wisps of sandy brown hair blew in the slight breeze. "And this here's got to be Jeremiah, his brother!" he said, touching the hair. He knelt down and carefully rolled the body on its side. The ground somehow preserved enough of the face to make it barely recognizable. The man stared at the face and slowly nodded his head before letting it back down onto the ground. He looked over to the other body, and at the great spear still stuck in its ribcage and shook his head. This body had laid face up too long. Nothing remained of its clothing but ripped shreds of faded linen. Besides, some beast had devoured half of its face. "Don't know who that could have been," the man said. "My God it's worse revisiting this place than it was on that day. These poor souls didn't deserve this."

"No," Jenkins said. "No one did. But we've a lot of ground to cover this day. The battlefield proper is a mile or so up river. We best get these men on a cart and keep going."

Heads nodded and a cart rolled to the bodies.

Bending down two men tried to lift the shriveled body of Lieutenant Ross but fell back in disgust. Arms fell out of dried and loose sockets and the paper-like skin crackled. They stood, took a few steps back, and stared down in horror of what they had done.

"Don't fret," a voice called from behind the party. Abel Yarington strode through the distraught men carrying several two-tined pitchforks in his arms. "Figured they'd be all dried out," he said, looking down at the bodies. "That's why I figured to bring these along." He passed two of the pitchforks to the men. They gently placed one under the upper torso and one under the lower torso and picked up the body in unison. It stayed intact, much to the men's relief.

"Thought you were going to stay back at the ferry?" Jenkins asked Yarington.

"Got bored," he said. "Least ways my man's watching it. It'll be there, don't ye fret. But these here's my people too, ye know. Wouldn't be right but to lend a helping hand, and anyhow, it seems ye all need it. Man should go to the grave in one piece, if'n it can be helped."

"I agree," Jenkins said, "and I'm grateful, too, thank you."

"Told ye not to fret," Yarington said. "Now let's get at it! Like ye said, a lot of ground is yet to be covered."

Jenkins walked to the spear sticking in the other

man's ribcage and stared at the lone feather dancing in the wind on its handle. He took the feather in his hand and angrily ripped it from the spear. Throwing it to the ground he stomped it into the earth before yanking the spear from the man's chest. He gripped it tightly on both ends and brought it down hard on his knee. Its crack sounded loudly across the silent field of carnage. He threw it to the side and grabbed his rifle, gesturing forward with its barrel. "Keep a sharp eye!" he said. "All of you! If you see anything suspicious shoot and ask questions later. There's no one on this side of the river that we can call friend. This I assure you, so let's get at it!"

The men marched onward, though slowed by the increasing amounts of dried and shriveled bodies. One by one they painstakingly lifted the brittle bodies up by the pitch-forks and loaded them onto the carts. Soon groups of two men with forks strayed all over the fields by the road, accompanied by an equal amount of Jenkins' men to guard them against the ever present enemy. All feared and knew the enemy's prying eyes to be upon them from distant shrubs and trees, but nonetheless kept focused on their task, determined to bury as many of the men as they could find.

The groups of scattered men followed the bodies until they funneled around a bridge, bringing the party back together. For a moment they stopped to catch their breath while Jenkins sent a party of men across the bridge to scout the area beyond.

"Carts are getting full already," a civilian with a pitch-fork reported to Jenkins.

Jenkins looked anxiously ahead to his men across the bridge. The dots of cloth in the fields beyond the bridge betokened more bodies lay ahead. He nodded his head at the man and examined one of the carts nearest the bridge. Gazing upon the growing heaps of shriveled humanity in the carts he shuddered. He had known each and every one of these souls, and now witnessing their remains he felt a sad relief he could not recognize any of their corpses. He bent down and touched the pick and shovels stuck up under one of the carts. "We will have to stop and bury them soon, even before we reach the battlefield proper," he said, standing straight again on the approach of one of his scouts.

"All clear, sir," the man reported.

"Very well," Jenkins said. "Let's get at it again."

Up the road they went, collecting and loading bodies until they lay in heaps threatening to spill over the top rails of the carts. Noticing the full carts, Jenkins ordered a halt and climbed over to a slight knoll by the side of the road. "Here," he said, thumping the butt of his rifle down on the ground, "is where we shall bury them." He looked all around the green grass surrounding the spot and at the tall trees offering some shade. The river stretched below them across a green plain on the right. In all it seemed a proper place for one to spend eternity. Nestled in the valley they so loved in life, it offered a serine place to rest in the comfort of mother earth.

Jenkins himself strutted to a cart and pulled the first pickaxe from underneath it. Without turning to order any of the surrounding men, he strode to the spot, paced a few steps to center himself, and with a great swing struck the axe into the ground. Soon every shovel and pickaxe from the carts joined him in excavating a great wide hole in the earth.

A distinct call- a loud gobble-perked all heads in the direction of the noise. Pickaxes stopped in mid-swing. The gritty sound of shovels moving dirt ceased. Once again the call sounded in the still air. Rifle locks clicked to full cock and rose to the shoulders of Jenkins' alert soldiers.

Jenkins himself stood silent and still. He slowly

lowered his pickaxe and listened.

The call sounded again, this time further down the road.

More rifles turned toward the noise.

"They ain't no turkeys!" a voice finally announced. "But I bet they're wearing feathers just the same!"

Jenkins struck the pickaxe in the ground with one swift thud and stepped from the hole, reaching for his own long rifle. He lifted the weapon to his shoulder and stared in the direction of the disturbing sounds.

"Do you want us to check it out?" one of his soldiers asked.

"No," Jenkins said, turning and walking up the road. "If they're there in them woods let them stay there. We're here to collect the dead. I am not going to let the threat of a few of those devils spoil that! I had a hell of a time convincing Colonel Butler it was safe to come over here as it is, so let's get at it!" He waved a few of his soldiers ahead. "Sergeant Baldwin," he called behind him. "You stay here with about a half dozen or so to guard the diggers while I take the rest ahead."

"Yes sir," Baldwin said, posting his troops in a wide circle around the nervous civilians digging the hole. "You heard the Lieutenant!" he said to the diggers. "Get at it! We's ain't going to let them stop us, besides, if'n they was here in any numbers they would have been all over us already. You all know how they is. Daylight's burning! Let's go!"

Some of the diggers grumbled at the brash sergeant but after his glaring eyes caught theirs' they thought better of it. They dug.

Jenkins spread his remaining men out in a wide arc surrounding the carts and burial party plodding up the road. They worked swiftly and steadily, with each man watching out of the corner of his eye while he worked. Many of them checked the pistols stuck in their belts and twisted them, wanting them loose and ready to fire at a moment's notice. Because of the vastness of the field the party soon split into two; one covering one half of the field while the other covered the other half of it.

Their steps only slowed at the remains of Fort Wintermoot with the ghastly figure perched among its charred timbers. The burned figure of a man stood slightly bent forward, his hands still clenched in tight fists at his antagonists after all this time. The steel prongs of two-tined pitchforks stuck in his feet and into his side. The man no doubt died in defiance of his enemy. The horror of the brave man's death flashed in each of the men's eyes staring at his body in shock and disbelief.

"That's got to be Captain Bidlack," a soldier said. "The story of his torture is true, every damn bit of it, and then it looks like more! He fought them so they had to pin him in the flames with pitchforks!" The man's bulging eyes gazed down at the decapitated corpse laying just before the burned ruins of the fort. "And that there's got to be Captain Ransom's body, as well!" He carefully lifted a knee buckle from the decaying corpse's leg. "Them are his fancy knee buckles fer sure, they is," he said. "He was known fer his buckles, now they tell us of his demise, poor, brave soul."

Jenkins stared in blank horror at the bodies. "Collect them," he finally said, remembering the two brave men he had known dearly in life. Apparently they had died as they had lived. His eyes caught the glimpse of the sun lowering just behind the trees to his right. "The day grows long," he said. "We, gentlemen, do not want to be caught on this side of the river at nightfall. Let's get these brave souls buried so they can finally rest in peace."

A cart hurried ahead and two men gently lifted Captain Bidlack's charred body from the ruins. One pulled a prong from the side of his body. "Look's like they stuck him time and time again," he said, "left this one in his hip."

"Yes," Jenkins said, "just get him out of there so we can be on our way." A disgusted grunt turned his head toward a few frustrated men tending to Ransom's body.

"Can't find his head," one of them said to the stern-eyed lieutenant. "Lord knows what they did with it, the bloody rascals!"

"Just collect what you can," Jenkins said. "No one can blame you under the circumstances, least of all me. Now let's get these carts full of the dead back to the grave so we have time to cover them properly!"

A call from further back along the road caught their attention. They rushed down a few rods to find men standing around a large rock. They stared in shock at the bodies arranged in a circle around it.

"What is this?" Jenkins asked.

"Torture circle of that half-breed witch Ester," one of them said. He lifted his pitchfork and pointed it toward the rock. Bits of red still shone in the crevices and cracks on it face. On one particular spot bits of flesh and other matter lay among a huge splotch of red.

Jenkins slowly paced around the rock, looking down upon the bodies. Though shriveled, several of the skulls appeared to be crushed. Cuts and other signs of misuse showed on their withered and dry skin. What happened here made his stomach lurch. He turned his head away and looked to the river for the longest moment before turning back to the men. "Load them in the carts," he said, overcome with grief. "We must be quick, the sun shall set soon."

One of the party motioned him over to the cart. He

looked down at a body to which the man pointed.

"It's Captain Durkee," the man said.

Jenkins looked down at the body and raised his lower lip. The body's head jutted back, locked in a painful position bearing witness to his dear friend's pain right up to his last moment. The empty, hollow, sockets of his eyes stared toward the heavens. What horror these men witnessed played at the very depths of his soul. He turned his head away and looked with empty eyes to the man.

"Look to his hand," the man said, thinking his stare needed an explanation. "Captain Durkee lost a finger in life, now it identifies him in death."

"They were all brave," Jenkins said through the growing lump in his throat. "Every man on this field was brave and should never be forgotten."

"I'll give you that, Lieutenant," the man said, turning to help lift some of the bodies onto the cart. "I'll grant them all that, for sure."

The other carts soon converged around the ring. Each man glanced at it with the same disgust before Jenkins ordered the whole party back to the grave site.

Sergeant Baldwin and his men's eyes lit up at the sight of the returning carts, bearing witness to their growing apprehension since they departed. "The calls are becoming more frequent," the sergeant explained to his lieutenant. "Was getting a bit antsy," he added, looking at his fellows. "All of us was for sure getting antsy. We're glad to see you."

Jenkins nodded his head and waved the carts past him to the grave. The men, sensing a growing sense of uneasiness on the part of the sentries, worked all the faster at emptying the carts. Soon they placed the last body, Captain Durkee's, unceremoniously atop the others. Shovels promptly went to work covering the huge grave while the anxious eyes of the soldiers watched the woods all around them.

With the last shovel full of dirt the sound of feet and the backs of shovels tamping down the earth atop the grave turned the guarding soldiers' eyes behind them. The sinking sun grazed the tops of the trees to the west. The shadows of the forest grew deep, seeming to close in on them.

Jenkins strode to the head of the grave, sensing the need for someone to say a few words, but feeling anxious for the safety of his command at the same time. "Well," he said, bowing his head and removing his hat, "here they are, many a brave soul whom died for liberty. We knew them all as son, father, grandfather, uncle, brother, and friend. Many of us here marched with them to this very field where they shall forever rest. Let their rest be peaceful, and most of all let their place in our hearts, and our history, never be forgotten. It's true we haven't the time, or perhaps the proper speaker for such an occasion, a preacher or such, but we have done our task here under the threat of the enemy breathing down our necks and howling from the woods. Yes, we all have done our part this day, so let it be to those whom shall reap the rewards of the great and noble sacrifices made here to commemorate these brave fallen souls, who died with them on their minds. What happen here should never be forgotten and I pray most heartedly to God himself that it shall never be. Dear God bless this ground and the bodies lying within it. Kith and kin I pray our posterity shall remember them, and their sacrifices. In that they shall live again. In that the ideals for which they died shall live again. Let all of us never forget, never forget. For that would be a tragedy far greater than any suffering felt by these brave men upon this field. Let their memory live in the hearts of men and the liberty for which they fought shall never be forgotten. I pray this for all standing here and lying in the hollowed earth of this field. No holier spot of ground exists than where defeated valor lies, crowned by mourning's glory. Amen."

With that, the solemn march of the burial party back to the ferry began. Each man walked silently, watching out of the corner of his eye for the same enemy lest he too be left on this field dead. With feelings of relief tinged with the sorrowful memories of those whom had fallen they stepped onto the ferry and filled the canoes.

The beautiful Susquehanna wound before them in the twilight. Its swirling waters caught many of the crestfallen eyes watching it wind past them to the sea. More eyes turned from the thought of the grave behind them and to the hopeful and relieved faces beaming at them from the opposite shore.

Women, children, and their fellow soldiers, all stood waiting anxiously for their safe return. The sight of the new and stout fort rising high on the bank behind the welcoming faces spread smiles of relief across many faces. Perhaps their comrades had not died in vain, they mused. Perhaps they would be remembered after all, and with that their own struggles, also.

But still the memory of that field would never be forgotten as long as they breathed, they promised one another, and they also promised to carry on in the light of the courage which shone from their fellows' great sacrifice. No, their memory lived, as Jenkins said, as long as liberty still lived in the hearts of men, great and small. They knew this without a doubt as they spilled from the canoes and ferry to the welcoming arms of their brethren and loved ones. Wyoming lived as long as they breathed. It lived as long as their descendants breathed.

But shadows still cast themselves across the light of liberty, and none the more greater in Wyoming than the shadow of the great Six Nations. That shadow penetrated so deep it cast itself across the hope shinning within the souls of the Wyoming settlers' hearts, no matter how intense the light of liberty glowed from their hearts.

Could hope alone prevail against the Six Nation's tomahawks?

Could this dreaded *curse of the tomahawk* ever be broken?

"Camp Wioming, Octo. The 3d., 1778

"Colo Hartley takes the opportunity of Returning his thanks to the officers and Soldiers Volluntiers and Others under his command on the Late expedition for their Good Conduct and perfservation during that Tolesome and dangerous March amidst Hunger Wading of River at Midnight.

"Marches no Complaints were heard all was Submifsion and Resignation in Action several Of the Continental officers difhtinguished themselves Capt Boone And Capt Champlane of the Voluntiers deferve particularly to be Named-Capt Franklin with his Voluntiers from Wyoming Were Very useful in this Expedition In short with Very few Exceptions the Whole detachment have acquited themselves With the Highest Reputation-and they have this Further Satisfaction to know They have saved the lives of many and served their country Sergt Allison and Sergt thornbury for Action are appointed Enfigns in Colo Hartley's Regiment."

"Oct. 30.

"Dear Genl. (A. Wayne)-You will hear of a splendid expedition we have had up the waters of the Susquehanna-In the actions we had with savages I never saw better choices of ground than they made to attack on-but the last time we outmanouvered them."

"Fate ordained that I was to go to make war on the savages of America instead of on Britain."

"It is hellish work to be fighting those devils."

"Your most obedient and humble servant,

Colo. Thomas Hartley"

"Fort Augusta 7th October 1778

"Sir

"The 5th Inst. Coll. Hartley Returned from an expedition he carryed on against some of the small Indians towns on the North Branch of the Susquehanna, where he was informed there was a party of Indians and Tories Assembled, but they being appraised of Coll. Hartley's march by a party of warriors he met comeing to the West Branch; Whome our People fired uppon and shot their Captain dead uppon which the Indians fled Imeadiatly and alarmed the Towns Coll. Hartley was Bound for, so that they had time to put their families and chief part of their Effects out of the way before he arived there, and when he came to Tiaoga where he took some Tories Prisoners, they informed him of a Town calld Shamung about ten or twelve miles from there where there was a Body of Indians Tories & Regulars in Garrison as good as Six or seven Hundred, Coll. Hartley after Consulting his Officers thought it most Expedient to Return Back without Attempting Shamung, and so after destroying Tiaoga & Shesiken and bringing off fifty or Sixty head of Horned Cattle and some Horses they got there beside several other articles our People Brought them in Canoes,-

"In the meantime the Indians was Collecting a party to intercept Coll. Hartley on his march to Wyoming, which they accomplished and fired on our People in front in this side of Wyaloosing, where the Indians had waylay'd our People among a parsel of Rocks as they were marching through a piece of Narrows along the River side, but Coll. Hartleys People Returning the fire briskly made the Enimy Give Way, and marched but a little ways furder when they were fired on again in the Rear and after a brisk fireing on Boath Sides for Some time the Enimy Retreated-

"It must be acknowledged our People beheaved with Courage and Conduct, in bringing off their Wounded all their Cattle and pack Horses, suppose the Enemy followed all the Way to Wyoming and scalped four of Coll. James Murrays men after they arived there, as for a more minute account of this Expedition I Refer you to Coll. Hartleys own letters to the Board of Warr & Executive Council-

"But in the whole it was well Conducted considering the number of men that went with Coll. Hartley, not above two Hundred and fifty which shows that Officers and men beheaved with spirit in bringing with them five Indian scalps besides several more of the Enimy Killed. Col. Hartley's loss was seven killed and Eight wounded includeing those that was killed at Wyoming.-

"As for the Inhabitants of this Country they seem very much afraid at present, hearing of such a large Body of the Enimy being so nigh as Shamung, and all the Militia that was here from Lancaster County & Berks gon, as their time has Expired, and none here but part of Col. Hartleys Regiment, sixty men of Col. James Murrays Company of Six Months men, and about one Hundred of our own Militia which is doing Duty in several parts of this County. Which is no way adiquit to the security of the same, as I am certain the one half of this County is left Vacant and not more than one third of the Inhabitants that lived formerly here is putting in any fall Crop this year, so that Distress & misery must Ensue-if no Continental Troops is Ordered up here this fall nor no Militia from other Countys Bordering of us, I am afraid a number of those that has brought their familys back will leave the County again.

Colonel Hunter,
commanding, Fort Augusta,
Sunbury, Pa."

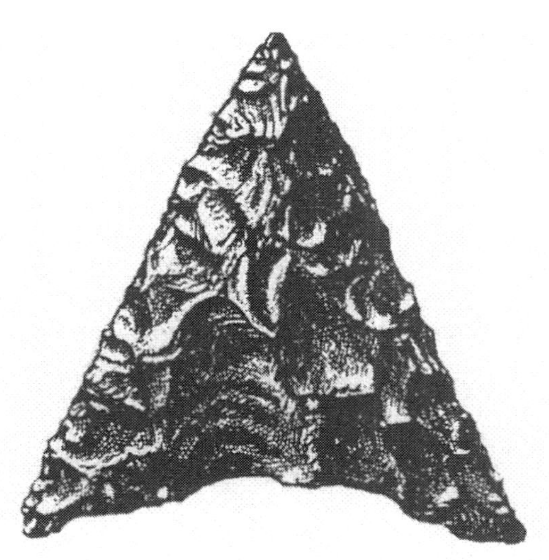

Index

Sources: *History Of Bradford County by David Craft, History of Bradford County by H.C. Bradsby, The Susquehanna Papers edited by Robert J. Taylor Old Tioga Point and early Athens by Louise Welles Murray, Early Times along the Susquehanna by Mrs. George A. Perkins, Draper Manuscript Collection State Archives, Madison, Wisconsin, by Lyman C. Draper, Mary Jemison by J. Seaver, Annals of the Buffalo Valley by John Lynn, History of Lycoming County edited by John F. Meginness, Tri-Counties Genealogy and Historic Sites by Joyce M. Tice, Loyalists Narratives of Upper Canada by Talman, Historic Pennsylvania Leaflet No. 40, The Settler, A Quarterly Magazine of History and Biography by the Bradford County Historical Society, Wilderness War by Allan Eckert, History of Wilkes-Barre and Wyoming Valley by Oscar J. Harvey, Mrs. Jane Whittaker's Narrative, Life of Brant by Col. Stone, Wyoming by G. Peck, Historical Address at the Wyoming Monument July 3, 1878 by Stueben Jenkins, Joseph Brant Mohawk Chief by J. Bolton and Claire Wilson, Indians in Pennsylvania by Paul Wallace, A Connecticut Yankee in Penn's Woods, Charles E. Myers, The King's Rangers by John Brick, The Susquehanna Frontier by J. Wilson and Linda Fossler, History of the 8th Light by Gargano, Indian Villages and Place Names by Dr. G. Donehoo, Iroquois in the American Revolution by B. Graymount, The History of the Seneca Indians by A. Parker, Pioneer America by C. Drepperd, Te-A-O-GA Annals of a Valley by Elsie Murray, The State of Westmoreland and The Pennamite-Yankee War by Richard Irby, Cry of the Tomahawk by J. Miller, Pioneer Life by J. Wright and D. Corbett, Pioneer and Patriot Families of Bradford County by Clement Heverly, Luke Swetland's Captivity by Merrifield, History: The King's, or 8th Regiment 1768-1785, History of Luzerne County, Lackawanna, and Wyoming Counties by W.M. Munsell, History of Wyoming by C. Miner, Penna Archives Vol. 6, History of the Towandas by Clement F.Heverly, Frontier Forts of Pennsylvania in the Wyoming Valley by Sheldon R. Reynolds, North and West Branches by John M. Buckalew, Big Indian Raid, Leader Corning N.Y. Oct. 23 1978 by Ellsworth Cowles, Sullivan Expedition, Prologue Marked, Leader Corning N.Y. Sept. 26 1978 by Ellsworth Cowles, The Pennsylvania Line 1775-1785 by John B. Trussell, The Pennsylvania Militia by Samuel Newland, Beyond Philadelphia, The American Revolution in the Pennsylvania Hinterland edited by J. Frantz and W. Pencak, The Wyoming Valley by F.J. Stefon, A Sketch of the History of Wyoming 1830 by I. Chapman, The Susquehanna by Carl Carmer, Pennsylvania's Susquehanna by E. Singmaster, The Pennsylvania German in the Revolutionary War by Henry Richards, Old Tioga Point and Early Athens Pennsylvania by Elsie Murray, Indian Wars in Pennsylvania by C. Hale Sipe, Indian Chiefs of Pennsylvania by C. Hale Sipe.*

Made in the USA
Charleston, SC
12 April 2010